THE FISHING WATERS OF SCOTLAND

MORAY McLAREN AND WILLIAM B. CURRIE

THE
FISHING WATERS
OF
SCOTLAND

JOHN MURRAY

This book was designed and produced by
Rainbird Reference Books Ltd
36 Park Street London WIY 4DE

First published 1972
Reprint (Revised) 1978
John Murray (Publishers) Ltd
50 Albemarle Street London WIX 4BD

Printed in Great Britain by
Robert MacLehose & Company Ltd
Printers to the University of Glasgow
and bound by
Hunter & Foulis Ltd
McDonald Road Edinburgh

House editor: Yorke Crompton
Indexer: Ellen Crampton
Design and maps: Crispin Fisher

ISBN: 0 7195 2586 1

CONTENTS

5

U.D.N.

The first edition of the book noted the coming of the epidemic of U.D.N. (ulcerative dermal necrosis) to many Scottish rivers. In the late 'sixties and early 'seventies this disease took a heavy toll of salmon and sea-trout in such rivers as Tweed, Nith, Spey and waters of the Loch Lomond system. Happily, the stocks of fish are showing signs of strong recovery (1977). Outbreaks are less severe and are localized. The cycle of disease would seem to have run through and we expect it to clear our rivers in the near future.

p. 33: The Ewes Water joins the Border Esk at Langholm. The White Esk joins the Black Esk some ten miles above the town.

p. 49: Nith sea-trout in good numbers and weights have been reported during 1977, indicating some recovery of the fishings.

p. 77: The Endrick suffered badly from U.D.N. and its stock of sea-trout declined seriously in the early 'seventies. In 1977 a clear recovery was noted, although runs appeared later than formerly giving the best fishing early in September. Salmon are still low in numbers.

p. 90: An important rainbow and brown trout fishery has been established in Loch Fitty, near Kingseat, Dunfermline. This loch is excellently organized and has good boathouse facilities, including a tackle shop and snacks. Ideal for club fishings. Good bags in May, June and July (rainbows) averaging about one pound.

p. 90: Loch Leven has largely recovered from its fish decline. Numbers of large fish have been caught in recent years, some over four pounds in weight. Smaller fish of three-quarters to a pound are increasing in number.

p. 176: The Helmsdale beat record was broken in July 1977 with a catch of twenty-six salmon to two rods. The interesting thing about this bag was that nothing was on the bank by lunchtime.

p. 176: In 1977 a series of good trout lochs in the Badanloch area, eight miles above Kinbrace, were opened to public day fishing. They include Badanloch, Loch Rimsdale, Loch Coire na Mang, Loch Fearnan and others. Boats from the Badanloch fishing office. Excellent wild trout fishing in remote hill country.

p. 178: Charles C. McLaren has retired as the hotelier at Altnaharra and is now running an angling resource centre in the village, complete with a tackle shop, programmes of fishing, accommodation and fishing instructions.

SALMON AND TROUT LEGISLATION

There is still no law to protect private trout fishings adequately. Until legislation allowing proprietors and clubs to invest in their fishings with a suitable measure of protection from unauthorized anglers is passed, trout fishing in Scotland will remain less well developed than it might be.

W.B.C.   1978

KEY TO THE MAPS

Throughout the book, wherever lack of space on a map prevents Loch from being spelt in full, it is shown as L.; where Lo. appears after a name, it means Lodge. On the frontispiece map, C. stands for Clackmannan, Dunb. or D. for Dunbarton, and K. for Kinross; W. L., Midl., and East L. indicate the three Lothians. The list below gives the page numbers of the maps.

ILLUSTRATIONS

Acknowledgments to photographers appear in brackets and the page numbers of colour plates in bold type.

FOREWORD

The fishing waters of Scotland have been written about by many angling authors. This is not surprising, for Scotland has a greater range of game fishing – salmon, sea-trout, brown trout – and, at best, a higher quality of it than any other country in Europe. Nor is it strange that so many writers on the Scottish scene in general should have praised the entrancing beauty to be found in various of its lochs and rivers.

Yet it is curious how few books have attempted to describe the fishing waters of Scotland as a whole. In 1853 Stoddart, in his *Angler's Companion*, covered a large sector of the country; Grimble's remarkable work *The Salmon Rivers of Scotland* gave in 1899 a detailed technical description of our salmon fishing; and Calderwood, writing in 1921 *The Salmon Rivers and Lochs of Scotland*, brought Grimble up to date with an admirable account by the Inspector of Salmon Fisheries for Scotland. There have been works from lesser pens too, most of them guides on where and when to fish; and it has been interesting to see, in the last few years, not only a guide to the 'ticket waters' of all Scotland published by the Tourist Board and revised every year, but also several excellent and detailed area guides covering accessible waters in given counties.

This book on the rivers and lochs of Scotland is written principally from the angling point of view, for both its authors are keen anglers, and between them they have fished in most waters of the kingdom. Though we might have written a book that aimed at comprehensiveness, we chose not to attempt such a task. No one could cover in a single book that would be readable, or even portable, all the rivers and burns, lochs and lochans, of Scotland. Our policy is to characterize a wide and representative selection of our angling waters and bring into view the tremendous resources that Scotland has in this one aspect of her country life alone.

Naturally our book contains descriptions of fishings that involve each author personally. Thus areas of particular detail, and moments of reminiscence, contribute to the total picture. Yet even in comprehensiveness we may at times have achieved something. When writing of the Hebrides, for instance, we have brought together what is probably the first extensive description of their fishings.

The waters of Scotland have contributed to our song, poetry, legend, and history – did not the burn of Bannock give its name to the battle that established our nation, if only for a time, as an independent kingdom? Our way of life in Scotland continues to be influenced by our lochs and rivers to a notable degree. This link with Scottish society is recorded in our book.

We deal with the rivers and lochs of Scotland in the following way. We begin with Tweed and move across to the western Borders and the fishings of Dumfriesshire and Galloway. Next we take in Ayrshire; the fishings of central Scotland, including Loch Lomond, the Forth, and Loch Leven; and then the Highland waters, dealing first with Tay and their western areas in Argyll. Eastern districts, including the Aberdeenshire Dee and waters of the north-east, are described, including the Spey. The fishings of Inverness-shire, Ross and Cromarty, Sutherland, and Caithness follow, and in four chapters at the end we describe the Inner and Outer Hebrides and the Northern Isles.

Each author has written separately about the waters he knows best, excepting the Tweed and Galloway areas, which we deal with jointly. Although differences in treatment and style might well identify the writers, we thought it wise to be explicit, and each of us has put his initials after the chapters that he wrote. This arrangement has made it possible for us to write of personal events, using 'I', without losing each other's fish or playing hide-and-seek with the reader.

If our descriptions convey something of our deep sense of pride in Scotland's rivers and lochs, and of the immense pleasure we have found in travelling and fishing through our own land, we shall feel that an important goal has been reached. If our writing makes others want to travel and fish through Scotland, we shall be doubly rewarded. Finally, if we have conveyed to native and visitor something of the Scottish scene, something perhaps of the intangibles that cause men to delight in hills and flowing waters, in sweeping moorlands and rippled lochs, we shall consider our book well worth the labour that its writing has involved.

M.McL., W.B.C.

Chapter One

THE TWEED

We begin with the River Tweed for the following reasons.

Tweed is the first major river that the visitor to Scotland from the south is likely to see. True, there are important rivers well south of Tweed in Ayrshire and in Galloway, but they are not so immediately or dramatically encountered; moreover they are somehow district waters, and do not 'belong to all Scotland'.

This brings us to the second reason. Tweed is the only river, perhaps the only water (apart from Loch Lomond), in which all Scots feel an immediate proprietary interest. Tweed, Tweedside, the whole basin of the river, is a district different from all others, Lowland or Highland; yet the remotest Hebridean, Highlander, or even Orcadian or Shetlander feels, each in his degree, that he has a stake in Tweed and its countryside, popularly named the Borders. Had it not been for this bastion between England and Scotland, our country would not once have attained the status of an independent kingdom. That independent kingdom is gone, but our nationality remains; we owe this to the 'battles long ago' fought in the borderland and in the countryside of the River Tweed. Scots law would not still be operative, the national Church of Scotland would not still be national, and Scottish customs would not still prevail in the remotest island or north-western glen, had it not been for the Tweed borderland and the men and women who lived there.

These words are written in Edinburgh, from which Tweed and her countryside with her tributaries are easily reached. We feel a close relationship to her, but we should never think of claiming Tweed as belonging especially to us in the sense that Glasgow rightly claims the Clyde. Edinburgh Castle lies in the heart of our capital, but it belongs to all Scotland. So it is with the River Tweed.

Our third reason lies in the word 'angling'. There are perhaps a few better salmon rivers in the mainland and islands of Scotland, certainly better rivers for sea-trout and brown trout, but the all-over quality of angling for game fish is in Tweed so high that it has a unique place in all the angling waters of Scotland, whether river or loch.

The fourth and last reason for putting Tweed at the forefront of this survey has nothing to do with angling, but is potent nonetheless. In song and story, Tweed, its countryside, and the tributaries of its basin have surely produced more that is remarkable than any other river in Europe.

Spenser wrote the ever-memorable line:

Sweete Themmes! runne softly, till I end my song,

and there have been some charming verses and prose passages about England's great river. We should also remember that what some hold to be the most perfect sonnet in the Petrarchan form in English was composed by Wordsworth on Westminster Bridge, as it were in mid-stream of Thames. The Germans have a strong romantic devotion to the Rhine. They have eulogized it in speech and print – but what remains memorable to those who are not Germans? Nothing, save a traditional popular song and a few poignant references in Heine's *Dichterliebe*.

Tweed in this matter overwhelms them all. Enough to mention the Border Ballads, most of which sprang from Tweedside and the tributaries of Tweed. The best of these have joined the corpus of Western European poetry, and thus almost deserve the epithet of 'deathless' so frequently applied to them. Close by Tweed itself stand the Eildon Hills, where Thomas of Ercildoun underwent a mystical experience that he expressed in the poem describing his sojourn with the Queen of Elfland. In the original, and also in the verses that later formed the well-known *Ballad of Thomas the Rhymer*, there has come to us from Tweedside an incomparable poem. Merely to look at the Eildon Hills, with Tweed running sweetly yet mysteriously at their feet, is to recapture the purely local magic of Tweedside that Thomas of Ercildoun experienced and expressed.

Below and hard by the Eildons stands Abbotsford, the home that Sir Walter Scott built for himself and that still houses his descendants. Tweed runs immediately by Abbotsford, and on still evenings you can, from open windows in the house, hear its movement towards the sea. In his day Scott's genius influenced the entire literate world of the West, nor did the places and the men he wrote about come only from Scotland. But the inspiration of his genius was local; it came from his beloved borderland and from Tweed, which was for him the most precious stream on earth.

No one – angler, tourist, casual visitor, or resident – within the influence of Tweed can, if he has any sensitivity, be unaware of its romantic, historical, and literary past. Now for some more practical facts.

Tweed rises in a small spring called Tweed's Well in the southern uplands at the extreme south of Peeblesshire; it flows eastward into the

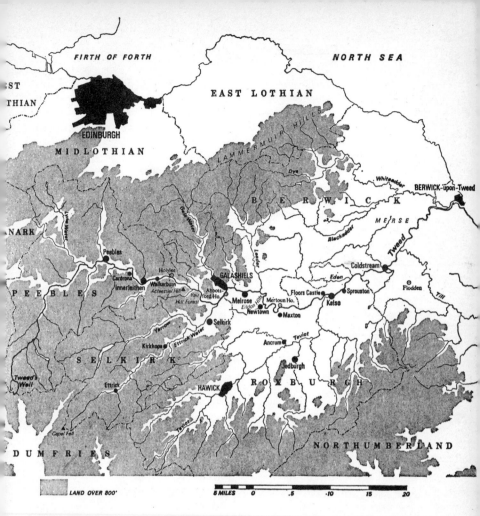

North Sea by the town of Berwick-upon-Tweed, and is, after Tay and Spey, the longest river in Scotland. Were a crow to fly direct from Tweed's Well to Berwick, it would pass over sixty-four miles, but the windings of the river among the Border hills make its length just over ninety-seven.

Because Tweed and Tweedside have been regarded as Scotland's bastion against English conquest, the popular phrase 'north of the Tweed' has come to mean merely 'in Scotland'. Geographically, ethnically, and administratively (as applying to the divergent legal systems of England and Scotland), this is far from correct.

Owing to the fact that the once outstanding port of Berwick changed hands forcibly between England and Scotland no fewer than thirteen times, and to the present anomalous system by which Berwick and its environs lie outside Berwickshire and Scotland, the last two miles of

13

Tweed flow to the sea through English ground. Above this English possession of Tweed, the river does indeed for sixteen miles act as a border between England and Scotland until it passes above Coldstream, where it retreats into its native land and becomes for its upper seventy-nine miles very much a Scottish river. Leaving aside the two miles in England, it will be seen, then, that only for about sixteen miles does the phrase 'north of the Tweed' strictly mean 'in Scotland'. For the first seventy-nine miles, 'south of the Tweed' (if such a phrase exists) would comprehend a large area of the most characteristically Scottish part of our Border country. But one example will suffice. Abbotsford, lying between Galashiels and Melrose, is on the south bank of Tweed. Is it conceivable that Sir Walter would have built the house he so passionately yearned for, worked for, and died in on any but Scottish soil?

Tweed rises at 1,500 feet above sea-level, and its drainage basin, contributed to partly from England as well as from Scotland, extends over an area of 1,870 square miles, again in this respect surpassed in Scotland only by Tay.

The scenic charm of Tweed is its own. To call it a Lowland river would be unfair, for it passes by many hills that would in England seem considerable; yet it lacks the majestic tumble, flow, and fall of many rivers north and west of the Highland line. Our forefathers would have called it much less 'picturesque' (a favourite word of theirs) than the rivers Tay or Dee. It is not as wild as they, and is more pastoral. True, it begins in upper Tweedsmuir in bare wild hills for fifteen miles; but thereafter it flows through cultivated land and by many Border towns that have long been of importance – three of them are associated strongly with the making of the world-famous cloth of Tweed.

Peebles, Innerleithen, Walkerburn, Galashiels, Melrose (where in the ruined abbey grounds the heart of Robert Bruce, king and saviour of Scotland, is buried in a hidden place), Newton St Boswells, Maxton, Kelso, Coldstream; and Berwick, which, though in England, is essentially a Tweed town of importance – all these proclaim that a vivid human life has long congregated and still congregates by Tweed. None of your wild Highland desolateness here! Its numerous towers and castles do, however, speak of the adventurous past. 'Picturesque' or not, Tweed combines much that is best of the Lowland scene with a hint of Highland grandeur further north. To enter Scotland by way of the Tweed valley is a splendidly comprehensive introduction to our country.

Tweed is richly fed by tributaries, both river and burn – perhaps more richly fed by well-known waters than any other river in Scotland. Leaving aside the River Till, which joins Tweed by running only over English soil, there is the Whiteadder, with its own tributary, the

Blackadder, well-known to trout anglers; the Teviot; Gala Water; Ettrick Water (itself contributed to by Yarrow Water, famous in song and legend); Eden Water; and Lyne Water and many other smaller streams. Of these we select for special mention here only Whiteadder, Teviot, and Ettrick. They will be dealt with specially when we come to angling. A word or two, however, must be said about these three as apart from angling: their sources, surroundings, quality, and where they join the greater stream that carries them to the sea.

The Whiteadder rises at 1,100 feet in East Lothian and pursues its course through the Lammermuir Hills into Berwickshire, with which it is mainly associated for its thirty-four miles of length. Just before entering Tweed, it passes through about a mile of English soil immediately above Berwick. In the Lammermuir Hills its surroundings are wild moorland; when it sinks into the flat land of what is known as The Merse, it has a gentler, more pastoral aspect. It was down the valley of the Whiteadder that James IV of Scotland in 1513 led his doomed army against the might of Henry VIII's England to the disaster of the battle of Flodden.

The catastrophic floods of March 1947 temporarily diverted the river, destroying much fish life. Despite this, and the river's easy access from Edinburgh, the landscape has hardly changed. The Whiteadder and its tributaries still provide delightful, if not highly ambitious, trout angling.

Teviot is a southern tributary of Tweed, yet it passes only through Scottish ground – in Roxburghshire. Rising 700 feet above sea-level, and just over twelve miles south-west of the town of Hawick near which it passes, it is fed by various burns or headstreams rising at an altitude of over 1,200 feet. Its immediate scenery is less wild than that of Whiteadder, but it is pleasing and variegated. In its upper reaches there are fastnesses both natural and artificial, reminding one of the fierceness of life in the days of Border warfare.

Ettrick Water is another southern tributary of Tweed that passes entirely over Scottish ground, rising and running throughout in Selkirkshire. It originates at the far south-west of the county on the banks of Capel Fell at an altitude of 1,900 feet. It pursues its winding course over nearly thirty-six miles north-eastward along the borders of Ettrick, Kirkhope, Selkirk, and Galashiels parishes. Descending through this part for 1,500 feet, it presents a lively and at times tumultuous appearance in characteristic Tweedside Border scenery. It has itself a number of tributaries, of which Yarrow Water is the best known. Ettrick Water passes by Selkirk to join Tweed between Galashiels and Abbotsford.

As an angler's water, Tweed is memorable. Of the game fish – salmon, sea-trout, brown trout – Tweed has impressive sport, with perhaps the exception of sea-trout, for, although the river carries a good run of them, many large, they seem to pose certain problems for the angler. But the salmon of Tweed, spread throughout an angling year from the beginning of February to the last day of November, provide magnificent sport, and the brown trout of Tweed, running to average weights that are second only to those of the Don in Scottish trout-river fishings, provide sport throughout the whole fishable length of the river, and for a good part of the trout-fishing season, which lasts from April until the end of September.

Tweed has other fish that are often the subject of debate between game fishers and those who take a wider view of fishing and include sport with coarse fish. In its lower reaches, from Kelso to the sea, Tweed carries stocks of roach, some dace, and some chub. There may well be other species, and one might predict pike and perch, but little is known of the figures for these fish. In the recent past, anglers from England have been allowed to fish certain parts of the lower Tweed for these 'coarse' fish, and some clubs have been able to cooperate with the Tweed commissioners by helping to net out and carry south to their own waters some of the roach that shoal in the slower pools of the lower river.

A special mention must be made of the grayling. Both lower and middle Tweed and several of the tributaries – including Teviot, Ettrick, and (to name two of the smaller tributaries) Lyne and Leader – have stocks of grayling. The grayling is an anomalous fish, by family a game fish – a salmonid with an adipose fin; but it is a coarse fish in appearance and by its seasons. Grayling spawn in spring, as roach do, and they are often caught by anglers in late spring or early summer, when trout fly fishing is at its best. Against the trout in the peak of their condition, the grayling, not yet recovered from spawning, are insipid creatures, discoloured and weak, and at times laughably easy to catch. Later in the year, however (in late summer, autumn, and winter, when the grayling is at its peak), the fish is a very worthwhile object of angling pursuit. November grayling fishers on Teviot trot a small worm down glides and gentle runs, and take large numbers of grayling of the pound class. Fly fishers in mild late summer weather may find that the 'trout' rise they are covering yields a grayling of over a pound. Whether it is a curse or a blessing for the grayling to complement the trout stock in Tweed and its tributaries, is under constant debate. Those who would have the grayling exterminated point out that the limited total food supply for trout is depleted by them. More seriously, they accuse grayling of gorging trout and salmon spawn. Not very much is gained

A selection of artificial flies: LEFT TO RIGHT Waddington Elverine (Thunder and Lightning), Yellow dog; Shrimp Fly, Hairy Mary; Kingfisher, Esmond Drury Logie, Green Highlander; Parker tube Hairy Mary, Teal Blue and Silver, Bucktail and Green; Stoat's Tail and Orange, Grouse and Claret.

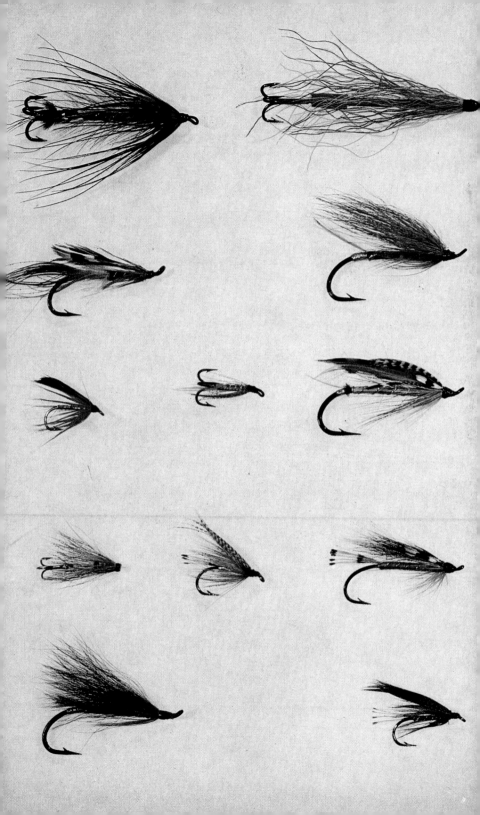

with the riposte by some game fishers that trout eat salmon spawn also. Logically this would lead to a river policy that tried to alter the balance of the stocks of Tweed towards salmon only. As a working compromise, grayling fishing in the winter months is encouraged by some clubs, and anglers are asked to kill all the grayling they hook.

The salmon of Tweed, like those of other prolific rivers, are difficult to classify in 'runs'. Traditionally one talks about spring, summer, and autumn runs, but anyone who has fished Tweed early and late knows how run merges into run and season into season with a richness that few rivers know.

If you were to fish on lower Tweed in February or March to enjoy the spring salmon fishing, you might hook small clean springers of eight or nine pounds, and occasionally you might add to the bag a magnificent spring salmon of the sixteen- to twenty-pound class. The larger springer is rare, and fish of the twenty- to thirty-pound mark are striking catches in spring. To some, the smaller size of Tweed springers is a drawback, and we have heard of Tay fishers who have referred to this class of spring salmon as 'tiddlers'. Some Tweed spring fly fishers do little to improve their sport with these small springers, fishing with rods of from fourteen to sixteen feet, heavy sinking lines, and, where permissible, heavily leaded tube flies and even lead shot pinched on to the cast. Deep fishing is necessary for springers in the cold waters of the 'fly only' fortnight in early February, but one feels that the dredging tackle used by some anglers defeats the whole idea of sport with the graceful little springers for which the lower Tweed is famous.

In spring, the angler who is not well advised by his boatman or ghillie might have difficulty in identifying the fish he catches as fresh, clean fish or something else. Taking as our starting-point the most obvious unclean fish, the kelt, we could describe a scale of cleanness of fish encountered on Tweed in spring. The kelt is the spawned salmon identified by its lean appearance, disproportionately large head, and ragged fins, its sore, distended vent and maggot-ridden gills. But some Tweed kelts mend well after spawning, and a bright, tinny silver appearance can make the inexperienced angler wonder whether his catch is clean (and therefore legally takable) or technically unclean. With true kelts – that is, fish that have shed their spawn – this is an open-and-shut case, but real perplexity can, for instance, result from landing a Tweed 'kipper'. The fish may be of twelve pounds, and silvery and clean, although it may have a distinctly larger head than the springer. There might be a bit of a kype showing. The fish may be full and high in the back and full and rounded in the belly. It is not emaciated, may have no gill parasites, and in some cases may even have sea-lice on its flanks, indicating that the fish has recently run up from salt water. But the fish is heavy with spawn. It is clearly making a

Summer salmon rise to the fly on Whirls Pool, River Tweed, near Melrose.

B

spawning run, and given a month or so might well have spawned and become a kelt. But as an unbroken fish, fresh from the sea when caught, it has not spawned. Some anglers return these fish as a matter of principle; others kill them, for they are fresh, admirable salmon. We cannot debate the finer legal points of this situation; we merely note that, on the scale of freshness, this anomalous fish is a common catch in early spring.

In all probability, Tweed spring 'kippers' are very late autumn fish or winter salmon of a distinct group. We have often seen clean cock and hen salmon of exactly this description taken in late November. Who is to deny that this remarkable river could carry an 'autumn' run of clean, mature salmon throughout the short close season, and present the angler with an autumn tail-end that in February merges with the beginning of the rod fishings of spring?

On most salmon rivers spring produces unspawned hen fish, but Tweed seems to yield a rather larger number than we have encountered, for example, on Tay. These hens, for reasons best known to themselves, have not shed their ova in winter when there was opportunity. They may be caught in spring still full and probably dropping back towards the estuary with the kelts. If left alone, they would probably absorb their unshed ova back into their systems and return again to the river with a future run to spawn naturally. In the hands of some anglers on Tweed their future is quite different. Some take these thwarted matrons as legitimate fish, and in the past some difficulty (and some considerable embarrassment) has arisen when commissioners or their bailiffs have arrived to find that a 'baggot', after its efforts in the fight or perhaps as a result of being carried up the bank, has started to 'spawn' posthumously. The angler is now in possession of an 'unclean' fish and is liable to prosecution.

In November Tweed produces a run of small grilse-like salmon of five to seven pounds, very silvery and with tinges of blue, and these autumn grilse produce excellent sport for late fly fishers. In spring these 'winter grilse' are often still in the river, and it appears to some that they are returning to the sea after wintering in fresh water. We doubt the validity of this argument. Having seen numbers of these fish in November, and again in Tweed and Teviot the following spring, and having examined them, we incline to the view that these are very early springers, which will remain in Tweed for almost a year before spawning with the other springers. We suspect that they move up in the spring floods to the remotest burn, and lie under banks and in holes in the bottom until the year turns towards autumn again, and their milts and ova mature, and they find a mate and spawn. The milts of these little winter grilse in spring are tiny, like those of springers, but the fish themselves may have lost something of their original brilliantly fresh appearance and turned during the winter into a deeper silver-blue. On Teviot we have seen four of these fish caught in spring on one short beat inside an hour. What splendid little fish they were! The locals call these fish 'blue backs', and they prize them as excellent catches of the spring. Some other rivers also have these 'blue backs', but not in such numbers as Tweed, Teviot, and Ettrick.

Tweed produces more fish between September and November, and again between February and the end of March, than it does at any time during the summer. One could argue that Tweed showed a kind of inversion of the legal view of the salmon fishing season. The law permits salmon fishing from early spring to late autumn. Tweed seems to carry its main runs from autumn right through the winter to the end of the next spring – that is, right through the close season. There are summer fish, of course. Fish run the Tweed in June, July, and August, and some beats enjoy sport with fish of ten to fifteen pounds whenever there is a freshet in summer to bring fish in from the sea. There are also the grilse – those sprightly adolescents of the salmon world. Such little salmon running in July and August may weigh six pounds and populate certain pools with fighting shoals, which can give superb greased-line sport. We have heard of thirty in a day in the pools of the Floors Castle stretch of Tweed above Kelso, and we know of some delighted ticket fishers on the Peebles Association water who have found grilse as far upstream as that by early August. But the commercial netting stations take the bulk of the grilse runs.

The most exciting part of the Tweed salmon season, however, is the autumn. This late-season fishing begins in September on the lower river, and reaches the Peebles district either later that month or in October and November, according to water-height and overhead conditions. Broadly speaking, the coming of the autumn fish coincides with the Tweed rule that there shall be 'fly only' fishing for salmon from the 15th September onwards.

Autumn fish can run large on Tweed – eighteen to thirty pounds; and from the autumn run all the really big individual salmon of Tweed have come. The reports of the net catches on the estuary confirm this. They often report a fish of twenty-five pounds as their biggest from February up to mid-September (when they stop fishing), but by the end of November many anglers will have had fish heavier than this, and others will have been seen, or hooked and lost, weighing ten pounds heavier.

Autumn fly fishing for this wonderful run of late fish is a kind of institution on Tweed. Some anglers fish Tweed only at this time. Others fish throughout the year, longing for the colder days of autumn when the larches of the Yair are golden brown, and the river, after a high wind, is full of floating leaves, 'yellow and black and hectic red'.

The river is also full of fish that are yellow and black and hectic red – the stale fish of earlier runs. Springers long tarnished by the stay in fresh water lie beside not-so-stained later summer fish and, almost miraculously, beside great silver fish fresh from the North Sea. These October and November days are memorable on Tweed. The big rods are out in force; the talk is all of large tube flies, Garry Dog, Thunder, or concoctions of one's own fancy. In the colder waters of November the flies are well sunk, and we have often on a bleak November day felt more at one with the scene through the sense of touch – the weight of the rod and the pressure of the stream on the line – than by the sense of sight. In November the air can be full of leaping salmon, disturbed fish, edgy fish, running fish, or just devil-may-care leaping fish, and the experienced salmon fisher pays little attention to them. The showy fish is not likely to be the taker. It is the brace of big fish, eighteen pounds or more, which have slipped up over the gravel bar into the pool at Ashiestiel, or Holylee, or Cardrona, that makes the fishing worth while. These fish take firmly, run hard, and fight with all the excitement of big salmon at any season of the year. We would say that they often show more dogged fighting power than any other salmon we could name.

Every river dictates the angler's best methods. The character of the pools, the degree of bank wooding, the amount of weed, and a host of other factors channel the fisher's techniques into a method typical of the river. Tweed is gentle for the most part, and above all it is wadable. The pools of its middle and higher reaches, from Galashiels up, are famous for their gravel bottoms, their evenly graded streams, and their generosity in not swallowing anglers. In these pools the autumn fish are sought by an ever increasing number who take to the water in breast waders, wield a long rod, and in the course of a day exercise more muscles more vigorously than many a farmer in the fields behind them. You can feel exhausted by a hard day in Tweed with the big rod in a fair wind, wading a stream that, though reasonably safe, is as tiring as any you have ever experienced.

Lower Tweed lords it in boats over broad pools. But Tweed boat fishing is active in a way that Tay boat fishing for salmon is not. On Tay one harls the bait, or (more accurately) the boat harls the bait, trailing it behind and dangling the offering over the lies as the boat is moved systematically across and down the pools. On Tweed you generally cast the fly or bait from the boat. The typical Tweed boat is broad in the beam, with an angler's seat rising like a mushroom from the stern. For a sight of this kind of fishing at its best, go to the riverside at Kelso and watch the Junction Pool being fished. The Teviot joins the Tweed at this point, and a superb pool is formed, with a fast stream pouring down from the Kelso cauld, merging with the Teviot stream

22

on the right side of a long wooded island and, losing pace, ambling into an apron of gentle streamy water that thins before flowing under the arches of the road bridge. The boat on this pool is rowed, and the working of the boat keeps it more or less stationary. Alternatively, on pools like Floors water, the boat may be controlled by a rope from the bank, and the boatman walks, rope in hand, down the side of the water as the boat otters out into the river and the angler casts his fly over the lies as he goes.

Tweed did not invent the tube fly, but has embraced it. The large tubes of Tweed are often gaudy, like the Garry Dog, with yellow and red hair mixed; local variants of every hue use hair from goats, cows' tails, deer, or girl-friends. Some of the most successful flies in this class are tied on a forged steel shank with a treble hook attached. These, of course, are not tubes but Waddington Elverine lures. Many a salmon falls to one of them on Tweed in Hairy Mary, Thunder, or Garry pattern. Some of the more successful local 'Waddingtons' on Tweedside are distinctly prawn-like in the water, with trailing fronds of pink and cream hair over mohair-dubbed bodies.

It is curious to compare today's flies with those recommended by Scrope in the eighteen-forties in his delightful book *Days and Nights of Salmon Fishing on Tweed*. There, traditional single hook flies were described and illustrated. Meg in her Braws was a fly with wings of bittern, a light brown turkey-like pattern and colour. The body was a brown hairy one of mixed wool and bullock's hair; a yellow throat was tied in and a yellow tail added. The whole fly, with its gold twist glinting through a forest of dullish natural colours, looked more like Meg in her hodden claes than in her braws. It has been argued that the Irish influence never touched the Tweed at all in its development of salmon flies. The Irish tied flaming reds, glaring blues and greens, and indescribable exotic blazes of colour that, in the Victorian and Edwardian days, greatly influenced Scottish fly fishing. Today's Tweed flies look like a latter-day Irish invasion, although there is still a strong tendency on Tweed to use black in the fly body even with brighter plumage and hair elsewhere on the lure.

In trout fishing, Tweed has bred a remarkable school of anglers, the fathers of which were men like Stoddart and Stewart. Stoddart was one of the inventors of the dry fly, and, if he did not actually precede Halford and the chalk-stream anglers who raised such a cult of dry-fly fishing in southern England in the nineteenth century, he must at least be credited with making an independent discovery. Stoddart, like others of his generation, was a wielder of the long trout rod (twelve feet was common), and he practised the remarkable art of fishing upstream wet flies. It is still widely in use. The angler, wading upstream and carefully reading his water as he goes, casts his flies rapidly over likely lies, searching the water for trout. He moves his rod up to take in the slack caused by the stream and, like someone never at rest, lays his flies gently and accurately on likely water, watching for the slightest sign of a rise. Out of this upstream style of fishing evolved Stoddart's floating fly fishing of the middle eighteen-forties. Stewart, writing later than Stoddart, remained an exponent of the upstream wet fly, and crystallized the art in his now famous book, which is still prescribed reading for trout fishers.

It was on lower Tweed at Sprouston that Canon William Greenwell invented the Greenwell's Glory. There never was such a popular fly. Today almost every angler fishing wet flies has a Greenwell somewhere on his cast. Dry-fly fishers use it throughout the year. Sea-trout are not averse to it, and, although it is not a salmon fly, we should hardly be surprised to find that it has addicts who dress it large for salmon. What is it that makes the Greenwell so outstanding a fly, not only on Tweed but wherever trout are to be fished? The dressing is simplicity itself. The wing is starling or inside blackbird primary; the body is yellow silk, or sometimes khaki silk ribbed with gold wire; the hackle is furnace (sometimes called coch-y-bondhy), and the tail, if one is demanded, may be fibres of pheasant or, in some variants, a yellow tag.

There is a standing joke about Greenwell's Glory. A novice angler reported a 'hatch of Greenwells' and was ridiculed because the fly is a fancy pattern, technically; it does not imitate any one variety of fly at a stage in its hatching. But the story of how Greenwell's Glory was created should wipe the smile off the face of ridicule. The Greenwell was tied in 1854 at the request of Canon Greenwell by James Wright, a famous Tweedside fly-tier, in an attempt to imitate what the Canon described as a fly that trout at Sprouston were taking in preference to the March Brown. Greenwell and Wright succeeded in making an imitation, not really of a specific Olive, but of a whole range of Olive duns. Used wet, as originally intended, the Greenwell represents the nymph of such attractive flies as the large dark Olive of April, which trout feed on so avidly. Fished, at the other extreme, as a tiny dry spider, the Greenwell can cover fish rising to the smuts, those minute flies of June, and kill them well. This last achievement is undoubtedly connected with the hackle, whose light points become virtually invisible, leaving the tiny blob of their dark roots as the imitation.

The Tweed trout fisher has various very well known flies, some of which can be traced back to notable Tweed fishers like Stoddart, Younger, Aitken, and Stewart. Such flies include Grey Hen and Rusty, Badger Spider, Greenwell, Blae and Black, and two spiders of the Stewart variety, Black Spider and Blae Spider, tied with suitable bodies in plain silk or ribbed.

The biggest trout of Tweed are probably in the reaches between

Kelso and Melrose. Here the trout have least competition from coarse fish, but the weight of water ensures protection. The May rise to assorted Olives on a water like Mertoun can be staggering. The June evening rise to smuts can be infuriating. You can take May fish on well-presented dry flies or on the carefully fished upstream wet fly, but you cannot do anything with June smutters. Their food is microscopic. You try to fish a small enough Badger Spider dressed parachute-style, hoping that the high translucency of the feathers will ensure that the barest speck of an imitation will remain. But smuttering trout are so often preoccupied with what amounts to surface 'soup' that it breaks an angler's heart to see the trout of Tweed so uncatchable. Early mornings tend to yield fish more easily in smutting season. Evenings are tremendous for activity, but desolate with frustration.

Clearly, to characterize fully the trouting of the Tweed would be to write at length on all the tactics of Scottish trout fishing. Tweed has enough trout fishing on its ninety-odd miles to keep an angler happy for a lifetime. In recent years there has been a careful stocking programme on its middle and upper reaches, and some attempt is being made to improve waters that the increase in ticket fishers has somewhat depleted. There is still, however, a tendency for anglers to take home far too many small trout from the Peeblesshire waters – fish that a stricter discipline would allow to reach ten or twelve ounces before being killed. Happily, there is now no trout spinning on Tweed, and, even if cannibals might be there, salmon flies and baits certainly account for them. Worming is allowed after the spring hunger period is over. All in all, splendid trout are available for the ticket fisher, particularly if he keeps off Saturdays. If the smaller stream is looked for, the Teviot offers ticket trout fishing from the Hawick and Upper Teviotdale Angling Association, which covers over 100 miles of Teviot and tributary trouting. Similarly, fat trouting in the Whiteadder is available by the day from the Whiteadder Angling Association. In this system of streams and burns the Blackadder should not be forgotten. Its trout are said to excel those of the Whiteadder, which it joins. We have seen baskets of good trout from each, but Blackadder, as a smaller water, shows up exceedingly well.

In short, for the trout fisher, Tweed is possibly the finest centre in extent and, to a large degree, in quality. The salmon fishing, particularly in autumn, can be outstanding; and, for the man able to take fishings on the fat lower beats of Tweed in the spring, summer, or autumn, sport with the larger game fish can be exceptional. Stocks of fish in Tweed are said to be the largest in Europe, and it is not surprising that, when salmon disease breaks out, as it has done several times in the last century, the losses seem alarmingly high. The outbreak of U.D.N. (ulcerative dermal necrosis) that occurred after the spring of

1967 took a considerable toll of fish, and was still evident in the spring of 1971.

Like any really big river system, with its variety of pools and streams, caulds and dams, major and minor tributaries, Tweed is too large to describe in one passage. Let us merely say that, even at its worst, it is incomparably exciting as a game fisher's stream, and at its best is a trout and salmon fisher's dream.

THE TWEED BURNS, AND BURN FISHING

About 100 burns from Scottish soil empty themselves into Tweed either directly or by contributing to tributaries or tributaries of tributaries. The Tweed valley is richer than any other locality in Scotland in that particularly native water, the burn. The number of burns in Scotland may not be incalculable, but they are at least beyond our power to enumerate. The burn, both as a feature of the inland Scottish water-scape and as the source of many a Scottish angler's first efforts in his sport, must be touched on somewhere in this survey. Where better than in this chapter on the richly burn-fed Tweed? We shall therefore now deal with all the burns of Scotland, named and unnamed.

'Burn' is given in the *Oxford English Dictionary* as an Old English word meaning 'A spring, fountain; a stream or river. In later use: A small stream or brook'. Old English or not, it is now purely Scottish and lingers for English usage only in place-names such as Bournemouth. In Scotland it is used by all classes of speakers to mean a small stream, and, if we were to seek a definition of its smallness, we might add that at certain seasons of the year a man could jump or even step over some parts of nearly all Scottish burns. A burn is for us a burn whether it glides through the pastoral landscapes of Fife or Ayrshire, or falls precipitously from a Highland mountainside. In general, however, the words 'a Scottish burn' evoke an image of surrounding hills and moorland, whether in the Highlands or Lowlands. Such are the burns of the Tweed valley.

Even among those small tributaries of Tweed there is diversity. Some are pastoral burns joining Tweed near the centre of its course; others, at the head of the river in the wild circumstances of Tweedsmuir, are moorland burns. But those that most nearly accord with the popular image are found running to Tweed in its lower reaches, and from the Lammermuir Hills, by which the river passes before it enters the North Sea. A few join Tweed direct; most reach it by falling into river tributaries such as the Whiteadder and Whiteadder's own tributaries, the Dye and the Blackadder. Since we must here take one group of Tweed burns as representative not only of this famous valley but of all Scotland, we choose those of Lammermuir. We do this for three reasons.

The first is the typical scenic charm of these burns; the second is the high quality of pure burn-fishing that they offer; the third is that, though apparently remote and undisturbed, they are easily accessible from Edinburgh and all east Border towns.

The Lammermuirs rise to 1,750 feet; but they attain their stature in a way quite different from all other large hill groups in Scotland. They rise gently, so that in a car or even on foot the ascent is almost imperceptible; a cyclist could traverse all the highest Lammermuir hill roads without once getting off – an impossible, or at least a highly disagreeable, feat among most other Scottish hill groups.

This slow ascent, descent, and ascent again of the Lammermuirs gives them a soft beauty; yet there is nothing pastoral about them. The moment you enter the Lammermuir territory, you are in moorland scenery entirely heather-clad, with a few farmhouses, few but direct roads, and nearly as few pathways through the heather. The sound of the cock grouse is the commonest bird-cry here; and you might walk for miles among the lesser byways without meeting another person. Yet all this is but little over twenty miles from Edinburgh.

In such circumstances, then, the many Lammermuir burns run to sink into Tweed's northern shore. They run between banks of heather, with here and there a waterfall, here and there a pool, and occasionally a long but visible glide. There is no grandeur about them, as in some Highland streams – no silvery flashing falls from the heights, no foaming swirls. But no lover of moving inland water could resist their purely visual appeal.

As with all moorland waters, they are peaty, but are not so much so as to present the tannin-stained appearance you will find in the waters of such peat-Saharas as the Rannoch Moor in the Highlands. The angler will note with approval the freedom from excessive peatiness. The trout that lives in peaty waters loses much of his attractive look, and is so deeply stained that he might have spent his life in a teapot. Indeed, for size, most really peaty trout could get into a teapot.

The sight of the Lammermuir burns will delight any Scottish angler, if only because they will arouse memories of boyhood. Most of us began our trout fishing in burns; and, as the decades pass and leave the sixties behind them, we look back upon the burns of our boyhood with affection and 'find again our fourteenth year'.

But it is not only Scottish anglers recalling their youth who should look with interest at the waters of Lammermuir. To the sixth sense of every true angler the burns here positively proclaim the presence of trout. They are there in large quantities, and often in quality, in size, and of a strength not to be despised.

All the same, most trout that you see flickering about in the pools and glides, those that come most greedily to the fly or worm (the only alternatives in burn fishing), will be little fellows, some scarcely more than fingerlings. If they are lightly hooked, they should as soon as possible be shaken back into the water. If not lightly hooked, they should be removed with as little touch of the scalding human hand as possible, to avoid damage to the protective slime on their bodies.

The seasoned angler may smile when we add that the burn fisher is at liberty to keep the quarter-pounder and perhaps the three-ouncer, but nothing under. He will smile with less comprehension when we admit to a certain pleasure in striking and hooking even these little trout that we put back again. They are a sign of life in these waters, and, if the day be bright and sunny and the waters low, they present a tribute to your skill in keeping out of sight and in casting the line accurately upstream into these heather-hung rivulets. Moreover their presence and activity lead you to hope that their bigger brothers are there somewhere hidden under bank or stone, and not yet in evidence only because they have learnt to be more cautious.

Indeed, in all the Tweed burns that we have fished from boyhood, but particularly in the Lammermuir burns, these bigger brothers have always proved to be there, and with patience and skill they can be lured to the hook. Where do they come from? Are they native fingerlings who have stayed in these upper waters, and grown large on the plentiful trout food that comes down to them from the moorland banks, or on the flies that in summer abound there? The answer in most instances is No.

The bigger trout, the distinctly 'keepable' burn trout, and certainly those of the kind that would be keepable in any larger waters, may have been hatched here, but they have gone downstream in middle life or youth, to be tempted back by special elements, and have remained here for a while and in hiding. These elements include the breeding instinct that leads them upstream in autumn. But this is unusual; for nearly all trout, having laid and fertilized their spawn, drop back again in winter to the deeper, more spacious river waters that provide their true living conditions. Some few that have laid and fertilized in the burns may have stayed, but the majority by far have been drawn temporarily upstream by the lure of spring or summer spates, when all the waters on the hill-sides are swollen with several days' rain.

These spates fill the burns with what is to all trout the most deliciously fresh food – worms: wriggling worms, not yet drowned, that have been newly washed out of the banks from their native soil; large lob-worms; brandling worms from dung-heaps, yellow and red; ordinary red worms; grubs; and especially that succulent yet to us disgusting creature the docken-grub, which lives in the roots of thick vegetable matter by the waterside; and other grubs and insects of all kinds.

The spates cause all this tempting food to be discharged from the burns either directly into Tweed or into its tributaries. In the river or rivers, the good-sized trout that has any sense does not wait lazily for the feast to flow into his mouth, but pushes upstream and up-burn finding fresher and still more delicious food as he goes. Then the spate stops, the burn falls to normal; yet he may feel inclined to stay where he is, for he may be in a fair-sized pool near which he may very well have been hatched. Perhaps infant memories haunt him. At any rate he is in comfortable circumstances, with a tolerable degree of worm and grub food coming down, and, even on the brightest day and at lowest water, plenty of floating or drowned flies, which he can snatch at with greater authority than that of the contemptible fingerlings and fish under a quarter-pound that are his only rivals.

But he has seen the great world of Tweed or Whiteadder, or both. He has learnt that the brown trout of whatever size has many enemies – the most formidable of these are men. This pool or glide may be comfortable enough, and sustaining him with its food, but it lacks the depths to which he had resorted in the rivers. He then becomes adept at finding large stones and shelving banks to hide him. He is clever at disappearing in these comparative shallows, and does not dart about like the foolish fingerlings and quarter-pounders. However cautiously you may approach one of these burn pools when the spate has fallen, you will never see him disporting himself with his juniors.

'Nothing but minnow-trout here!' exclaims the visitor as he comes to one of these pools and sees it alive with darting little shapes. But you know better; you know that, in nearly every one of these Lammermuir pools, at least one larger and definitely keepable trout lies hidden. He and his companions of his own kind can run up to well over a pound; sometimes really sizable brown trout are caught in these moorland pools. There is a peculiar pleasure in landing them in such unusual conditions, especially as one goes burn fishing as a rule without a landing-net.

The easiest method of burn fishing is to use worm or native bait when the spate is rising, the sooner the better and certainly before the full flood has come or is falling. In these circumstances it is almost impossible not to make a killing of keepable burn trout. It is not so much a crude as an elementary form of trout fishing. But occasionally it can be enjoyable and, in spite of its discomfort, rejuvenating. The spates themselves, even among the Lammermuirs, are few and irregular. If you happen to be there when one is rising, go out and enjoy it.

We recall just such an occasion that happened in the year before these words were written. One of us was staying at a Border hotel by the Lammermuirs after a full night's plump of rain.

'You ought to go up into the hills and try the burns with worms,' said the proprietor, indicating on the map a rivulet that looked no larger than an inch or so of thread.

'I haven't gone small burn fishing with a worm since I was a boy.' Was this but a defence against the need to dig for worms and climb the hill-side in the still driving rain? Perhaps, but it was countered by: 'Be a boy again'.

The worms were dug for and entinned in moss, inadequate waterproofs put on, and wind and rain and hills encountered. In the end, wet to the skin, cold but happy, the angler returned with not only a creel but a capacious fishing-jacket pocket stuffed with sporting – and how edible! – brown trout.

Something between forty and fifty years, including two world wars, had been blown away in the wind and rain and at the burn-side. The man had been a boy again, such was the gift of this rare experience – and its essence lay in that very rarity.

A less elementary, indeed comparatively skilful, form of burn fishing is to use the fly upstream when the spate has fallen and retreated, yet not to the extent of reducing the burn to its normal midsummer size. The keepable and larger trout will still be there, but will have been gorged with worm and grub. Their languid appetites or curiosity, however, may still be aroused by the sight of a small but very naturallooking fly skittering across or just underneath the surface.

It is better to cast up-burn, but, if you keep decently out of sight, downstream can be effective. The skill lies in the approach, and in casting the line from a distance to hit the narrow waters at exactly the right place between the banks of heather. Once a burn trout has gone for your half-wet, half-dry fly, striking is unnecessary. He has taken you or he hasn't. The still post-spate but quickly running water, and the trout's desire to dash for safety, will do the trick.

But there is one skilful and arduous form of burn fishing that offers unique rewards. This is to fish imperatively upstream with a small worm on a bright summer's day (or long summer evening, if you want to make it slightly easier) when the water is low.

The skill is twofold. First you must push to its utmost limit the business of keeping out of sight. You must scan the proposed territory from afar, decide in advance on your pools or small runs of water, and then approach each spot from well downstream with exaggerated caution, if necessary kneeling or on 'all threes'. Second, you must take what is for burn fishing a long line and cast it so that the bait falls into the exact spot without the smallest splash – and do all this with so slow, so easy, yet so large a gesture that the worm does not come off the hook in casting. As the worms that are all but essential for this bright day, low water, and upstream burn fishing are brandlings, or of the small, odorous, soft-fleshed kind, this is a most delicate point.

The pools in any burn worth fishing in bright summer day conditions never really become shallow, however tenuous the trickles of water that connect them. They can indeed retain a respectable depth, but their surfaces, though moving, are placid. It is no good just flinging a worm somewhere near the top of the pool, even if you have kept well out of sight; the splash will alarm. You have to hit an exact target from as far below as you can possibly get; and that target is the tiny waterfall that feeds the pool. Only then, to the watchful eye of the keepable trout that has stayed here since the last spate, will it seem that his food is approaching him in a natural way. Tender worms, as keepable trout well know, don't drop splashily out of the sky into the body of the pool; they come through the food-hatch of a very small waterfall perhaps only inches wide. You have to hit that hatch with a bait that is liable to come off at the slightest jerk.

Never seek to make your cast easier by putting even the smallest lead pellet above the hook. The weight of the fragile bait alone must carry your cast. If you succeed in hitting the food-hatch, the force of the water will push the bait at once to the bottom of the pool, to be carried naturally towards you by the lower currents, which are the most mobile. In so doing it will also naturally pass any deep-hidden sheltering stones, or be sucked by the side of shelving banks where the bigger fellows lie.

As the bait approaches you, keep as much as possible of the line out of the water; and, if it suddenly stops, do not strike or even faintly pull. If it has not been arrested by a stone, stick, or weed, but has been taken, you will be rewarded by the sight of the line moving cautiously but steadily sideways or, better still, upstream. This sight of your line moving against the water is the most agreeable in all burn fishing; indeed, it has a high place in all the pleasures offered by angling in Scottish inland waters. Savour it, partly for pleasure, partly because it is wise to do so. Something has taken your tender-skinned little worm into his mouth, and he is making away with it to a deeper, remoter place, maybe to chew and swallow it. Let him for a brief space, and then strike – but strike gently.

He may turn out to be anything: a fingerling who has audaciously taken a vantage-place in the deeps beneath the waterfall. But, if you have kept clean out of sight, managed your line well, and hit the target dead centre, the odds are that he will be something worthwhile: a half-pounder, a pounder, or a fish well over a pound.

Of course, even in a really good-sized burn pool, there will be little or no chance of playing him in the sense of letting your line run out so that there is much sound from the reel, but you will have great fun in keeping control of him as he dashes about the pool. And control is necessary. He knows deep recesses and obstacles that you cannot see.

You must keep as tight a line on him as you dare until you've got him to the bank or under the net – supposing you have taken one with you.

If you lose him, even after a dash lasting only a few seconds, the pool will have been temporarily ruined. For a few hours there will be no point in trying it again. Not only will the one you lost be in a sulky rage, but every other inhabitant of the pool will have been put on his guard.

Such are the pleasures, by no means all humble ones, of burn fishing. They may be enjoyed in every part of the mainland and, to a lesser degree, on many of our islands. They are pleasures that can be gustfully enjoyed by a lad not yet in his 'teens, and by those far older who have still the energy to scramble and stalk through heather and about hills.

M.McL., W.B.C.

Chapter Two

THE BORDER ESK

An angler's impression of a river depends partly on the way he first comes to fish its waters. I approached the Border Esk from Teviotdale. This has for me created an anomaly; I can now drive over the Esk at Longtown, near its meeting with the head of the Solway, and hardly identify the river with its middle reaches at Canonbie and Langholm. Thinking of the Esk like this, biased by its fishings, is an example of what I have called 'fisherman's Scotland', a country as much of the mind as of physical fact.

Teviot and Esk are not really alike as fishing waters. One flows east into Tweed, the other west into the Solway Firth. Teviot is a salmon river with a splendid head of trout and grayling. Esk is a salmon and sea-trout river; in its middle reaches lie some of the best summer sea-trout waters I know. But it was at a memorable angling club dinner at Hawick that I received my first invitation to fish the Esk near Langholm, and it was at Hawick that I first heard descriptions of the magnificent night fishing for sea-trout that the river could give. Further, every trip I have made since then to fish the river has been by the route that crosses the Teviot at Ancrum, passes through Hawick, and follows the Teviot for some miles west, before picking up the hill burns that flow west to the White Esk and its junction with the Black Esk at Langholm, where the best reaches of the Border Esk begin.

If you were to ask me the colour of the water in the Border Esk, I would say 'gin-clear', but with two reservations. One, that in a summer flood it can run any colour from tea to dark brown porter. Two, that even in the clarity of low summer water the Esk has a suggestion of green in its gin. It is a river that I remember more than any other for the ease with which you can study fish in it. On one of the beats I fish below Langholm, there is a path by the river with a thin screen of bushes shielding you from the fish. At one point you can peer round the end of a bush into the pool beyond. What a sight! Scores of sea-trout lie on the shingle and reach in ranks to your left up into the fast water of the stream, disappearing as the surface cuts off your vision, and to your right they reach in what seems like hundreds to the darker water in the dub of the pool and the glide at its tail. The Esk is a river for seeing fish and, if you care, for counting them. You can approach a pool in the dark, knowing that there are sixty sea-trout and two salmon lying in a certain part of it. Embarrassingly, when conditions are against you, you can fish it for an hour without a take.

Fishing clear water like this at night demands care – almost as much care as a darker, tumbling river would demand in broad daylight. I creep along the banks of the Esk when I am night fishing, and when I wade I do so gingerly. On the Esk, darkness is only a compromise between the impossibility of clear, still daylight fishing and the abandon that sea-trout show at times in night fishing on other waters. The Esk sea-trout respond well to being stalked in the dark, and any angler who wants more than an occasional fish to take his flies should survey his water carefully during the day, and should plan his approaches to the sea-trout streams and pools before the light goes.

In recent years the sea-trout of the Esk have been returning plenti- fully to the river, although U.D.N. has taken a heavy toll. It is some- thing of a surprise to find that 100 years ago they were barely men- tioned by Stoddart. He looked at the Esk with a trout-fisher's eye and seemed to find it a little disappointing. In comparison with Tweed trout in the halcyon days of the nineteenth century, this may be justified. But are we to believe that the recent harvest of sea-trout taken from the river is a fairly new phenomenon? If it is, the credit for the development must go to two things: management of the river, with a careful eye on the pollution problem at Langholm; and a more liberal attitude on the part of Solway netting – again a reflection of management.

Esk also has a name for salmon fishing, both early and late. The earliest spring fishing, and the best, in Scotland has always fallen to east-coast rivers, and some would say that there is no genuine early spring salmon fishing at all on the west-coast waters. A glance at the January and February figures of the Carlisle Eden, and at the growing catches on the Nith under the improved fishings enjoyed there recently, would disprove this. One can detect an upsurge in the spring salmon fishings of Solway, if not on the west coast as a whole, while some eastward-flowing waters are experiencing a recession of the early fishing. Certainly April can be a good month for salmon fishing be- tween Canonbie and Scots Dyke, and I have seen excellent conditions there at Easter for spring fly fishing. I should perhaps mention that it is one of the black marks against the Esk that, on a water splendidly suited to fly fishing, some local clubs allow spinning for spring salmon.

The late autumn fish of the Solway, the 'grey backs' of the area, run the Esk and can provide splendid sport with really big fish in autumn. Fish of over thirty pounds are taken from time to time (a thirty-seven-

A sea-trout is netted at Skipper's Bridge on the Border Esk, near Langholm.

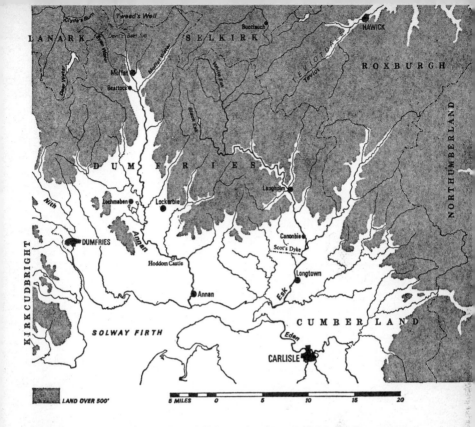

LAND OVER 500'

pounder was the 1970 heavyweight), and a brace of fish in the upper
'teens or mid-twenties of pounds would not be at all unusual in
September or October. In a river with a total course of some forty miles,
fish of this size seem very much larger than the big fish of a mammoth
river like Tay.

The Border Esk fishings are, to my mind, marred by a tradition of
worming. I say this knowing that there is a minority of local anglers
who fish the clear-water worm for sea-trout in a way that ranks as an
art. I have seen one of the Buccleuch keepers fishing clear-water worm
in this way; his was a superb skill, and he demonstrated a very great
knowledge of the water he fished. But, if you look over the bridge just
downstream from Langholm, you will note on the right bank of the
river at the head of that lovely sea-trout pool a ledge of rock. On it I
have seen lines of anglers drowning worms in a way that does little
credit to the splendid fly fishing of their river. Worm fishing can be
anti-sport as well as super-sport. The Esk deserves the latter.

The best sea-trout fishing of the Esk falls in June and July. One
friend of mine has had double figures to his own rod several times; in
recent seasons I have been lucky enough to have two really fat nights
under delightful summer conditions. There have been other nights when

The Irvine House water of the Border Esk sometimes yields large sea-trout.

the Esk, full of fish as it was, has failed to produce sport. I dread clear nights with a bright moon, when the summer sky suddenly chills and the warm river steams all night. In these conditions sea-trout will not rise. I hold that it can never be dark enough, nor still enough, for the night fishing of Esk.

Two or three anglers fishing the Esk have recently been trying out sunk fly fishing for sea-trout in a new way. I have experimented with a sinking line and a small fly fished very deeply and slowly in the gentler tails of the pools. Another angler has found that a sinking tip spliced to his floating line brings tremendous sport, and yet another insists at times on using a heavy fly with a floating line. All three attempts to sink the fly have yielded the same result – much larger fish than average have been taken. Fifty years ago Grimble noted specially that the Esk had produced a sea-trout of five pounds. In the last few years I have heard of six fish heavier than this, and two have been between seven and eight pounds. My own best is just short of five pounds. This slow, deep technique of fishing small sea-trout flies is for the still reaches of the night, when the sea-trout have ceased to take interest in the flies fished near the surface. It is not universally successful, but it is clearly a taker of big fish and a stop-gap method for the doldrums when the Esk, like any other river, appears to rest.

Another technique that I have had great sport with on the Esk belongs to the 'scuttering' fly fished in the late evening for sea-trout. I tie a parachute Kingfisher, about No. 10, to my bob and fish this across the surface in such a way that it leaves a wake. Sea-trout sometimes leap wildly at this fly, and on one evening I had five in quick succession at it. The quiet, hot July evening is the time for this – when sea-trout are moving freely in the tails of the larger pools, making circles rather than wild splashes.

The Border Esk is in a very sheltered valley, and I have occasionally left an east coast that was clothed with haar, at a temperature far too low for evening fishing, to find that the Esk had a still, hot evening that lacked nothing but the nightingale to give it a richness all too seldom found in Scotland. For me it is as delightful a stream for night fishing as one could dream of. It is a liberal water – on occasion a prolific one; and, although its fish may not run to the averages of some larger waters, the Esk, with its two-pounders in streams and pools full of good fishing character, is most memorable.

W.B.C.

Chapter Three

THE ANNAN

Once the Annan was a far better salmon river than the Nith. The tables are now turned, but that is not to say that the Annan has declined. On the contrary, it too has greatly improved in recent years. It is the Nith that has changed, as the chapter on that larger river will show. Annan, however, has in the last forty years changed its pattern of sport. People used to say that it had no spring fish in its waters. Now, from the opening day in February, you are likely to find fresh salmon there. I have seen a bag of three springers taken on the opening day from the Annan – shapely, silvery fish of twelve to sixteen pounds, the harbingers of a whole year's sport.

The coming of springers to the Annan in increasing numbers should not obscure the fact that this river is principally a summer and autumn water with the predictable Solway pattern of runs. Grilse appear in late May, but more fully in late June and July. Summer salmon come up with the floods from late May onwards, and shoals of sea-trout occupy the pools. The 'grey backs' of autumn run Annan too, bringing into it some of the heaviest salmon of the year.

I think of Annan in terms of the middle beat at Hoddom Castle, which I have so much enjoyed fishing. There the river has a gravelly and rocky bottom, with some deep dubs in the pools formed by shelves of the sandstone on the bottom, or by a series of pot-holes that have joined up. This is marvellous sea-trout water. The fish find sanctuary in the deeper parts during the day, and in the evening they range up and down the streamy flats, rising to night flies and providing the best fly-fishing sport of the year. Sea-trout in Annan do not run large, but they may often touch three pounds. In June and July they are fresh and willing takers, but as the season goes on the willing ones are usually the smaller fish – the whitling (or herling) of Solway, bright little trout of some half to three-quarters of a pound. They can be good fun on light tackle, but the larger sea-trout of the earlier part of the summer are superior fish in every way.

Annan has one strange claim to fame. It is a rich river with some deep, slow pools, and in these slower parts chub grow large. The

British record rod-caught chub, a fish of ten pounds eight ounces, came from the Annan. At night, when you are fishing fly for sea-trout, you sometimes catch a chub. I have seen a four-pounder taken in this way. You can often tell that your colleague has hooked a chub, for he will normally express his disappointment by cursing the coarse fish. I remember once hooking a fish on the Duke's Pool at Hoddom and finding it sluggish. I called to my friend, fishing a little way below me in the dark, that I had hooked a chub. What a waste of time! I hauled in the unresisting fish and netted it with little ceremony. It turned out to be a sea-trout of nearly two pounds.

Annan flows through rich country with arable fields on its banks. The principal disadvantage of this is that the river can rise into floods where mud stains the water to the appearance of milky coffee. In spate it becomes (like the Nith) a wormer's water, and many sea-trout fall to this lure in summer. However, as a fly-fisher's water, in ply, it provides splendid fly fishing for salmon and sea-trout, and it has very good brown trout too. Waters rich enough to support big chub are rich enough to support big trout. I have tried unsuccessfully to tempt some of the big trout of the Annan in the dubs near Hoddom, but they seem to have learnt that a floating fly is a snare. These fish, some of which must run to several pounds, challenge the trout angler and yet promise him a basket to be recorded with pride. My game book is still empty, and to the best of my knowledge the big trout are still rising in the deep pools of Hoddom.

The Annan rises from a spring in the uplands within a mile and a quarter of the source of the Tweed. This in turn is hard by the source of the Clyde. The old rhyme has it:

> Annan, Tweed and Clyde
> Rise a' out o' ae hill side.

Those, however, who have taken the trouble to tramp the moors to find if this is true report a deception. The Clyde really rises at the source of the Daer Water, ten miles away from the source of Tweed; but a tributary of the Clyde, named Clyde's Burn, does rise very near Tweed's Well. I wonder whether Clyde's Burn was named to keep the romantic notion alive after the coming of detailed maps.

The principal tributary of the Annan is the Moffat Water, a spate stream that flows down beside the Edinburgh–Dumfries road from the Devil's Beef Tub to Moffat and Beattock, where it joins with the Evan and Annan. The trip down to the Annan from Edinburgh, leading you to the Devil's Beef Tub, is a splendid experience. There the moors suddenly cleave and drop sheer to the valley of the Moffat Water. Your eye, looking down from the dizzy height, follows the valley away to the south-west, from moorland to trees, from rushes to fresh fields. As with so many of the best views in southern Scotland, it is like coming into plenty after the starker scenery of the moors. In this land of plenty, seen shading off into the haze on a summer morning, runs the Annan, and beyond it the Nith. As a west-coaster, brought up in Ayrshire, and having roamed the south-west corner of Scotland fairly widely, the sight of the hills rolling down to the valley of the Annan and Nith makes me think I have suddenly arrived in a land that I know well. It is a land of still, warm evenings, of soft rain and of the mildest winters. East of the Devil's Beef Tub, to my adopted home in Edinburgh, there lies a land of crisper climate, brighter sun, colder nights, and east winds that can cut through most calculated layers of wool. Your wardrobe for the west would include at least one oilskin raincoat; for the east, it would include at least one sheepskin.

We usually travel down from Edinburgh on a July evening to fish Hoddom at night. We can, as with the Border Esk, leave in coldish conditions and descend into the valley of the Annan to find midges and soft night-fishing conditions. But, equally, we can leave Edinburgh bone dry, with hardly a chuckle in the burns, to find the Moffat water red in spate, completely ruining our chances of sport.

It is curious that in the valleys of the Annan and Nith there is hardly a single loch. The lochs of the Southern Uplands lie much more to the west into Galloway and Kirkcudbrightshire. It is a sad loss, for a loch in arable country is usually rich, and its trout grow large. In the moors further west a loch is often acid, and then its trout, though they may be plentiful, are small. But Annan is splendid fishing, in any terms.

W.B.C.

Chapter Four

THE NITH

At the beginning of the century, when Augustus Grimble was writing *The Salmon Rivers of Scotland*, he said this about the Nith: 'It would not be difficult to give an average of fish killed on any of the Nith waters – next to none would be the best description for them all. I am afraid that salmon fishing in the Nith is entirely done for. It is full of pike and grayling, which ought to be destroyed as far as possible, but the proprietors appear to take no interest in the river, few of them being anglers. For the last seven years it has been going back yearly, and 1900 was the very worst on record, and not a dozen fish killed on the whole river.' Grimble was quoting 'a gentleman who knows the river well'.

By 1921 little had changed. Calderwood, in his *The Salmon Rivers and Lochs of Scotland*, declares: 'Unhappily, the fisheries have been allowed to sink to a very low ebb'. In a splendid account of the Nith, he outlined the decline through pollution by mills at Dumfries and elsewhere, through over-netting, and through blocking of the ascent of the salmon up all the major spawning tributaries by small mill dams. What should have been a good second-class salmon river, or even a first-class one, was a sporting nonentity. The Annan was a far better salmon river and commanded far more in rents than the Nith.

I have started this description of the Nith on a note of woe because I have a remarkable tale to tell. Nith, through the efforts of the Nith Fishings Improvement Association, has come from being a river with a total annual catch of under a score of salmon to being one that in 1966 showed a return of 2,251 salmon weighing a total of 21,948 pounds, 559 grilse weighing 2,556 pounds, and 9,502 sea-trout weighing 22,671 pounds. Perhaps no other river has ever in Scottish history made this kind of recovery. If not, it reflects all the more credit on the foresight, energy, and devotion of the Improvement Association, which, for thirty-three years before that return, had been nursing the river back from oblivion.

Nith has always had the name of being a salmon river that is late in bringing sport to the rods. Once it was held to be little more than an autumn stream, and few people would have thought of fishing before

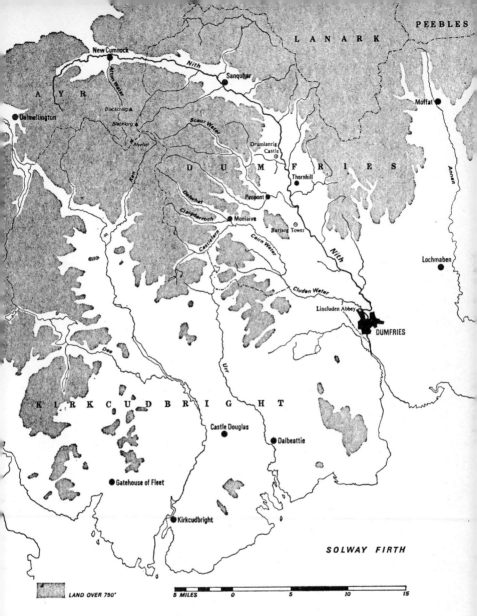

the end of May. Now Nith is regarded as a spring river with a growing run of fish, some of which are so early that rods fishing the previous November have had fish immature enough in spawn to be deemed the first of the springers running. It has been calculated that fourteen per cent of the total salmon catch in 1964 were spring fish, and fifty-nine per cent were autumn fish. In the following year twenty-three per cent of the run were springers and forty-two per cent were autumn fish. In

1966 twenty-seven per cent were spring salmon and only thirty-nine per cent of the year's catch were autumn fish. Bear in mind that these figures are associated with an increasing number of salmon returning each year, and you have a suggestion that the Nith is not only emerging as a river with a splendid total catch, but as one with an ever-rising spring catch – and that today is extraordinary. Many anglers and proprietors throughout Scotland think that the spring run on many of our earlier rivers is giving way for a larger summer and autumn run. Clearly the Nith is a river resurging into prominence.

The sea-trout fishing of the Nith in recent years has become almost a legend. I know rods who live on the water, and who fish the river at least every alternate night, and bring in, from the month of June onwards, fish of up to six pounds. This is from association water. I can think of rods who would gladly pay steep rents for fishing of this quality. A summer night on the Buccleuch waters can be a memorable event, with fish, as dusk deepens, plopping up and bringing sport to almost every rod fishing the water. Sea-trout shoal in the river, and at times it looks from a high bank like a scaled-up version of the Border Esk, where fish pack the tails of the pools and give the impression that a stone thrown in would not reach the bottom.

Nith is a river of good volume, and in times of rain it can rise to give alarming floods. A drawback is that the floods of the river are often yellow, with an opacity that makes fly or spinning tactics useless. Worm fishers tend to exploit the floods, and in periods of high water many of the sea-trout caught are taken by a continuous massacre. Nevertheless, worming in floods is not to be worried about to the same degree as indiscriminate worming with heavy tackle in lower water, when worm can be the cover for stroke-hauling or can be the cause of some anglers' monopolizing the pools.

The Nith rises in the hills behind the Ayrshire town of Dalmellington, and it first flows east; then, receiving the waters of the Afton near New Cumnock, it turns south and makes its way through Thornhill to Dumfries, some fifty-five miles from its source. For almost the whole of its course, the river is a pastoral water with fields and trees, holms and gentle banks, that give it a sweet style. However, at the beat called The Linns, above Drumlanrig Castle, it runs through a series of gorges, with rocky pools and rapids not unlike those of some Highland waters. This stretch is difficult to fish, but it holds and yields good numbers of salmon. Elsewhere one has the impression that the Nith is a river for the overhead-cast fly, and can be approached easily from a farm road, even by car. It is easily waded (except for the impossible Linns), so long as you look out for the odd sandstone ledge with a pot-hole or a cleft in it likely to plunge you well over the head after one false step. Nith shares the difficulty of ledge hazards with the Annan.

An angler wades with his net in fast water at The Cauld on Ettrick.
OVERLEAF *Devorgilla's Bridge stands staunchly against Nith floods.*

As a brown-trout river the Nith does not raise any eyebrows, and perhaps it should be accepted that as a salmon and sea-trout river it ought not to encourage competition from brown trout. But a stocking programme has been successfully carried out by many clubs on the river. I have taken my best Nith trout while fishing for sea-trout at night. In most cases I thought I was into sea-trout. Some of the fish, running to near a pound (I know there are better ones), were well-marked and well-shaped, and I would not sniff at a day's trouting on a water with fish like this. Of course, where Nith is fished by day, if possible one tries for a salmon.

The Nith was badly hit in 1966 by the outbreak of U.D.N. In the winters of 1966 and 1967 dead and dying fish were reported. These were mainly salmon and sea-trout, although brown trout were also affected. U.D.N. is a disease that thrives in cold water. During the summer of 1967 the river seemed to be almost free of this scourge, but it took hold again during the autumn of that year and is still with us in the spring of 1971. It is lamentable that a river that has been rescued from the brink of annihilation and brought so far towards first-class fishing should be struck by this pestilence.

It must not be supposed that the Nith is failing to produce fish. Far from it. Angling continues as usual, but, so far as the quality of stocks and spawning reserves is concerned, the disease, most prevalent in colder waters, can kill off the fish that have escaped the lures of the angler and the normal hazards of the summer months. They are thus lost to the river on the very point of spawning. This loss, the marginal one, is the unkindest cut of all.

Since the record 1966 season rod catches on the Nith have declined. In 1968 anglers took 830 salmon, 266 grilse and 3,377 sea-trout. These figures are a sad reflection on the magnificent 1966 catches. However, 1969 brought an improvement in the salmon catches, and this continued in 1970, when anglers took 1,444 salmon and 666 grilse. Unfortunately, the improvement in salmon catches is not matched in the sea-trout totals. From the splendid return of 9,502 sea-trout in 1966 catches slumped to 2,753 in 1969 and 2,812 in 1970.

Nith has good stocks of grayling. Some anglers would dispute my use of 'good'. Let me confess publicly: I fall into that sub-set of anglers who like grayling and do not turn up their noses at a chance to fish them, provided it is with fly and preferably in crisp autumn weather. They are handsome fish, good eaters, and at times blissfully free risers. When they are in a river, I feel they should be enjoyed. It serves little purpose to fret at their presence, for they can be very difficult to eradicate. Nith grayling can run to nearly two pounds, and in streamy water they give a good account of themselves.

Of the tributaries of the Nith, the Scaur Water, flowing down through

Grilse and sea-trout frequent the Fleet at Gatehouse in late summer.

Penpont, is notable. It is a splendid water, with its share of good brown trout, sea-trout, and the odd salmon in its lower reaches. This little river was once useless to salmon and sea-trout because of a cauld near its mouth. This was removed, and the water has thrived ever since, providing valuable spawning-beds for the migratory fish.

The Cluden Water, called the Cairn Water from its middle reaches up, is one of the main lower-course tributaries of the Nith. It flows into the main river on the right bank about a mile above Dumfries near the ruins of Lincluden Abbey. This charming little river is universally known for its association with Robert Burns. In his song *Ca' the Yowes to the Knowes*, he draws a portrait of the pastoral peace of the river, its tree-covered banks, its abbey with its towers:

> We'll gae down by Clouden side,
> Thro' the hazels spreading wide
> O'er the waves that sweetly glide
> To the moon sae clearly.

It is the headstreams of the Cluden (or Cairn) that one sees near Moniaive. There the river draws its waters from three hill burns: the Dalwhat, the Craigdarroch, and the Castlefern. All are fed from the same moors behind, which also give birth to the Ken, and they are dominated by the three hills Blackcraig, Blacklorg, and Alwhat, all over 2,000 feet. The Cairn in its middle and upper reaches is a perfect trout stream, and in summer and autumn it is a fine sea-trout water with some good salmon casts, particularly in the lower reaches. There is association water available on the Cairn along its many miles of good water.

The Nith and its tributaries are connected with some famous names in angling. In 1812 the poacher Jock Wallace caught a salmon of sixty-seven pounds in Nith, and the story goes that he ran it from eight in the morning till six in the evening, and landed it with only two strands of his hair line still intact. The fish was weighed and witnessed at Barjarg Tower, and a certificate with appropriate witness signatures was issued. This beat by a short head the present salmon record held by the late Miss G. W. Ballantyne of Caputh for a fish of sixty-four pounds caught in the Tay in 1922. Why should Jock Wallace's Nith fish be forgotten? And why indeed should we doubt the reality of that still larger fish, the salmon of sixty-nine and three-quarter pounds taken by the Earl of Home in Tweed in 1835? There is documentary evidence for that too (see Calderwood, 1921, page 22). It is rather irksome that the present British Rod-Caught Records Committee should doubt many records of long standing, especially those with careful verification before witnesses.

The really big fish of the Nith are autumn runners. The local name for the big autumn fish, common throughout the whole Solway area and up into Ayrshire, is 'grey back'. One might say that Nith is the best river for them. The season there is specially extended to the end of November, for many of the better autumn fish do not appear until the last few days of the autumn. Of course, by this time the springers may already have spawned, and great discipline is required in angling, for fishers not to take the gravid fish nor the early kelt.

In summing up the quality of the Nith and its fishing recovery, let me quote two sets of figures. The first is a Tweed figure. The average rod catch for the whole river during the five years 1916–20 was 2,500 per year. At this time the average total rod catch for the Nith may have been somewhere around twenty-five fish per year. In 1966 the Nith catch was 2,251 salmon and 559 grilse. I doubt whether I could find words to convey the wonder of this achievement by the Nith in our time. It is an example to all Scotland of what can be done by co-operation between proprietor, angler, and local authorities. A desert has been made fruitful; a part of our natural heritage has been saved from the abyss.

W.B.C.

Chapter Five

GALLOWAY

Galloway is the most strongly surviving of the 'provinces' from the ancient Kingdom of Scotland; it also bears the most obvious signs of this survival.

To begin with, it is composed of two counties, the stewartry of Kirkcudbright and the shire of Wigtown, while all other ancient provinces have declined, at least on the map, to shires and one at least to a small shire. As the most southerly part of Scotland, hanging from the south-west into the Atlantic Ocean and the Irish Sea, it has a geographical unity surpassed in Scotland only by some island groups.

Its appearance is distinctive, and, when he enters it, the traveller feels he has reached a special part of Scotland. In its southerly position, close to England, it belongs to the Border and Lowlands district of Scotland. It has nevertheless much upland and even mountain country. Some of its most impressive hills are 2,500 feet high, the equal of many Highland ranges.

This scenery is also most attractive. The hills and mountains do not bear the usual heathery tint, but are a vivid russet, which made R. L. Stevenson, in his celebrated lines dedicated to a Galloway man (S. R. Crockett), speak of the 'wine-red' moor. By contrast the agricultural land is a vivid Irish green. Galloway is a haunt of Scottish artists.

It is also a haunt of anglers and lovers of Scottish waters, and it has some distinguished lochs and rivers. We shall proceed westwards and southwards through the province, taking lochs and rivers as we go. We can include only those waters that are outstanding or particularly representative. This is necessary in Galloway, which has a wealth of angling waters.

We take first Loch Ken, because of its great size and pleasing appearance, though in the past it has had only a limited appeal to anglers. This appeal is likely to increase.

Loch Ken, lying north-west to south-east, splits a large part of the stewartry of Kirkcudbright in two. It is over fifteen miles long and at its widest about half a mile. Lying between the Cairnsmore of Fleet to

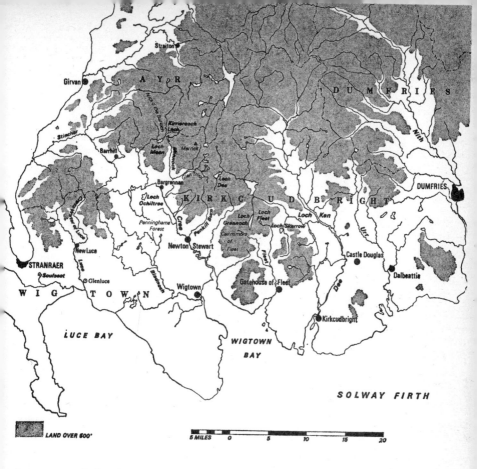

LAND OVER 600'   5 MILES   0   5   10   15   20

the west and the fertile plains north of Castle Douglas, it is finely situated and presents, though in a different way, a lochscape almost as beautiful as Loch Lomond.

The average trout or salmon angler, seeing it for the first time from the roads that run on either side of it, will be strongly tempted to try his luck in it. Until recently, however, he would not have had much chance among the few game fish – salmon, sea-trout, or brown trout – that somehow managed to exist there.

The reason was that they had strong competition, unusual in Scotland, from large, voracious, and multiple pike. We cannot resist mentioning that the unofficial record pike for the British Isles was captured in Loch Ken near the end of last century. It weighed seventy-two pounds. A pike of this size and in good condition, as this one was said to be, might well have been as dangerous to a bather in this inland water as a shark would be in the sea. It could not have killed or eaten an adult bather, but its teeth could have inflicted grave damage.

In the last few years the hydro-electric authorities, who in Galloway are cooperating with the game-fish anglers, have declared war on the Loch Ken pike. They have opened their warfare by the use of traps and nets, and in a recent period of five years have been responsible for extracting from the loch and killing no less than twenty tons of pike.

This has resulted in the emergence from obscurity of large brown trout up to three and four pounds, sometimes over. These larger and older fish obviously existed in Ken water when the pike's reign was undisputed, and their agility must have allowed them to escape. Of more interest for future angling prospects has been the appearance of three-quarter-pound trout that have grown up during the period of the pike's recession. Tickets for angling may be obtained from local hotels and angling associations, but there is a good deal of all but free fishing to be obtained by asking permission from farmers who own land on the banks.

Further to the south-east and upon the borders of the stewartry, the Dalbeattie Angling Association has the rights over various stretches of the impressive Urr Water. Grilse, salmon, and sea-trout run here; moreover there are brown trout in the river and in the reservoir about two miles from Dalbeattie. This is also stocked annually with Loch Leven and rainbow trout. Visitors may procure tickets for angling from the Angling Association. One cannot leave Dalbeattie without mentioning that in 1967 there was a run of salmon in the Urr that surpassed anything within the memory of the oldest local anglers. Since then, however, disquiet in the whole Solway area about the salmon disease (U.D.N.) has to some extent also involved the Urr.

Moving westwards, we come to a district shared between Gatehouse of Fleet and Newton Stewart. It contains two notable rivers and some lochs. Angling tickets for the Gatehouse part can be obtained from the Cally Estate office; for the Newton Stewart division, from the angling association in the town.

Gatehouse is a little town of great charm standing near the mouth of the Water of Fleet, surrounded by agricultural land and under the shadow of the most 'wine-red' moors in Galloway, the Cairnsmore of Fleet. Mrs Murray Usher, the proprietress of the Cally Estate, takes a keen interest in angling and all sporting activities. She is by descent a member of one of the oldest families in the province.

She has recently stocked the Fleet with Danish or Baltic sea-trout, which can run to a great size. Even in the three- to six-pound range they are distinctive, beautifully and compactly shaped and with deep bellies. One of these magnificent fish was taken in the Urr in 1967, weighing fourteen pounds. There are also grilse and salmon in the Fleet; but, as these do not always get on well with the sea-trout, the management are encouraging the latter.

Only certain stretches and banks of the Fleet are available to the public. Details can be obtained from the Cally Estate office in Gate-house. Fairly wide at its mouth, the Fleet narrows to an attractive small river in the upper stretches amongst the hills. On the Fleet, night fishing is best, but day fishing can be fruitful during the constant spates, which must be seized as they come, for the forestry plantations in the upper part, with their efficient drainage, induce rapid rising and falling of water.

The most attractive loch in the Gatehouse district, both scenically and from the trout angler's point of view, is Skerrow. This island-studded water has boats, is just the right size, and is well up amongst the Cairnsmore hills. Remotely situated, Skerrow can be approached by the Forestry Commission road (keys are obtainable from the Cally Estate office). Fly fishing only is allowed. The average weight is three-quarters of a pound, but three-pounders have been taken.

Lochs Grannoch and Fleet are worth mentioning, though the average weight is not quite up to Skerrow standards. On a fine day those and other lesser lochs in the Gatehouse area provide a feast for the lover of scenery.

The Newton Stewart district is focused on the River Cree; we deal first with some lochs further up among the hills. The little Kirriereoch Loch, far up, is remarkable. It can be fished for brown trout most successfully on the day that trout fishing begins. We should add that this is a characteristic of Galloway inland waters. The mild climate and rich feeding of the province allow trout to regain condition very soon after spawning. One of the present writers on a recent visit to Galloway was treated by two trout anglers to a vivid description of fishing on Kirriereoch on the 15th March. Despite the prevailing mild climate, this happened to be a day of frost and snow. The edges of the little loch were fringed with breakable ice, and there were flurries of snow. Nevertheless trout up to a pound were coming well to the fly in con-ditions that one might suppose would have been utterly hopeless anywhere else in Scotland.

Other lochs worthy of note in the Newton Stewart Angling Associ-ation's control are Loch Ochiltree (did Walter Scott name one of his celebrated characters after this loch?) and Loch Dee. The former has been restocked, and trout running to two and a half pounds have been taken. Loch Dee provides angling not quite up to this standard, but is remote and in splendid scenery.

Anglers from Ayrshire quite commonly drive down to the Cree for the first spring salmon of their year. Cree, like other Solway rivers in recent years, is a water with a distinct spring run developing. In the recent past the first salmon has come from the waters in March and (rarely) in February, although in a water with a spring run like Cree there is always the chance on the opening day in February that the pools might contain an odd winter-run fish. However, it is in the later spring fishings, of April and May, that Cree shows its best sport. These are months in which the neighbouring Stinchar hardly draws in a fish.

On the drive down the Barrhill road from Ayrshire, the Cree itself is encountered as a sluggish moorland stream. It flows from Loch Moan above Bargrennan, and it wends its way through rushy pools to the High Bridge of Cree on the main road to Newton Stewart, where it takes a turn southwards and brisks up in current for some miles. It continues to run attractively between its 'flowery banks', as Burns sang, winding among trees and presenting many a vignette of Galloway scenery, until it is joined by the Water of Minnoch some seven miles above Newton Stewart. At Penninghame begins a stretch of over two miles in which the river forms what is virtually a loch (indeed, some call it Loch Cree), before the current brisks up again for the passage through Newton Stewart itself and the outflow into the long, meandering estuary with its silt and sandbanks leading to Wigtown Bay.

The Minnoch is encountered close beside the hill road from Ayrshire – one could come either by Straiton or by the Nick o' the Balloch. It is a hill spate stream, gradually forming better and deeper pools until it receives the Water of Trool, rumbling down through the Glen of Trool, with steep tree-clad slopes, a sparkling loch, and behind it the majestic slopes of the Merrick (2,764 feet), the highest point in the Southern Uplands.

Salmon run the Minnoch in numbers probably equal to those of the main stream of Cree; but, for character, the Minnoch is much to be preferred. The rocky pools, the gravelly streams, and the clearer water are thought by many to be better fly-fishing water. The Cree has a great deal of peat-staining in its streams, and we have fished for its salmon, along some of the upper waters particularly, in dark pot-holes in the peat with slow streams that could hardly work the fly. Lower down, of course, the Cree changes, but the Minnoch runs as a cheerful gravelly river for almost its entire length.

At Newton Stewart the Penkill Burn joins the Cree, and this small stream has for long had the reputation of being the sea-trout water of the system. However, with the increase of sea-trout numbers in the Solway rivers generally, more are being caught in the Minnoch and Cree. But some of the best fly fishing for sea-trout in the area is still on the Penkill Burn.

Like other Solway rivers, the Cree has greatly improved in recent years as a salmon water, and now it offers a really worthwhile prospect of spring salmon sport. The Minnoch is largely in private hands, but the Cree itself offers several stretches with club ticket facilities, and some waters still in the hands of farmers who may let a rod fish for a day, either for a small rent or gratis.

A glance at the map will show that the most westerly and southerly part of Wigtownshire lies well out to sea, and is connected with the rest of the province only by a fairly narrow strip of land. This strip is a part of the shire known as the Machair. Readers of our chapters on the islands will become familiar with the Gaelic-derived word 'machair', which means a shell-sand area on a raised beach, with rich grasses, flowers, and (above all) rich fishing lochs.

Such indeed is the now fertile strip connecting the Rhinns, or most westerly part of Wigtownshire, with the rest of the shire and the province. Geologists tell us that the Rhinns were once an island, and that the waves and tides of the Atlantic used to move over this now fertile strip of land. Their statements can be confirmed by anglers, who will find certain lochs, now well inland, supported on bottoms of sandy soil exactly like that which is found on the seashore.

Pre-eminent among such lochs is Soulseat. It is shallow, its waters are crystal clear, and its bottom is of pure silver or slightly golden sand. It is well stocked with rainbow and brown trout that fight in the best tradition of machair lochs. They run to a goodish size, but few exceed two pounds. If, however, you are into a half-pound Soulseat trout, and if he does not show himself on being hooked, you may believe that you are connected with a pounder or more until you get within sight of him.

Tickets for angling in this district may be obtained from the Stranraer and District Angling Association in Stranraer.

Before we come to the Water of Luce, which is in this district, we cannot forego the pleasure of mentioning the delightful-sounding Lochnaw or Black Loch, which lies in the northern part of the Rhinns. We have never cast a line on it, but have heard such enthusiastic descriptions of it that we can, in good conscience, pass that enthusiasm on.

It is a very small loch in beautiful surroundings, fringed with flowering rhododendrons and other plants that in any other part of Scotland would be considered exotic. At one time a powerful Wigtown family put up a castle on an island in Lochnaw. In the seventeenth century, however, when more peaceable times came, the castle was dismantled and rebuilt some two miles to the west on the mainland. You may still row around the Castle Island; if you care to land there, you will find traces of the original building.

The average size of trout in Lochnaw is three-quarters of a pound, but some run into the class of a pound and a half or even two pounds. In its own kind, the sport is good here; but all who have fished this, one of the most southerly angling waters in Scotland, grow lyrical about its beauty, which is of a luxuriant kind not often found in our country.

Permission to fish Lochnaw may be had on application to the hotel by the water's bank.

The Water of Luce flows down from the moors of Ayrshire to the sands of Luce Bay. It is a small river with the character of a spate stream. However, it holds a good head of resident brown trout in its middle and upper regions – one of the present writers can remember a magnificent day's trouting on the beat below New Luce, where the Cross Water of Luce joins. It also has a very fine run of sea-trout from June to October and a good run of grilse and small summer salmon. Although it is near the Cree, the Luce does not share to any extent the spring run of fish for which the Cree has become noted. But in autumn the pools of Luce fill up with fish, and they can be well into the 'teens of pounds. For a smallish spate river, this is magnificent fishing.

The Luce is a peaty stream, and after rain it can be as dark as any Highland water. Its sudden spates tend to run dirty for a short time, then to settle down to a dark sherry colour and stay in it for long periods. Many prefer to fish the Luce salmon with a worm, searching the smallish pools and pot-holes in the middle and upper reaches, but some find the Luce excellent as a fly water. For sea-trout fishing at night there are few small streams with the sport the Luce has. In summer, in low water, the sea-trout come well to night fly tactics, and, when the finnock (or whitling, as they are locally called) come up-stream, the flies are sometimes torn to pieces by the smaller fish.

This is a delightful stream flowing for almost its entire length through unspoilt Galloway scenery. Its banks are rushy and rocky, giving way below New Luce to riverside holms and meadows of some quality. The lower reaches are set in gentle Solway coast scenery with good stands of trees, plenty of wild flowers, and rich pasture lands. At Glenluce the river narrows and flows under the main road to Stranraer, before winding its way into the sands of Luce Bay, where its excellent sea-trout thrive in the estuary.

M.McL., W.B.C.

Chapter Six

AYRSHIRE WATERS

Anglers quite often say that they know the waters of a certain area 'like the backs of their hands'. I should like to put it on record that the back of my hand is a mystery to me, although I have looked at it every day for many years; similarly, the waters of Ayrshire, which I have fished from my boyhood, are to me still something of a mystery, and have a perpetual fascination. I love the lochs of the wild southern moors, where the shores ring with the cries of the whaup and the speely (curlew and oyster-catcher); I enjoy burn fishing in the middle of rich pasture land; I return season after season to fish for salmon in the Doon, Girvan, and Stinchar; I long for my next chance to fish the excellent trout of the Ayr.

Ayrshire yielded me my first trout, when I was only eight. It gave me my first real fishing education, on the admirable streams of the Ayr. The county gave me my first salmon as a boy; in short, it brought me up into the world of game fishing in conditions that could make me hope for a good bag, and yet could provide a sufficient challenge, and sufficient heartache, to make the better fishings of the Highlands seem splendid by comparison. In a word, Ayrshire found me, formed me, and informed me about fishing. I was lucky.

Straddling the Southern Uplands and the low, fertile plains of the Clyde estuary, Ayrshire is clearly divided into two regions. The Doon seems to join them most effectively.

The river finds its beginnings in the moors above Loch Riecawr, although there it is not called Doon. In origins at least, the Doon is a river of the Southern Uplands, and for over twenty miles it remains so. It gathers itself in the long, cold waters of Loch Doon; it pours through the barrage at the north-western end of the loch – a barrage put up in the 'thirties in one of the first hydro-electric schemes in Scotland. From there the river runs like a Highland stream for about five miles towards Dalmellington, coursing down the Ness Glen. At Dalmellington a flooded moss loch, the Bogton Loch, kills the river's pace and starts the Doon on about five miles of moorland wanderings in which it looks, often, like the 'dead' waters of a Highland river. Past

Waterside, down as far as Patna, this character of the sluggish moorland stream is maintained; but then suddenly, as if at a signal, the
river changes character. It enters a richer valley and picks up pace. It
runs streamy, through boulders; it forms pot-holes and shallow pools
and as a fishing water improves immensely. This fast, streamy character
is maintained past Hollybush, Dalrymple, Auchendrane, and Doonholm, save that as the river gains in volume in its lower reaches it forms
pools that are larger and deeper, but never of any great length except
where artificially long dams, like Doonholm, hold the current back to
provide salmon and sea-trout sanctuaries.

Below Doonholm, the river continues streamy until the final dam at
Greenan, the tidal weir, forms the last long pool, and the river runs
over the weir to provide a small tidal reach, which spends itself in a fan
of distributaries over the sands and mussel-beds of Ayr Bay, just south
of Ayr. Thus the Doon links the hilly south with the fat plains of the
central part of the county. Doon is a sheep river in its upper and
middle regions and a dairy-cattle river in its lower stretches. These
divisions are the essence of Ayrshire, and in its fishings the Doon seems
to hint at the richness of both.

It can be a wonderful salmon water. I remember days on Nether
Auchendrane when you could find a run of summer fish in the pools
and take a brace or more before lunch. I love the way Doon fish sometimes rise to your trout flies, and often are to be tempted on tiny Dee
tubes like the half-inch Stoat's Tail. One of the finest fishers of the lower
Doon, a man who could take sixty and more salmon in a season, during
summer reduces his fly size at times to No. 10 – that is, to trout size.
Usually one fishes larger flies, and I have always taken the No. 4 fly,
say a Hairy Mary or a Blue Charm, as the 'home' size for the river. The
Grey Turkey is a fly that had its origins in the Ayr district, and some
fishers swear by it as a Doon fly, but I have always inclined towards the
hair-wing versions of the dressings I name. I have seen excellent
slaughter done on small plain-winged flies like Pheasant and Yellow,
but I have never persisted in fishing this local fly, partly because I am
fascinated by the action of hair in the water. Jeannie, in its low-water
dressing, has followers on the Doon, and on a floating line it can do well
in summer. Tradition has it that a blue hackle improves the chances of
the Doon fly. Perhaps my Blue Charm has what I would define as Doon
appeal, with its black body and its blue throat-hackle. I also like a
Stoat's Tail wing with gold twist on a black body and a hot orange
hackle at the throat – a perfect fly for the darker waters after a spate.
Thunder and Lightning, with its combination of hot orange and blue
hackles with the black body I describe, is also an obvious choice.

I started my salmon-fishing career with a spinning rod when I was
a boy. I took a fair number of Doon fish spinning in spates, and it was

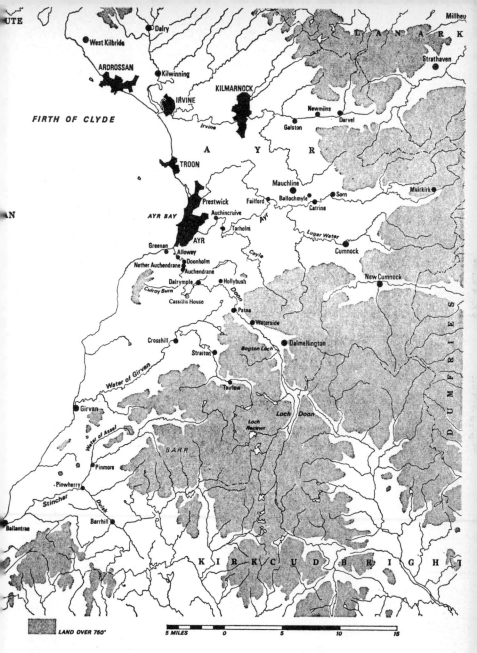

several seasons before I managed to get myself a good salmon fly rod of twelve foot six and a No. 4 silk line and seriously fly-fish the Doon. That, in my view, began salmon fishing proper. But I shall never forget the first fish I ever took in the Doon on spinner, in the most public of pools in Burns Monument tea-gardens, Alloway, with the old bridge above and the new road bridge below and the gardens around full of sightseers and hotel guests. I hooked an eleven-pounder and called to the gardener (a Mr Spain, a retired keeper and a charming man) that I was into a fish. He produced a gaff apparently from the middle of a rose bush, and in due course had the fish out on the bank. One of the hotel guests near me, jumping up and down with excitement, was a Prestwick woman, a Mrs Veitch, who was on the point of having twins and had come out to the hotel for a quiet last few days before her confinement. I hear the twins were none the worse! I fished that pool several times in later years and took sea-trout from it, but never again touched a salmon in it. For me at least, however, it will always rank as a pool among pools, productive, exciting, and memorable; and I can think of pools that have yielded me far better fish and yet that I would not rank so high.

The Doon has an odd flow, for it is a river with a compensation water arrangement, forming part of the hydro-electric scheme centred on Loch Doon. Compensation seems to me a good thing on the Doon. It runs sweetly in summer when uncompensated waters dwindle and stagnate, and I have taken salmon several times at this compensated level. Floods on Doon are often 'wee dirty spates', and last a comparatively short time. There is no doubt that the river has lost many of its long-sustained spates, which in the earlier years of this century must have made superb conditions for sport. Yet the river's small dirty spate was noted by at least one writer in the 'twenties, and it appears always to have been typical. The Culroy Burn can flood the lower river and bring a small muddy spate down when the upper river is still running clear. Yet the Doon today, with a judicious release of freshets arranged at the loch dam, can still have marvellous bursts of summer sport when other waters in the district – the Ayr, for instance – are languishing in low water.

Doon fish do not run early. I know of March fish, but they are in historic isolation. April fish are predictable, and May fish can be depended on in the lower river at least if the right water conditions exist. June brings the first big summer runs in, and these continue throughout July and August until the end of September, when one is apt to find the pools full of reddish fish until the grey backs of the autumn begin to run. Fish of well into the twenties of pounds come out of the sea after about mid-September, and they are the finest fish of the year for the river. The average Doon fish is about eight pounds, with a few summer fish of around twelve to fourteen. The grey backs are fish of seventeen to twenty pounds, and in the smallish pools of the Doon they appear enormous. A twenty-five-pounder is really big for the water; and, although fish into the thirties have been taken, they are very rare indeed.

The sea-trout of the Doon, I have found, are hard fish to tempt.

They run in good numbers in July and August, but they seem to obey local rather than universal rules for taking the fly. Some evenings you will land half a dozen in rapid succession, and on others you will fish hard for nothing in pools well stocked with migratory fish. Fastidious sea-trout are not new to angling, but in many seasons I have found Doon fish to be excessively individualistic about conditions. They seem to like a fly as large as No. 8 where, on similar rivers, I would have predicted a fly much smaller. They can be good fish of two and a half pounds and better, and there are odd reports of larger fish that have fallen to worms and spinners, and even occasionally to fly, but the best sport of the year is with the mixed bag of whitling and smallish sea-trout of up to a couple of pounds that July and August bring to the Doon.

There is considerable local feeling among the angling community that the Doon is suffering rather badly in its estuary from over-netting. The development of fishing in the estuary after the Second World War has an unhappy history. There have been mammoth catches with a sweep net in the very restricted estuary below the tidal weir, and in recent years the netsman, using an amphibious vehicle to carry his net quickly round fish in the sea at the mouth of the Doon, has seemed to be exploiting the river in the worst way. The tidal weir at Greenan is said to be now useless, and is to be removed. This has been said for several years, and still not a stone has been taken away. Perhaps by the time these words are read the weir will be gone. I sincerely hope so, for the Doon is the sweetest river to fish, and provides some really sporting pools on its lower and middle waters for the fly fisher. To mention only four beats, Swallow braes, Doonholm, Auchendrane, and Cassillis, one could say that challenging and productive fly fishing is carried out on smallish pools of great character. Trees make for difficult casting, and the switch and spey casts are virtually *de rigueur*. I have, for instance, watched Major Bruce Kennedy fishing his pools at Doonholm, and have delighted in the skill with which he can speycast and rollcast his way down the water, raising and hooking a salmon in the most difficult lies. That is real fly fishing – the essence of the Doon.

The other two rivers of southern Ayrshire are Stinchar, entering the sea impressively at Ballantrae, and the Water of Girvan, flowing to the Firth of Clyde through Girvan town twelve miles north of the Stinchar's mouth. Stinchar is a flash flood river of great distinction. The story is told of an angler who was fishing in dead low water at Pinwherry and taking nothing. The post office van drew up on the bridge, and the postman asked, 'What sport?' 'Nothing,' came the reply. 'Well, it's raining up at Barr, and all the folk are getting their fishing rods out,' said the postman, 'so ye'd better wait.' The angler waited, and, sure enough, down it came – a roaring flash flood. He waited until it began to settle and clear a little (only a matter of a couple of hours), and had the pleasure of taking several good sea-trout before his day was done. That is typical of a hill-stream, and it is well known that for fat bags on Stinchar – impressively fat in the middle and lower reaches – you need a friendly keeper to telephone you, and you must drive to the river immediately if you are to find it in ply. Local people say that in recent years the flash characteristics of the river have been aggravated by the coming of forestry drainage.

The hill land above Barr was once a great sponge, retaining the water and rationing it out in its floods over a longer period than we now enjoy. This complaint is laid at the door of hill-drainers everywhere in Scotland, and there is no doubt that the régimes of many hill-waters have been altered by the new drainage. But drainage does mean more effective freshets, and this can bring sport on for productive bursts where, under the old régime, the water would hardly have moved with a shower of rain. Freshets, of course, are marvellous for bringing sea-trout up in lowish water in July, but are irritating when they come during a day's fishing to unsettle salmon that were on the take. I have hooked salmon just as a freshet was coming down, and I am sure these rising-water fish are bonuses. The 'bonus' fish, however, is usually the last of the day, for the freshet of the Stinchar and Girvan can often be rather dirty, and the yellow waters of an Ayrshire spate are usually fit only for worm-drowning and heavy spinning.

Stinchar is a late river, providing its best sport from late July right on to its extra late closing in mid-November. The late closing of this river reflects the late running of the 'grey back' – the larger autumn salmon; and, every autumn, fish in the upper 'teens of pounds enter the river from October onwards, making for some excellent sport right up to the last day of the season in November. No other Ayrshire water is open so late, although Girvan and Doon also have a run of grey backs. Clearly no Ayrshire river can claim to be a spring water, although an occasional salmon enters some rivers from the beginning of February onwards. Tales of springers usually come from inexperienced fishers, who mistake the bright, well-mended kelts of the early spring for clean fish. I believe there may be March fresh fish on Stinchar, but I would never really expect the first salmon before late April, and I would not predict the sport of Stinchar to yield steady interest before June.

The excellent run of whitling and sea-trout that make the Stinchar a night fisher's dream come mainly in July, and sport continues throughout August with the taking of some heavy bags. Largely, fly is fished for the nocturnal sea-trout, but (and this is not to my particular taste) an increasing number of anglers fish fly and maggot in the dark, or trot worms in the low summer river at night. With a beautiful little stream like Stinchar I am obviously a faddist, and plead for fly fishing, with

Angling success on Stinchar depends on its depth, which rises and falls quickly.
OVERLEAF *The Girvan in spate provides sport at a moderate price.*

light tackle, as the sea-trout are not large. A three-pounder is really good, and your bag is more likely to have in it fish of a pound and a half. You might at times, however, take a dozen fish, and on a bumper night the sport might go steadily all night through.

Stinchar is not a brown-trout river, although, as with many Scottish rivers, there is a resident stock. They are modest fish, and a trout of half a pound would be good, by my reckoning. However, the main tributary of the Stinchar, the Duisk, which joins it just below Pinwherry, is quite an interesting bit of hill-trout fishing. The Duisk also has half-pounders here and there; but, with trees to add hazards for casting and attractive dark pools in the peaty water to add mystery, it is good trouting as far up as you can fish it, right past Barrhill.

Above Pinmore, where the Assel river joins it, the Stinchar is really quite small unless swollen by rain. Above Barr, it becomes a stream with only pot-hole lies for its salmon, and it takes on the character of a hill spawning stream. Fishing a salmon from a hill water like this can be either great sport, with a trout rod and a small fly, or a travesty of fishing, with great worm tackles raked through tiny pools where fish are known to be lying. I am aware that certain proprietors are very careful about their regulations, and it might be inappropriate to appeal for greater concern over the salmon in the head-waters of the river. Living with the angling community of Ayrshire, however, taught me to expect a minority who would drag a large worm tackle through anything from a bathtub to a falls pool if they suspected there were a salmon lying in it.

In some respects the Girvan is rather like the Stinchar. It is small, and it begins in the same hill country, virtually in the same peat-bog, as its more southerly neighbour. But the Girvan flows north, and from Straiton downwards takes on a more Lowland character; it also provides some splendid pools on its middle reaches, where salmon fly fishing is a delight. The salmon of the Girvan do not run above Tairlaw Linn, which lies some five miles above Straiton, and in some ways this is an excellent thing. The local club guards its fishing at Straiton jealously and well; the local River Board bailiff is, to my mind, doing a splendid job in caring for and improving the stock of the Girvan. It is such a pleasant stream, and its salmon, running from about March onwards, provide some really good fly fishing that is very well worth preservation. Lower down the river from Crosshill to the sea, there is some excellent sea-trout and salmon fishing on the pools, and night sea-trout sport can be delightful. In this area certain stretches manage their fishings well, and provide fly waters that are as good as any small salmon river in the south of Scotland; but there are other waters where spinning seems to be the only form of angling, or where the worm is barbarously dangled in tiny pools, although it would be far better for

Inch Fad's best sea-trout drifts lie round the shores of The Island.

sport if the water were left to the fly. Worm fishers dwell long and tend sometimes to monopolize pools. Fly fishers at least move through, disturbing the water little.

The Ayr reaches the sea about a mile north of the Doon, and sometimes one muses on what would be the result if these two rivers, so close at their mouths, merged to make one large stream. It would be a river of something like the size of the lower Nith, and would certainly provide excellent salmon fishing. The Ayr, however, is slower, gentler, richer than the Doon – almost entirely a Lowland river with a fertile arable course. It reaches the sea through Ayr harbour, and it makes what seems to me a poor meeting with the tide. Harbours never bring salmon in happily. The threat of pollution is always there, and the water is constantly disturbed. Nevertheless the Ayr has a substantial run of summer and autumn salmon, and some of its lower and middle reaches produce very pleasant sport, particularly after spates when the water has added briskness and a little colour.

The lower reaches of the Ayr, around Auchincruive and Tarholm, have good holding pools; some are of the 'weil' type where there is a dub of considerable depth in the rock. There are delightful gravel streams, and on various of them, and on the glides formed between pools, there is excellent sport with trout and grayling and, on summer evenings, with sea-trout. In my early years of fishing I was fortunate enough to have permission to fish at Tarholm, both downstream of the bridge on some excellent trout water and on the short stretch above the bridge below the junction with the Coyle. I had some great fun there with salmon, and I saw excellent fish taken on fly and spinner in the falling water after spates. The trout in this part of the river run large, and fish of up to two pounds are reported every season. It is a great dry-fly water, with the richness that marks a fat stream. Weeds trail in the slower glides, and long sandy and gravelly streams merge with the darker depths of pools. Trout plop up tantalizingly under the trees and produce demanding conditions for deftly presented dry flies or carefully worked nymphs.

The middle reaches of the Ayr at Failford and Ballochmyle find the river cutting its way spectacularly through a bed of red sandstone. The bluffs of stone plunge into pools with pot-holes and whirlpools in which lie some of the finest trout I have ever longed for. I have caught a few and have been defeated by many more. These fish lie, fat as sows, sucking in flies from May to September; catching them is as skilled a piece of dry-fly fishing as you will find anywhere. Rich fields lie beside a rich river, as so often happens with really good fishing.

Above the Mauchline area at Catrine, the river flows through a small milling town, and a dam across the Ayr prevents the salmon from running further. At present there is a movement to have this old weir properly breached, thus opening up for salmon fishing the attractive stretches of the river at Sorn and even beyond. Possibly this can now be done, but there have been difficulties for many years. Certainly the salmon, gathering in numbers below Catrine weir, are pillaged by poachers, and the stock of spawning fish on which the Ayr depends is considerably reduced. Whether it would be safer above in the thinner waters of Sorn and Muirkirk stretches is a matter for debate. Local anglers there are divided. Some want the Ayr left as a good trout stream (which it is, above Sorn); others feel that the presence of salmon would only bring in salmon-hungry anglers with poachers hard on their heels. In my view, salmon in the Ayr need greatly improved spawning facilities to boost their numbers, and I would argue strongly for the full breaching of the Catrine dam.

The tributaries of the Ayr include the Lugar Water and the Coyle. The Lugar can be a good trout stream, but like the Ayr itself it has suffered pollution by coal slurry from washing-plants at coal-pits nearby. The whole Ayr is affected, and the Lugar has been at times badly hit by this filth. So has that once excellent little trout stream, the Coyle. However, with the running down of coal workings in the area, it is likely that the menace will be reduced. The vigilance of the local Purification Board and the efforts of the A.C.A. have in recent years created vast improvements, bringing the Ayr and its tributaries into better condition than they have been in for some years. It is very desirable that the Ayr should be further cleaned up, for with its tributaries it is not only a trout river of distinction, but it has the potential of a good salmon and sea-trout stream with an interesting character in its slower, deeper pools.

North of Ayr, the Irvine, running down from Darvel and Newmilns to Galston, Kilmarnock, and Irvine, was very much improved as a fishing water after an extensive sewage scheme was introduced in the 'thirties. Now the river has a growing run of salmon and sea-trout. It always carried a splendid head of trout, particularly in its Galston, Newmilns, and Darvel reaches. The Irvine is a Lowland river, rather like the Ayr in many ways but probably still better as a trout river. One could often see splendid fish feeding between the walls of the lace mills in the 'valley' towns, and, although these trout were nobody's fools, they were the source of fly-fishing interest for several prosperous little angling clubs. Now with cleaner water, a run of salmon and sea-trout, and greater rod pressure than ever before, the management of the Irvine fishings is being carefully handled. An association of clubs has been formed – a first step towards an integration of stocking and fishing policies that will greatly help the river.

W.B.C.

Chapter Seven

THE CLYDE AND LOCH LOMOND

If you associate the River Clyde with Glasgow, you are right, but you are not thinking like an angler. The river from about Bothwell down is a polluted stream, becoming, as it runs through Glasgow and into the tidal reaches in the Clydeside area, perhaps the most polluted stream in Britain. In its middle and upper reaches, however, it is a clean, productive trout stream of the most distinguished kind, with good trout, difficult fly fishing conditions, and a tradition of fly fishing that has marked it out from other rivers as a kind of aristocrat of trout fishing in its area.

I think I can claim to have seen the last salmon that ever tried to run up the Clyde through the pollution of Glasgow. I was a very small boy, in Glasgow with my parents, when we found a crowd gathered outside the window of Sawers's fish shop in Howard Street, just off St Enoch Square. In the window was a great glass tank in which a grilse was moodily swimming around, gaped at by mere humans. This fish had that day been taken from the Clyde at Jamaica Bridge, where it had been seen in distress. Someone had had the idea of keeping it alive, and Sawers's nearby provided a glass tank. That fish was probably the last of an era, and the more I reflect on it the more I am sure that it was not a Clyde returning salmon at all. It was probably a sick Loch Lomond fish (or even a Cart fish) that had missed its way and found itself in the Clyde at Jamaica Bridge. Except for that memorable one, it is fifty years since the last salmon was taken from the Clyde, or rather from its polluted tributary the Kelvin; and it is nearer 100 years since the fish ascended the river in any numbers. Clyde, which would rival Tay for summer and autumn salmon at least, is dead as a salmon river – and the cause is simply man's filth. That a river should become an open sewer is disgusting, but the Industrial Revolution turned many streams into sewers. Some of these waters have been revived, or are being revived, by the purification boards and the A.C.A.; others have gone beyond recall. Lower Clyde is probably one of them.

On the middle and parts of the upper Clyde there is trout fishing of quality, which is looked after by the Clyde Angling Protective Associ-

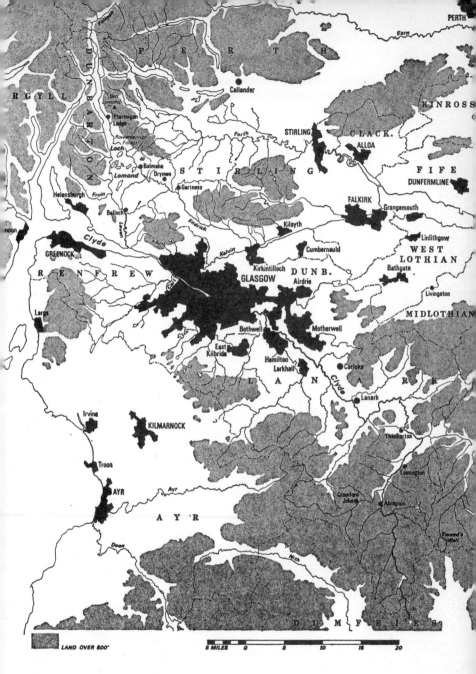

ation, a group of clubs with fishing interests on the river. They deserve praise for the way it has been saved from the worst effects of indiscriminate fishing (although a great deal of 'free' fishing is still indulged in) and pollution. They have acted against polluters through the A.C.A., and have pursued the concerns of good management with commendable zeal. They issue tickets for fishing the river; a day's sport might include trout of well over a pound, some grayling, and some coarse fish.

The fly fishing in waters of the Lamington, Thankerton, and Abington areas is in a tradition on its own. The trout are shy, but are often keen takers of wet and dry fly. In the clear waters of the Clyde, fine tackle and small, lightly-dressed flies are the order of the day. This is the river of the 'single hair', as our forefathers would have described it, fishing with a cast of flies tied to a single strand of horse hair. Today it is still a river of 'fine and far-off' techniques. The tiny No. 16 flies, tied locally, are fished (by the experts) on nylon of breaking strains down to a pound and a half. The patterns at times imitate local hatches – for instance, the McLeod's Olive, the Sand, and the Cow Dung flies; at other times they are the intuitive representations of local fly life tied from local bird plumage. The Clyde is the river of the Lark and Grey, the Corncrake, the Hen Blackie, and the Blue Hen. Each of these flies, tied Clyde-style, has a very short body-dressing, a fine, light wing, and a minimum of hackles. Some Clyde flies seem to have only as many strands of hackle as the real insect has legs! Clyde patterns fish well not only on Clyde, but throughout Scotland, wherever there is a call for small flies and care in dealing with educated trout.

But the Clyde is also famous for its natural bait fishing. Local anglers have shown me how they fish the 'gadger' – the larva of the stone fly, sometimes called the Scottish mayfly. This creature, an inch or more long, is common under the waterside stones of Clyde in May and June. It is fished on a very light bait tackle of two hooks mounted Pennel-style, and it is most successfully fished by floating the bait down the streams during the dusk and dark.

Another fascinating Clyde tradition in natural baits is 'stick bait', the larva of the caddis fly. This worm-like creature lives inside a tube of sand, fibres, and other debris. Clyde anglers extract the larva and fish it on amazingly fine tackle, trotting it down to trout. I saw a picture of a four-pounder that fell to this succulent and skilfully fished natural bait.

Clyde fishers also use natural minnow and clear-water worm. In connection with this last bait, something of a problem is arising. Those who fish for grayling in autumn and winter, using a small float and trotting the worm down to grayling shoals, have adapted the float and fixed-spool reel style of fishing to trout during the spring and summer. Some anglers resent having float fishers operating on good fly water; *vice versa*, some float wormers dislike the deep-wading tactics that fly fishers sometimes use on Clyde. Clearly some compromise must be sought locally. At present Clyde continues to fish well for both parties.

Above Abington, the Clyde is a clear, brisk stream with good trout requiring, if possible, even more skill in their capture. I have happily waded this stretch from Abington to Crawford, and I have made a resolution to wade some year right up to the head of the river, fishing as I go, and from there to cross over the hill to strike the headwaters of the Tweed and fish down to the main road at Peebles. Clyde and Tweed, as stripling rivers, are very close neighbours. Together they transect southern Scotland in a great diagonal from the western end of the Highlands to the eastern borders with England. Their difference is partly due to man, for, where the Tweed has remained primarily a non-industrial valley, the Clyde has attracted the core of Scottish heavy industry, with resulting damage to its waters. But let us thank heaven for the upper Clyde at least, where the whaup still cries its wild cry and the sound of sheep in spring fills the angler's ears as he casts his flies on a pure stream.

Loch Lomond survives both its nearness to the largest centre of population in Scotland and its reputation as a beauty-spot. It is visited and revisited by ever increasing numbers of people. Its waters are boated on, swum in, boiled in camp billy-cans, and fished in. Yet the sight of the 'bonnie, bonnie banks' is still stunningly beautiful at times, and the waters of the largest loch in Scotland are improving year by year as a salmon and sea-trout fishery. It now rates high as a game-fishing water of Scotland.

Like any other large salmon loch, it yields its fish to those who know its waters well. Salmon are not deep-water fish, and the depth of water most likely to yield fish to the fly or to the trolled bait is not normally more than six feet, and is often only two or three feet. Look at a map of the loch, and you will see clearly that its northern end is steep-sided, with Ben Lomond plunging down into a narrowing Highland valley. This is deep fishing, and there is little suitably shallow salmon water round its shores. Look to the southern end of the loch, and you will see that Endrick Water, the principal feeder of Loch Lomond, winds sluggishly through rich alluvial fields before it joins the loch. Off the mouth of the Endrick is a bank of silt, providing some of the best fly fishing for salmon and sea-trout in the whole loch. Here, from May onwards, boats drift and redrift the productive bank, and there are records of six and seven fish in a day that have come aboard to a well-fished fly, particularly a well-fished dropper.

The whole of the southern shore is profitable salmon fishing – if you know the lies. The islands off Balmaha yield good salmon and sea-trout sport and provide also some picturesque drifts. Further up the Balmaha bank, Rowardennan has some delightful bays and points, many yielding salmon to the trolled bait and, less frequently, to the fly. Off

each burn mouth from Balmaha to Ptarmigan Lodge, there is a miniature 'Endrick bank', and those who watch will find the salmon lying in
the shallow water year after year. Often these salmon show freely, and
will not take. I have spent a week trying for fish of this sort, only to find
that with a change of weather they rose stupidly to a chance fly thrown
by a newcomer.

One of the pleasures of fishing Loch Lomond is to be found in late
summer, searching the shoreline for finnock, using a light trout rod
from a carefully handled boat. These gay little fish, and sometimes
better sea-trout, can be picked up by the persistent angler all along the
Rowardennan shore. Unfortunately there are few brown trout to keep
your flies busy, and you may have to endure rather long periods of un-
productivity. Occasionally you take a trout of half a pound or so, or
(rarely) one of a greater weight, but it is the migratory fish that provide
the sport.

In Loch Lomond there is a great variety of fish, not all of them
angler's fish. There are huge pike (the currently accepted record pike
for Great Britain, forty-eight and a half pounds, was caught here);
there are perch, roach, and some say carp. There is also that interesting
'Ice Age herring', the powan. This is a whitefish, not unlike the whitefish of Scandinavia, but different in some details. It is a shoal fish that
moves on summer evenings, making attractive dimples on the loch and
leading many an inexperienced angler to think that the trout have
come on to the rise in force. I have hooked but not landed powan on a
small fly. Occasionally they come to the net, but, as with the whitefish
of Finland, although they may take the fly, their mouths are so tender
that the fly tears out. As a piscatorial curiosity, however, they are of
great interest, and a splendid biological survey of the fish has been made
by the scientists of Glasgow University in their *Studies on Loch Lomond*;
those who wish to follow up the matter should do so there.

The Leven, which empties Loch Lomond, flowing from Balloch to
Dumbarton and the Clyde estuary, is itself a popular fishing river. It
has some of the best early fishing for salmon in the Lomond system; and
the biggest salmon of the year, of up to and over thirty pounds, come
from the Leven. They are superb for colour and shape, but they are not
by any means plentiful. The Leven provides some good summer salmon
and sea-trout fishing; and, although it is rather over-fished, as most
good association water now is, it still offers one of the best pieces of
ticket fishing near Glasgow.

Water is a valuable commodity; even in wet Scotland, water supplies
for domestic, industrial, and hydro-electric purposes is becoming
always scarcer. Loch Lomond is now the source of a new central
Scotland water-supply scheme, providing water for the new town of
Livingston and other places, and the level of the loch has been raised

some inches by a staggered barrage over the Leven near Balloch. This may radically affect the Leven itself, and could produce difficulties for running fish, although no one really knows yet how the coin will fall. The scheme has been the subject of a public inquiry at which the angling interests were well represented by the Loch Lomond Angling Improvement Association; but the objections to the scheme were turned down. Clearly, the amount of compensation flow down the Leven is of the greatest importance to a loch almost entirely dependent on migratory fish for its angling sport. It would be a gross sin against the conservation of natural resources for any reservoir changes to spoil this loch. A recreational and scenic area like Loch Lomond is without price, and to impair the angling in a water that lies at the doorstep of a populous city like Glasgow would surely be unpardonable. Adding to the difficulties, the Hydro-Electric Board is now surveying sites for a possible pump-storage scheme.

The Endrick is the principal feeder of Loch Lomond, and is itself a delightful angling water. It is also spectacular, for on its lower reaches, some three miles from Drymen below the village of Gartness, there is a fall that makes the running salmon leap dramatically in their ascent of the river. These 'Pots of Gartness' draw spectators from far and wide, and give endless Sunday amusement for layman and angler alike.

As a night sea-trout water, the Endrick can be marvellous. I have netted a thirteen-pounder taken on a fly at night, and have myself been lucky enough to take a fish of nine and a half pounds on fly. Salmon can also provide some merry moments on the Endrick, but in recent years I seem to have found far more response from the sea-trout. One bag of them caught by Mrs Elspeth Mitchell above Gartness on a well-known pool she owns deserves mention. This most ardent of lady anglers, fishing in the dark between half past nine and a quarter to midnight, took eleven sea-trout and one grilse weighing altogether forty-three pounds eight ounces. She was fishing with her hard-worked trout rod of nine feet six, and using her own technique of fishing a smallish fly moved slowly and very near the bottom. That night the fish seemed to go mad, and she described the sport as hard work for two hours. On the same pool her guest was also working hard, and he grassed seven fish during that period. Of course, the Endrick does not very often yield sea-trout in these quantities, nor in the very large sizes I have mentioned, although on many nights I have had from its waters an average weight of nearly four pounds per fish. It can be an infuriating river, with fish behaving like trapeze artists and completely ignoring your flies. The Endrick is a water of distinct moods, and the angler should be philosophical, for fretting on the banks only unhinges you, and makes you miss the first solid take when it eventually comes.

Loch Lomond has other feeders, of which the Falloch should be noted. It is a late-running water with somewhat patchy sport, although again, in a giving vein, it can dazzle. Fruin Water, joining the loch on the west side not far north of Balloch, is another stream that draws up from the loch runs of sea-trout and some salmon, although not in the proportions in which the Endrick does. Yet there are some good pools on the Fruin that local anglers know how to fish.

In sum, to the angler Loch Lomond is more than a romantic name. It is a water to be respected, giving sport with migratory fish that can make this loch the equal of many lochs further north whose claim to fame is less well earned.

W.B.C.

Chapter Eight

THE FORTH, THE TEITH, AND THE TROSSACHS

When one reads of the Forth as the fifth largest river in Scotland, his immediate reaction is to look for the misprint. Itself, the River Forth is an inconspicuous stream, wandering down through mossy banks from its headwaters in the north-eastern side of Ben Lomond and from streams in the hills behind lochs Ard and Chon. But this attitude to the Forth lies really in a peculiarity of its name. The Forth above the junction of the Teith is smallish and dull, but below the Teith it has much greater character.

There are in fact three main sources of water for the lower Forth, the river you see at Stirling, where it begins to meander through a long sandy estuary and join the long Firth of Forth, which extends on the north to the tip of Fife and on the south to North Berwick. These three water systems extend back into the Perthshire and Stirlingshire Highland areas, and they include on their courses several lochs of some interest to the angler. Let us consider these three systems individually.

Taking first the central line of feed to the lower Forth, we discover a river and loch system that we can trace back up the River Teith to Callander, to Loch Venachar and Loch Achray, and to Loch Katrine above. This is one of the famous tourist routes in the southern Highlands, and is popularly known as the Trossachs. It is a wonderful route, with the road winding along the banks of Venachar and Achray to a junction, one of whose alternatives leads south-west over the Duke's Pass to Aberfoyle and the other to Loch Katrine. For anyone who has loved Sir Walter Scott's *Lady of the Lake*, this is a most rewarding district, because here he will find Ellen's Isle. Here too he will find the romantic hinterland of Rob Roy McGregor, and a hundred other associations with the incidents and characters that Scott made famous. The angler too finds some interest in the Trossachs.

Glasgow Corporation uses Loch Katrine as its principal, and much applauded, water supply. Few large cities in the world have a flow of soft, pure water like the 79,000,000 gallons a day that Glasgow takes from Loch Katrine. For reasons best known to the Corporation itself, public angling was not allowed on Katrine, although councillors

79

fished it. I doubt whether public health was involved, for the Corporation in the past allowed pleasure-steamers to ply on the loch. Now Loch Katrine is under the control of the Lower Clyde Water Board, and fishing permits are issued for a limited number of boats. There is no bank fishing.

The lower lochs of the Trossachs chain, Achray and Venachar, are fished to quite a large extent – particularly Venachar, the larger one, where in recent years there has been a considerable increase in the number of boats for hire, and where the local club, helped by the Callander Council, has made the water an attraction for visiting clubs and individuals. Achray is less well developed, although boats and permits are readily available locally. Achray has some delightful trout, well coloured and well shaped, and I have seen some baskets of a dozen or more for one rod during a June day. Like its neighbour, Venachar, Achray is an early loch and fishes best before the middle of June. In some years Venachar yields its best fish in late March or early April.

Both Achray and Venachar have been noted as salmon lochs. Venachar, being nearer the river, used to hold the best head of fish, and there are records of not more than fifty years ago that thirty-seven salmon in a year were taken there. In recent years, the capture of a salmon in Venachar or Achray would be newspaper history, for it is a most rare occurrence. This is not entirely due to the difficulty of ascent into the lochs, but in part is almost certainly due to the decline in the runs of salmon up the Teith – a decline caused by the gross pollution of the esturial waters of the Forth.

Loch Drunkie, which nestles in the hills to the south of Venachar, is an angler's loch that has fished well in some recent seasons. It is now a Forestry Commission loch, and is drained by a burn into Venachar. Drunkie trout were about the half-pound average, and had the name of being very red in the flesh and excellent table fish. I hear that this loch also is less productive than it was, probably because there has been too great a rod pressure on it recently. I have heard that it suffers from the set-line fishing so many visiting anglers resort to in Scottish lochs. It is stupid to fish with a legered worm, but many an 'angler' seems to think that fishing is a time for brewing up tea round a fire and playing cards while his worm lies on the bed of the loch working for him. He catches a few fish, often quite small ones, and they are mutilated by swallowing the unattended worm. If only such 'anglers' knew the delights of fly fishing! It could moreover be argued that set-line fishing with the rod laid down on a forked stick by the lochside is illegal, and could be punished under the 1951 Act. But this and many other questions of trout fishing are under review in the findings of the Hunter Report, which may well direct our new legislation for the larger benefit of trout fishing.

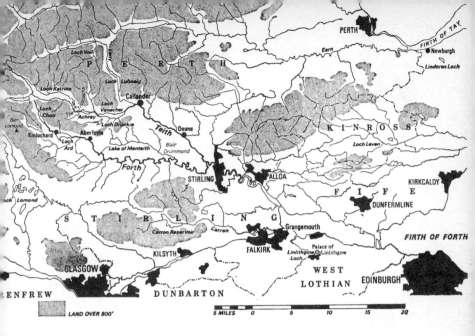

It is regrettable, to put it mildly, that the Hunter Report has been allowed to languish on the shelves of St Andrew's House in Edinburgh for so many years. Published in the autumn of 1965 after a searching investigation by Lord Hunter and his committee, the report contained 127 suggestions aimed at reforming and improving the shape and legislation of Scottish salmon and trout fisheries. Some of the proposals might be impractical from a financial point of view alone; others are certainly not. Over the years, queries in the House of Commons from M.P.s have been fobbed off by inconsequential ministerial statements, although action of some sort is always promised 'in the future'.

The water flowing down from Katrine and Venachar joins the River Leny just above Callander and forms the Teith proper. This makes a fine stream with good pools and a streamy character in places. Between Callander and the junction with the Forth the best of the Teith fishings are to be found. This was once a delightful spring river, with a quality of salmon that even the Tay had difficulty in bettering. The Forth and Teith have always enjoyed the reputation of showing big fish. One of my friends had a thirty-pounder from the lower Teith at its junction with the Forth. I know that fish well into the twenties have often been taken in spring from the Teith, and no doubt some still run the river. But there can be no denying that this lovely river, the Teith, is suffering from the effects of the Alloa and Grangemouth pollutions of the Forth estuary. That such foul discharges should be allowed to continue, when there is an Act to prevent it and to provide a remedy, is disgraceful. The Forth Purification Board should take stronger measures to secure the purification of the Forth estuary and the rehabilitation of the Teith and the Forth as salmon rivers. Not only have catches dwindled on the Teith in recent years, but the fish themselves have at times proved inedible through contamination by oil. Further, I know of at least one case where an estuary netting station on the Forth has become uneconomic because of oil-tainted fish.

The Forth and the Teith are principally spring rivers, and March to April provides the best sport of the year. Salmon seem to run the river early enough to be right up the Leny in Loch Lubnaig by the opening date. Venachar also, like Lubnaig, was held in the past to be a very early water, mentioned by Calderwood as a miniature Loch Tay. Later in the season, by July, the lower Teith can still be a good place for sea-trout fishing, particularly in the Blair Drummond water below Doune. This sport used to tide the river over from the spring run to the coming of the autumn run. As with the Tay, the salmon of Forth come in again in late summer and make up the stock.

I do not mean to suggest that the Teith does not produce any salmon at all. The local waters at Callander provide an odd springer, often an odd brace, to local men spinning the club water in March. Further up the northern arm of the water system, the Leny, there are several productive pools with both springers and later fish. In addition, Loch Lubnaig still from time to time yields salmon, but there is an obvious case for the regeneration of the whole fishery to a level at which it might once again rank as a really good spring fishery. In its position near the centre of industrial Scotland, the Teith, regenerated, would be worth a great deal in rent.

The Leny system, making up the northern watercourse of the Teith–Forth system, draws its main waters from lochs Voil and Lubnaig. There is trouting in both these waters; but, of the pair, Lubnaig deserves the lion's share of mention. The Forth Federation of Anglers, an association of some thirty clubs in the whole Forth area, has taken a keen interest in the development of trout fishings on Lubnaig. Before the Federation's action, that loch was perhaps the most misused in Scotland. The Federation surveyed it, started a progressive restocking policy, put new boats on the loch, and managed it. In the last few seasons results have started to appear. Lubnaig, from being a fished-out water poached by everyone who could get to its banks, is now a water with genuine trouting to offer in surrounds as rich as those of any Highland loch.

While we are recording the virtues of the Forth Federation, we ought to mention Linlithgow Loch, on which it now has the fishings, and which it has restocked. This fascinating water, lying hard by the main street of Linlithgow and making a splendid setting for the Palace of Linlithgow on its shores, is one of the richest, greenest waters of Scotland. It has in the past produced huge trout, but, through the encroachment of coarse fish and pollution, it was virtually wiped off the fishing map as a trout water. Since 1964 the loch has been in the hands of the Federation, and in 1966, after a suitable restocking period, was opened to the public. Its first season produced some superb and handsome trout of three and four pounds. Its second season again produced some marvellous fish, described by one of my friends, who has persisted in fishing Linlithgow until he caught several, as the 'finest trout of my angling life'. The desired six-pounder was taken in May 1968, and fish of five pounds are in the records. These big Linlithgow trout are hard to tempt, and are best fished in the spring and early summer, with the evening as the most popular time. They tend to want large flies very well sunk. Bank fishers have had a big share of the sport, for a deeply sunk fly can be fished most effectively from a shore. Tickets to fish Linlithgow are easy to get, and boats may be hired without too much difficulty. I am sure Linlithgow is going to be one of the most talked of trout fisheries in Scotland. I salute the excellent work undertaken by the Forth Federation on both Linlithgow and Lubnaig, and uphold it as an example to other groups of angling clubs in Scotland.

The Forth itself, the most southerly of the system's three main sources of flow, draws its waters from lochs lying behind it in the hills, lochs Chon and Ard principally, and from hill-burns flowing off Ben Lomond on the south and the Highlands to the north. Loch Ard is the main angling interest. It is an early trout loch and, although it is never a hearty loch yielding very many fish, it is a loch to which anglers return many times in April and May. Its trout are fine-looking and often run to about three-quarters of a pound. I have a great personal liking for the Kinlochard end, and I have found its trout rising well in May and June evenings when a dry fly may be the best lure. On a cold spring day, however, Loch Ard can be a dour place to fish, and many a club has returned to the pier at night feeling that a double whisky and a roaring fire were urgently called for if life and limb were to be kept together. Loch Ard, like any other water, repays study. It is not a prolific loch, but it does yield fish. It is cheap to fish, and it is in a beautiful and readily accessible place. I consider it well worth a spring day or two, and do not rate its success entirely on the weight of the basket.

The Forth is a sluggish river between Aberfoyle and its junction with the Teith above Stirling. It holds trout, although of no great quality; it holds pike and perch in some of its slower reaches, but it also holds sea-trout and salmon. The salmon are usually wormed out when their lies are found, but anglers have had some good sport with fly in some of the brisker pools. No one would call the Forth a great salmon river. It is, in geological and angling terms, a river in eclipse. It has lost much water since it cut its original valley in prehistoric times, and, more tangibly, it has lost water from its headstreams to the Glasgow water supply system. But it still produces fish and is very cheap to take a day on.

One of the waters closely associated with the Forth, and now enjoying a revival, is the only lake in Scotland, the Lake of Menteith. It once was a good trout fishery, but it reverted to pike and perch largely since the Second World War. Now it is regularly restocked, and the pike are closely controlled. The water grows big trout, and since the experiment began in August 1967 the lake has produced some lovely baskets of rainbow and brown trout, showing excellent growth rates. In Menteith fish appear to be putting on better than half a pound in a summer. This is a lovely water. Of its own islands, the one with a priory on it makes a delightful background for a day's drifting, reminiscent of the Castle Island drifts of Loch Leven. Leven, Linlithgow, and Menteith are all green waters. They grow trout well; they produce excellent fly life. They make a splendid trio, for all are associated with the river or the estuary. Few districts anywhere could boast such a group.

One last water in the Forth area asserts again the trend in this district towards good trout fishing, side by side with loss of salmon and sea-trout fishing. This trend is typical of any heavily industrialized area. The Carron dam, or reservoir, stands on the upper waters of the Carron river, a tributary of the Forth estuary. The river is a wreck through pollution. In its lower reaches it is a most disgusting water, a tribute to the filth of industry. On its upper reaches, however, has been built the water-supply reservoir for Falkirk and district. This is a fine trout water, and it produces trout of half to three-quarters of a pound (sometimes bigger) and often gives good baskets. A limit is thirty per boat, although this is seldom attained. Carron fishes well in May and June, and comes on again in late August and September. It is well worth a day in early summer, and, if you can wait until the evening, you might find it very rewarding for small flies and light tackle. Dry fly often fishes well if the wind drops away. Boats are available by prebooking, but no bank fishing is allowed.

W.B.C.

Chapter Nine

LOCH LEVEN

Few waters have the enormous prestige of Loch Leven. All over the English-speaking world you will find people describing a particularly good brand of trout in their lochs or rivers as 'Loch Levens'. Sometimes average weights of fish in really good trout lochs elsewhere in Scotland are said to have fish of 'Loch Leven size'. If someone is keen to impress his hearers on the sweetness of the waters of a loch, he might even say the loch was of 'Loch Leven quality'.

What is this loch that has become part of folklore? Basically, it is a Lowland loch extending to some 3,000 acres and lapping the shores of fertile fields in one of Scotland's richest agricultural areas. Geologists tell us that Loch Leven was formed, between the Lomond Hills and the Cleish Hills, when part of a glacier became trapped in moving down to the Forth. This trapped lump of ice caused the accumulation of glacial debris, which in turn formed the bed of the valley, flooded to the north and east of Kinross. The richness of the bed has been increased by the carrying down of alluvial material from the fields beside it. Loch Leven is a green loch – non-acid, even slightly alkaline at times, and forming algae, which give a greenish appearance to its waters.

But, in fishing terms, it is not only the bed that we find interesting. The shallowness of Loch Leven, with its average depth of only fifteen feet over its whole area, is a vital factor. Shallow, rich water means one thing: abundant fly life hatching from the silt. This Loch Leven most certainly has, with marvellous sustained hatches of fly keeping the trout from mid-April to mid-September and beyond.

There is a persistent rumour that the excellent trout of Loch Leven were imported from Loch Watten in Caithness about 100 years ago. Part of the myth that Loch Leven trout form a separate breed can be dealt with at once. Formerly a popular custom was to stock local waters with *Salmo levenensis* (Gunther's classification), but the biologist Tate Regan suggested that all British and Continental varieties of trout could be included in one classification *Salmo trutta*, and individual differences left to be explained as environmental. Dr Trewavas, as recently as 1953, supported Regan's view.

A Loch Leven trout in its home water is a beautiful fish. It is long and silvery, with a fine scattering of clear black spots down its flanks. Few, if any, Loch Leven trout have red spots. Their flesh is usually of a rich, reddish pink, and their bone structure is heavy and well developed. If you take a Loch Leven trout away from its home water, it gradually loses its characteristics, and, although its progeny revert in time to the undistinguished brown trout of the water that is stocked, there is definitely a short-term value in putting in good stock like Loch Levens. I have certainly fished lochs in Ayrshire in which Loch Leven yearlings had been stocked to supplement the local population of brown trout. You could take fish on successive casts, from the same area of water, one showing the silvery clear markings of the 'Levens' and the other showing the markings of the red-spotted, yellow-bellied local brown loch trout. Further, you could nearly always tell a Loch Leven trout when you hooked it, because it fought with such dash. On one loch I fished, those differences died out within two seasons. Loch Leven trout cannot seriously be considered as a separate race of trout. However, what anglers, as well as scientists, can say is that Loch Leven is a water patently apart from most others in Scotland.

Loch Leven trout grow quickly, and Malloch's table of growth rates made over fifty years ago is probably still true. Trout in Loch Leven aged two and a quarter years weigh about eight ounces; at three and a quarter years they weigh one pound; at four and a quarter, a pound and a half to two pounds; at five and a quarter, two to three pounds; and at five to seven years, two and a half to five pounds. Malloch notes that Loch Leven trout usually die or are caught before they are seven. He also argues that the altitude of Loch Leven, 350 feet above sea-level, holds back the trout growth through the food chain. Thus the loch, he claimed, could produce only an odd five-pounder and perhaps one or two in a decade heavier than this (ten pounds is the heaviest he noted). Had the loch been at sea-level, he concludes, it would have had still heavier fish. Elsewhere the Loch Leven trout have shown an ability to make a very great weight, and in the extreme case in New Zealand total weights of over forty pounds have been produced. These weights make fantasy reading to us. In an evening's fishing most of us are charmed to catch three brace of trout weighing a pound each. From our point of view Loch Leven is a productive and exciting water when it is on form.

Until about 1830, Loch Leven was a larger loch than it is today by some twenty-five per cent. Then, to produce a better fishery, and to make rich alluvial land available for farming, the level was reduced. After that the water was netted as a trout fishery, and was fished increasingly by the new leisured classes that the industrial revolution was producing. Eventually, in 1875, the netting of trout was stopped, and a

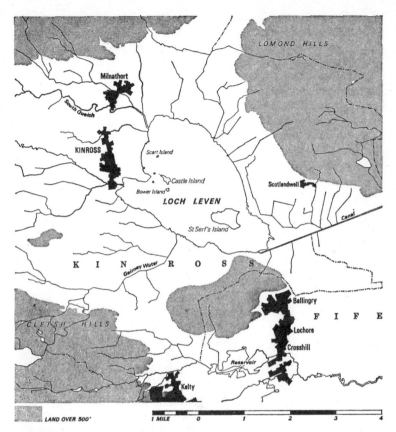

comprehensive stocking plan was introduced to make Loch Leven into
what was held to be the finest loch-trout fishing in Scotland. Speedy
gives a pen portrait of the early days of Loch Leven as a sporting
fishery in 1884. He describes the new boats (probably the same type as
we know today), the 'steady and superior class of boatmen', and the
courteous treatment anglers received from one, a Captain Hall. I
wonder whether present-day anglers will smile at some of this, reflecting
on their own experience of a modern Loch Leven under pressure from
enormous numbers of rods, and on occasion in the past employing
boatmen with – shall we say? – marginally lower virtues than those
that Speedy lists.

Speedy, however, notes two years of fishing decline on the loch, and
with a straight face he advocates that the price of fishing Loch Leven
ought to include a guaranteed basket. Thus the 'Company' might provide a tank full of trout from which the angler might select some to

87

make up his bag in the evening after a poor day's sport. This must rank as one of the silliest ideas in angling history, although the disappointment in Loch Leven's yields at times makes me sympathize with the feeling that produced it.

In a reasonable year, Loch Leven should yield some 40,000 fish, or about eleven fish of one pound to the acre. This is not spectacular. Other waters will produce fifty such fish, and small, rich ponds may produce 200 such fish to the acre. But, on a fishery with some forty boats, each carrying three anglers for two sessions each day (giving fishing on a full day to 240 trout fishers), this is still an impressive total. The best bag I have heard of in recent years was an evening's catch of sixty trout averaging one pound each to two rods. That was in the year of plenty, 1960. What a year that was for the loch! Over 80,000 trout were taken, more than twice the haul of the 'bumper year' noted by Malloch in 1908 – a year that 'far exceeded the catch of any previous year', with 34,000 trout accounted for. Even in 1966 the total catch was 50,000, but in 1969 had dropped to just over 19,000.

Is Loch Leven getting better, or is it merely responding to heavier rod pressure? I would guess that the loch had a heavier stock of fish in the 'fifties and early 'sixties than it had ever had. There has been no artificial stocking for half a century. Eighty thousand fish taken in 1960 represented an acreage yield of about twenty-three trout of a pound average per acre. Since 1960, however, things have looked back, and there is now grave concern at the state of decline into which this famous water has gone. I don't think it will do any injury to the name of Loch Leven if I recount my own experience of this decline since 1960, for I have fished the loch extensively since then, and have, with a rising degree of apprehension, watched a change overtaking it.

First, I have said that Loch Leven is a rich water. It appears that the richness is becoming its own worst enemy. It may be the result of over-fertilization of the water from chemical fertilizers washed in by burns, or it may be from same deeper cause of the loch's own chemistry, but there has been a progressive increase in the 'pea-soup' algae conditions that the loch has sometimes suffered in the past. There is an 'efflorescence' of algae, and the loch often becomes opaque and slimy; although trout continue to rise quite well at times, the quality of the fish often gives me cause for alarm. There are long eel-like trout weighing perhaps ten ounces or three-quarters of a pound where normally they would have been over twice this weight. These fish, once typical of the early part of a slow-starting season, can now be taken right through the summer. In some recent seasons the quality of the fish has risen abruptly in mid-summer and in the later fishings, and September has been like old times. But the fact remains that May and June, once the best months of the season, are now marked by kelt trout in some numbers. The better fish taken on Loch Leven are the smaller ones, half to three-quarters of a pound. These are the new fish, if Malloch's growth chart is right, and they represent the hope for the future. Sadly, it seems that some of these fish also are becoming emaciated in their turn. Why?

This question is being investigated by fishery biologists from Faskally Freshwater Laboratories, Perthshire. No better team could have been called in. Some twenty years of research on Scottish trout lie behind their work, and I have every hope that they will be able to find the reason for the decline in the Loch Leven stock. I trust that, when the cause is discovered, it will not prove too large to be treated. In a day of rising values in fishings, this would be a blow to all anglers, for, parallel with the disappointment in recent years on the loch, runs a desire for the excellent fishings the loch can give. Anglers will not easily forget the wonderful baskets of 1960, nor the occasional excellent patches of sport we have enjoyed since. Loch Leven is in the angling mind and conscience deeper than that. Further, a productive big fishery like Loch Leven is needed by the multitude of club fishers throughout Scotland, for it is their competition Mecca and, above all, the site of the national and international competitions.

A few notes on places and flies for Loch Leven might be helpful. There used to be two piers from which you left by boat. One was the Kinross pier, and the other the 'sluices' pier at the Scotlandwell end, which is now closed. I fished for many years at the Kinross end, and then found that the sluices end, with its beautifully treed shores and ready access to the drifts round the largest loch island, St Serf's, was superb fishing. One could drift through the narrows between St Serf's Island and the shore, with gliders from the local club swinging overhead like outsize gulls. This drift in May, with a Burleigh, a Dark Greenwell, and a Hardy's Gold Butcher on the cast, is as exciting as any Loch Leven fishing.

I like the shallows beyond St Serf's, where there is the largest extent of fly-bearing water I have seen on any loch. You can drift in a west wind from the buoy almost to St Serf's, and you could raise trout all the way. The islands of the loch are fascinating. There is Castle Island and its tower, in which Mary Queen of Scots was imprisoned in 1567. The other island beside this, Bower Island, is set in rather deep water for drifts, but I have seen a fly cast right in near the shore bringing up good trout. From Castle Island towards the little low island we call the Scart is a splendid drifting area. And from the Scart to the Green Isle and the burn mouth is another very productive region. Loch Leven is rich in shallow drifts. It is the drifting fishery *par excellence*. You can motor with your outboard to an up-wind start, and fish all day in a series of long, gentle drifts.

Many Loch Leven anglers fish four flies to a cast, but I have never used more than three. The bob fly and the dropper on the middle of the cast have a fascination for Loch Leven trout, and sometimes, with a 'parachute'-dressed fly on the bob, you can work the bob most effectively on the retrieve and have trout skipping wildly after it, showing you broad flanks of rich, deep spots as they swirl at it. A really worthwhile tactic is to drift down a 'slick' – a long line of spume on the rippled surface. These slicks trap innumerable hatching flies on their oily surface, and trout make short work of them. I have tremendous faith in slicks on lochs, and, given that the water below is not too deep for flies (and it never is on Loch Leven), this is my favourite lochscape feature for a drift.

I cannot end this chapter without reasserting my faith in Loch Leven as a superb trout fishery. It is accessible, near the cities (only half an hour from Edinburgh over the Forth Road Bridge), and there is urgent need for such a trout loch, especially for evening fishing. I shall continue to fish it, for I want to be on its waters when the revival starts. I can almost see it in my mind's eye now. I'm fishing with two of my friends. Someone misses a fish, and almost at once the bow rod is into a good trout. I miss a trout through watching the bow rod playing his. The middle rod raises a fish, and then hooks another – probably the one I missed. Before he can get his fish round behind the boat, where the bow rod is playing his still, and before I can reel in to let him pass, I'm into a trout too. There we are, three rods playing three hard fighting trout at once. Chaos! This is no fantasy. I have seen it before, and I live in the hope that I shall see it again.

Meanwhile, one development in the Kinross–Fife area is the clearing of pike from Lindores Loch, near Newburgh, on the Tay estuary, and stocking the water with rainbow trout, brown trout, and some *fontinalis*, American brook trout. This water has long looked a fertile place, but only in 1966 was it finally taken in hand by Mr Frank Hamilton and turned into one of the best lochs in these parts. Development like this makes one's hopes rise. Scotland has, ripe for such development, more than enough waters to make up for the increase in anglers. Fife itself could well use a new trout loch, for it is surprisingly unsupplied with fisheries. I expect great things of Lindores, and above all a pattern that others could follow to improve Scotland's fishing.

W.B.C.

Chapter Ten

THE TAY AND THE EARN

It takes an intellectual effort to think of the Tay as one river. It is at least three rivers and a loch. Its high origins, which you can trace west into the hills on the borders of Perthshire and Argyllshire, form a sizable river called the Dochart, which itself has on its course a whole range of paces, from rapids to lochs. The Dochart, roaring with some dignity over the Falls of Dochart at Killin, joins the deep, cold waters of Loch Tay, but the river emerging from the eastern end of Loch Tay becomes known as Tay.

From Loch Tay to Logierait and Ballinluig, the Tay is delightful, running through scenery that is half Highland, half Lowland. It is a salmon river with some excellent pools, particularly in the Grandtully area. Salmon run this water from the earliest fishing day in January to the last day of the season in mid-October. This is in no sense a remote upper section of the river, even if it is a good deal less in volume than the Tay below Ballinluig, where the Tummel joins its Highland waters to the Tay, making it the largest river by volume in Great Britain.

Below Ballinluig the Tay, in majestic sweeps, flows through the rich farmlands of Kinnaird and Dalguise, breaks through the Highland fault at Dunkeld House, and turns on to its more easterly course under Dunkeld bridge, down through Caputh, Delvine, and Islamouth to the most luxurious beats of Tay at Stanley and Scone. The river becomes affected by tides at Perth. The lower stretch of water, some ten miles in all from Islamouth to the sea, is a most wonderful area for salmon fishing, with some of the best spring sport and some extraordinary fishing in the later summer and early autumn months.

Below Perth, the river becomes esturial and spreads to form a tidal river often a mile or more wide, but still a river with distinct currents and huge pools, which are netted extensively for their salmon. In this reach of the river the Earn joins the Tay on its south bank. Whether we should regard the Earn as a separate river system or as a tributary of the Tay is an academic point. Certainly the Earn mimics the Tay by rising in the hills above its own large loch, Loch Earn. But it is true that the Earn also shows its own character, often much more of a Lowland one than that shown by Tay. Psychologically, however, the angler thinks of Earn and Tay together, drawing from the salmon of the same estuary. For these reasons I shall include Earn in this chapter.

One of the remarkable things about the Tay is that it has so few towns on its banks – from Loch Tay down to Dunkeld there is hardly more than a single house. Aberfeldy contrives (like so many other small towns) to sit a little way back from the river. Dunkeld is a Tay bridge town, straddling its important bridging-point with its smaller south-bank neighbour, Birnam. Eight miles below this, Caputh is a tiny village, set almost a mile back from the river, and Murthly, again a small but charming little Perthshire town, sits more than a mile away from the river and seems geographically not to be part of the bankside community at all. Stanley is a larger village standing on the south bank of Tay some eight miles above Perth, and no one would call it parti-cularly big, although the main street, as in several other Perthshire towns, strings out for over half a mile. Below this there is no riverside village until Perth itself is reached. This attractive capital city bridges the river at its lowest conventional crossing-point.

Tay is a very clean stream – volume for volume, perhaps less pol-luted than most other salmon rivers in the country. Its huge flow and its fast, stony character ensure this. Further, the Tay above Islamouth drains a comparatively well-scoured part of the country, and its floods are usually clear. Lower Tay gathers silt from the Isla and from its own lower course, and its floods are often muddy. I have seen the Tay at Caputh running ten feet up on the gauge at the bridge, but clear enough to see the bottom in three or four feet of water and, most im-portant, clean enough to fish. I have taken fish from Tay in a flood at seven feet six inches at this point, when the lower river was virtually useless because of silt turbidity. In this aspect of its character the Tay is typically Highland.

Another important feature of the Tay is that it is not a 'flash' river. It reacts only slowly to rain, and indeed may even react more to wind on Loch Tay than rain on the hills beside that vast reservoir. But, once raised, Tay can run high for weeks. Its flood pattern is probably one of the last remaining 'natural' régimes of the Lowlands or the Highlands. Many rivers that used to run in steady, falling floods, and give ex-cellent fishing in the clearing water, now rise and fall with tremendous rapidity as a direct consequence of hill drainage improvements. Tay gathers itself to a rise and usually comes up slowly, holds its floods im-pressively, and fishes splendidly for days on end as they settle and dwindle. An inch on Tay at Caputh bridge, of course, means that a huge amount of water has been added to its flow. Five feet of a rise at Caputh brings down a vast volume, increasing the Tay's flow by several times the amount of many a whole river system.

An angler on Tay brings his trout to the net.

Over its total length, including the estuary, the Tay harbours very considerable stocks of trout. These often run to several pounds, but anglers need not think that all they have to do is to get a day's trouting on Tay and catch fish of this size. The biggest Tay trout I have heard of recently have been taken, unromantically, on bait near the sewage-pipes at Marshall Street in Perth! There, a five- or six-pounder may not seem unusual. I heard of an angler who watched a local man fishing at this point with very coarse worm tackle, and hooking and bringing up a trout of about five pounds. The fish had to be cranked up some twenty feet of wall, and just near the top it kicked itself off. You might have expected the fisher to give a stream of curses, or at worst to throw himself into the Tay in despair at losing such a monster. Not a flicker of disappointment showed. The angling spectator, who was shaken to the core by seeing this huge trout lost, asked the local man whether he was not greatly disappointed at losing it. 'No' really,' he commented. 'Ye see, I've twa like it a'ready, and I've loast another fower.' Of course, cranking large trout up the wall of the river near the end of a sewage-pipe is hardly sporting fishing. I don't think I should want to take my five-pounders in this way, but it does prove something of the quality of Tay trout when man, inadvertently, adds a bit of protein to the fish's diet.

The angler's trout of Tay are lovely fish. They run to a pound or more, and they fish exceedingly well in the earlier part of the trout season. I have seen magnificent trout rising hard to Olives and March Browns at Logierait in March. In April there are some prodigious hatches of the Dark Olive and the March Brown, and dry-fly fishing for these good trout of Tay can lead to some memorable sport. The fish are at their least shy in March and April, but, as soon as evening fishing starts seriously (in May), the trout become tempting, though difficult. At this time of year many anglers turn to the natural minnow and, particularly, diving minnow to take the trout. From the gravelly runs of the middle Tay, trout of well over three pounds are taken on this bait every year. I have seen a basket of twelve averaging nearly two pounds each. This method of fishing, banned on some smaller rivers, is excitingly pursued on Tay. Often the angler wades deep, working his diving minnow into holes in the gravel of the stream. On a water as large as middle Tay, the bait seems to disturb the trout little, and they continue rising well to fly, but not necessarily taking the artificial kind freely.

The trouting of Tay is a great Scottish fishing potential, for at present it is almost wholly ignored by the tenants on most of the salmon beats, for the best reasons. With trout legislation possibly imminent, it appears that an imaginative and properly run plan could set up Tay as a trout fishery of note. Trout fishers on Tay need not be near salmon fishers on a beat; they need not spin (for that would certainly take

A spring day on Loch Tay at Kenmore gives memorable angling for two-pound trout.

F

salmon) or fish at night. In short, there is every reason to support development of the Tay as an organized trout fishery, side by side with the salmon fishings, once legislation makes control of the trouting possible. At present there is something like anarchy on the river as re-gards trout fishing. Where there are enough keepers, the casual trout fishers are well handled and, if they are uninvited guests, kept off. Where there are few or no keepers, the mobs gather, fishing by catch-as-catch-can methods and antagonizing everybody, particularly those sporting trout fishers who have taken the trouble to get permission to fish and who are often restricted in methods and times of fishing. It seems that, until legislation proper comes in, the Tay will not give its best in trout fishings.

As a salmon river, the Tay has no equal and few rivals. It has one of the finest spring runs in Scotland, and produces consistent sport from mid-January onwards in its main spring beats. A good lower beat may take between 250 and 350 springers before mid-May, when the boats come off. It may then take 150 salmon and grilse in the summer season, usually when the tenants are local men fishing at low summer rents. When the fishing tenants return for the autumn fishing about mid-August, the same beat may again produce 200 salmon before the season ends in mid-October. The spring fish average fourteen pounds each and better, many running to twenty or even thirty pounds. Numerous forty-pounders have been taken, and a few still heavier fish. The summer fish are in two classes: small summer ones of the nine-pound class and heavier fish of around fifteen pounds. These weights crudely reflect the early summer run in June and the continuing summer run of larger fish that people the pools of Tay from spring on-wards, giving sport with fresh fish throughout the summer. The grilse runs of Tay (which seem to be very much on the increase in the 'sixties) bring in fish of five to seven pounds. These can give flashing sport in July and August.

When the nets come off in late August, the Tay fills up with fish. Fresh fish with sea-lice on their flanks run the river right to the closing day in October, and other salmon, in varying condition but generally firm and takable, come in good quantities. The autumn run includes some very big fish, of thirty to forty pounds, and these are often for years the subject of anglers' stories, true and embroidered. In recent seasons, the biggest autumn fish has been a fifty-four pounder, but several in the mid-forties have been taken. Many more have stripped reels of their line and backing, have exhausted anglers, and have broken loose to become Tay legends. Miss Ballantyne's record fish of sixty-four pounds, taken at Caputh in 1922, was an autumn salmon. I tend to believe all I hear about big autumn fish, because there really are pro-digious salmon in the Tay, and it is a river with a great weight of

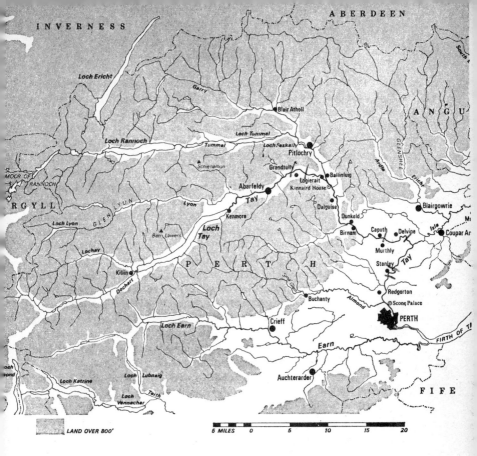

LAND OVER 800'

5 MILES   0   5   10   15   20

current. Oddly enough, on Tay, the big springer seems to be far easier
to kill than the really big autumn fish. There may be a good reason for
this, related to the temperature of the river and to other factors.

Tay salmon on the lower river are largely spun for, or harled from
boats. The process of harling, though productive, is hardly everyone's
idea of sport. The boats of Tay used to be double-manned by boatmen
operating two pairs of oars. Two anglers sat side by side in the fishing
seat at the stern, and they fished their lures at varying distances behind
the boat from two or three rods. The devon minnows, the plugs, the
large flies, and other lures were fished across the lies as the boat kept
its place on the current (often by vigorous rowing) and moved back
and forth across the stream to 'harl' the baits over the salmon. A boat
may fish carefully over a great number of lies in a day, and the salmon
that seize the lures undoubtedly see the baits presented in a most
attractive way. But it is essentially the boat that is fishing. The angler
sits beside the rods ready to act should the bait be taken, but he is not
actively fishing the baits. Further, the rods used in this method of
fishing are often provided by the ghillie. I have watched some very

coarse tackle indeed being used, with traces breaking at thirty pounds' strain or more. Tackle need not be like this, of course; but (sadly) it need not necessarily be any finer in harling. Add to this the modern outboard motor, making the ghillie's life as relaxed as the fisherman's, and you have a picture of harling that reminds you very strongly of the commercial rod fishing that one meets on salmon rivers in Norway.

Bank fishing the Tay is very hard work. The river is so large, and the lies are often very difficult to cover. A boat is an obvious necessity for reaching some of the water to be fished; and, clearly, boat fishing can be splendid for this purpose if it is used to provide a floating plat-form from which the angler casts. Many beats of Tay operate like this from an anchored boat, and the sport can be excellent, flies and baits being cast with the angler's own tackle in a highly skilful way. I am most certainly not averse to boat fishing. Nor, deep down, am I in principle against harling. I merely happen to be a hedonist in my fishing, and I feel that casting a fly over the Tay is a wonderful wading sport, and spinning the pools of Tay calls for good casting and leads to some very exciting fights. Harling often makes for easy living and easy fishing, without the necessity of knowing how to cast, how to hook a fish, how to follow and land a fish, or even how to tie a fishing-knot.

When the Tay in summer falls to show its bare bones, it is still a very big river. In fact, it is only when the river falls away to the lowest levels that some of the lies can be waded to and fished properly. This is when a long greased or floating line, fishing a small double-hooked fly, is ideal. It makes for magnificent sport. Fish lie in the faster water in June and July and can be hard fighters. Since one is often deep in the river wading when the salmon is hooked, it may be difficult to get out of the stream in time, with the reel screaming like a demented thing, and with eighty or ninety yards of line in play before you get to terms with your salmon. That is what you get from Tay! A fish of eighteen pounds, fresh from the sea, going hard down a fast run is without parallel in salmon fishing.

Loch Tay is a fishing world all on its own. The Tay runs its first springers during winter, and they make their way up to Loch Tay and by the beginning of January may be seventy miles from the sea. Tra-herne noted fresh salmon in Loch Tay in November. When the spring season opens on Loch Tay in mid-January, big fresh fish are taken. Many of them are well over twenty pounds, and there have been some catches averaging nineteen pounds over more than a score of salmon.

Fishing is largely done from the Kenmore end of the loch, although, in these days of outboard motors, almost any part of the loch can be reached. There are some excellent lies at the Killin end too, and off the Lochay river. The favourite bait used to be the gold sprat, but in recent years a wider range of lures has been fished, sometimes with great success. The Kynock Killer is well regarded here, no less than on the river fishings of Tay. This bait, invented by a man who lives at Logierait, is a plastic diving-plug, which looks for all the world like a large coloured ice-cream cone. The 'killer' dives when the current pushes on its 'lower lip' – a small diving vane; and it can search out lies in a most impressive way. It fishes with a wobbling, diving action, and salmon find it quite irresistible at times. Another bait of rising popularity in recent years is the Toby spoon. This long, sinuous, wobbling spoon is a great killer of spring fish on the River Tay, and it has its devotees on Loch Tay also. But the 'home' bait of the Tay is the wooden devon minnow. Usually, like the Spey devon, it is fished as a light shell rising and falling sensitively with the vagaries of the current; but some of the lower beats fish a weighted devon, either a wooden devon with a lead head or a lead belt, or a metal devon turned out of lead alloy. These heavy devons fish best where long casting is needed, and where heavy streams prevent the lighter baits from fishing deeply enough.

Of the tributaries of Tay, the Tummell, Lyon, and Earn are the most worthy of mention. Tummel is the Highland stream, deep, clear, and fast like Tay itself. Its waters form, above Pitlochry, the hydro-electric dam of Faskally, and this long blanket of water has robbed us of a beautiful reach of river, with splendid fishings in the wildest tradition of Highland sport. Tummel still fishes well from Pitlochry down, and it is a splendid fly water in May and June for the springers moving up from the lower river. Tummel is also a marvellous trout stream, particularly in April and May, when its trout rise superlatively to large Dark Olives. Fish of three and four pounds often fall to dry fly at this time.

Tummel itself once had an excellent tributary, the Garry, but the earliest of the hydro-electric activities left this river practically dry, and the subsequent work of the North of Scotland Hydro-Electric Board has finished it off as a river. Now it runs pitifully low from Blair Atholl down to its merging with Loch Faskally, though salmon still nose up its tiny watercourse late in the season. Above Blair Atholl the river is a stone quarry, nothing else. Its rugged, pot-holed bottom is bare by the roadside for everyone to see. Once this was a Landseer-painted river with foaming falls and turbulent, fast pools. Its destruction is a monument to the disgraceful exploitation of a river, to short-sighted planning, to the 'dust-bowl' mentality. This was the worst mistake of hydro-electric activity in Scotland, for later agreements helped to save most of the rivers affected by hydro-power generation, and, to be fair, the North of Scotland Board is now one of the most fish-conscious bodies in the land. It runs hatcheries, maintains rivers and fish passes, and counts salmon assiduously. But it also destroys, even though as little as it can, when it builds a dam. The day of hydro power appears to be over; capital expenditure on dams is now regarded as not yielding enough power in return. The day of thermal generation, however, is not by any means over, and the day of the atom is virtually here. The rivers of Scotland may not, perhaps, be further interfered with, and we may take comfort from this.

A short distance below the outflow from Loch Tay, the River Lyon joins the Tay on its north bank. This is a charming little Highland river, with runs of salmon in the late spring and throughout the summer and autumn. The Lyon often holds a splendid stock of fish by August or September and, in a rather frustrating way, shows the angler what he is missing, by spectacular displays of leaps and splashes. But these leaping Lyon fish seldom take. They are usually earlier-run fish already far on in spawn. Many may have taken up the redd lies that they will eventually spawn on. It is a blessing of nature that such fish become virtually uncatchable. The stock of Lyon fish is preserved by it. But Lyon can fish well in the late spring, with good fish, some of well over twenty pounds. Its deep, rocky pools are often hard to fish with fly or bait, and there is a local tradition of worming on some beats. This confirms its Highland status. Its scenery, however, needs no confirmation as Highland, for this is a region of great splendour, with hills like Schiehallion towering above a rugged glen through which a fine rocky river cuts its way down to the Tay.

The Earn, seen from the main road between Auchterarder and Perth, looks very like Matthew Arnold's picture of a 'foiled, circuitous wanderer'. On this lower half of its length, the Earn is a deep, clear, sluggish river with some salmon pools, many good trout that rise in its slower reaches, and an assortment of coarse fish also available there, including grayling, roach, and pike. In its middle and upper reaches, however, the Earn becomes a nice streamy water with good trout, sea-trout, and salmon fishing.

It is a river rapidly being rehabilitated, for certain local proprietors have joined together to form an improvement association, and they have shortened the season voluntarily, imposed certain restrictions on salmon fishing (they permit only fly fishing after the end of the spring), and in general kept a close eye on stocks and on fishing. The river seems to be improving as a spring water. The first fish of spring is often taken in February, and more certainly in early March. A fairly substantial run can follow this, and fish may run fresh until May. The summer is usually a rather slow time on the Earn, with low water and high temperatures advancing the growth of weed and staling the pools. But sea-trout run the river and provide some very good evening and night sport in June and July, although they are not really plentiful.

It is in the autumn, however, that the fishings of the Earn really come into their own. The autumn-run fish include some very large salmon of the upper twenties and thirties of pounds. Many later fish now ascend the river after the season has closed. Local anglers resented losing this run with the earlier closing date (the 15th instead of the 31st October), but it may well be to the great good of the river to leave the stale summer and spring fish alone from mid-October, and let the later-running fish have clear access to the spawning-beds.

Loch Earn, in these days, is not really a very good angler's loch. It does have stocks of trout and char in it, and there is some nice fishing for the trout in May and June on the southern shore, but the sailing and water-skiing fraternities have virtually monopolized the loch. In a way it is not an important loss. If Loch Earn had been really good, it might still have continued to fish despite the water-sports activities. But Loch Earn was poor – a hard, dour loch from which, many a time, one would come off blank. It is reasonable to see water sports concentrated on a loch we could well afford to lose, leaving some other waters like Venachar and Lubnaig to be properly developed as fisheries.

The Almond, which runs parallel to the Earn and joins the Tay just above Perth on the south bank, is not a very interesting anglers' river. It carries a good run of salmon in the autumn, and they are to be seen leaping at Buchanty Spout, but not very much fishing is done on this small spawning river. There are some trout, though the Almond is, generally speaking, a fairly barren river with a cold Highland feel. Its headwaters, reached by driving up through the picturesque Sma' Glen from Crieff, are attractive, but not really worth fishing except in a picnic spirit.

The Isla, joining the Tay above Stanley on the north bank, is rather like the Earn in its lower reaches, where the current is slow and the appearance of the river canal-like. The lower Isla contains some very big trout and grayling and, it is said, good pike. Further upstream the Isla takes on a more interesting character, and provides good trout fishing and some quite exciting autumn salmon fishing in the Meigle and Coupar Angus areas. The Ericht, which joins the Isla, is a minor salmon tributary, but it also has some pleasant trouting to offer anglers in the Blairgowrie district. Some very large trout have been taken in the deeper pools above the town. The Ericht is fed from the snows of Glenshee, and in its upper reaches provides some marvellous scenery. It is hill-burn country up here, and the Ardle and its tributaries and the Shee Water and its burns make Glenshee a wonderful area for hill-burn trouting.

This is the merest sketch of Tay. The details about a river like this would need a book to themselves. Tay embraces all the wildest and most prolific aspects of fishing; it runs the whole span of a year in its

January to October season; it yields fish big enough to talk about in any salmon circles in the world; and it can bring forth dreamlike quantities of salmon. One beat near Perth recently had in sequence a day of twenty-five, a day of fifteen, and a day of eleven. A good opening day on Redgorton may give ten to fifteen fish. A late summer day's fly fishing at Islamouth may basket a dozen or more salmon. At Caputh, tens and elevens are not unusual, especially after mid-August, when the nets come off. I know well the satisfaction you feel with a brace and a half of summer fish on the fly, or five fish to your own rod spinning in autumn. Long may we see the fly line uncurling in its cast over the summer streams, or feel the wooden devon fanning round in the currents of the pools. Best of all, long may we all enjoy the sudden stopping of the bait as a salmon takes, followed by the double pull as he shakes himself, then turns to run and make our rod buck and our reel scream.

Tay, Tummel, Earn and Almond, Dochart, Lochay and Lyon cover the largest water-catchment area in Scotland. It covers the heart of the southern Highlands, embracing such areas as the Rannoch Moor, and Glen Lyon with Schiehallion rearing its peak over Loch Rannoch and Ben Lawers over Loch Tay. But the Tay is far more than a Highland river, for it pierces through the Highland 'wall' (that impressive fault that transects Scotland) at Dunkeld, and from there flows through Lowland scenery and fertile country. I, who know Tay well, have often felt something akin to a primitive terror in thinking about its antiquity and vastness, as I have looked down from one of its bridges, say at Dunkeld or Caputh; have looked into its streams; and have let my mind boggle at the idea that, for longer than recorded history, myriads of salmon have forged up its waters to spawn.

W.B.C.

Chapter Eleven

ARGYLL

It would be fatuous to try to describe every fishing water in the county of Argyll. Not only are there many lochs and burns accessible from the main roads, but the county has tremendous resources of hill fishings. I remember walking from a point about four miles south of Inveraray across to Loch Awe, and counting twenty-one fishable lochs on the way. I fished four of them as I walked, and in each one had either a trout or a rise from a trout. As far as burns go, you have only to think of the great wealth of good trout burns that flow into Loch Awe to realize that again, in this one region of Argyll alone, there is water enough for a volume on its own. As a young fisher, I once spent a splendid holiday centred on Dalmally. I fished myself to the south into the hills above Cladich, to the north up that remarkably barren water the Strae, and on other days drifted the head of Loch Awe. It was a feast of varied trout fishing. Further down the 'leg of Kintyre' is another wide variety of burn and loch fishing, culminating in the waters round Campbeltown.

The richness of Argyll, however, is not only a matter of hill-lochs and hill-burns. The River Awe, draining the massive reservoir of Loch Awe, is a spectacular, if short, salmon river. The Orchy, the main feeder river of Loch Awe, is also an excellent salmon river from late spring onwards. North of this river and loch system lies the little-explored fishing country of upper Loch Etive, with waters like the Etive and Kinglass rivers draining wild hill country threaded by numberless burns. Appin and Benderloch are surprisingly dry areas in comparison with other parts of Argyll, but the Creran river, with a good run of migratory fish, is the focus of the area.

South of Oban we find ourselves again in a sub-area with tremendous fishing interest to which it lends its own character: the area from Loch Nell – a salmon and sea-trout loch of some potential – to the Euchar river at Kilninver (draining Loch Scamadale), where sea-trout and grilse run well in summer, and through that lovely tract of trout-loch country to Kilmelfort, where there are several anglers' hotels of some standing and antiquity.

Loch Awe always seems to me to have made a wrong decision at some time in its remote past, for at Ford it very nearly manages to drain west into a tributary of the Add and enter the sea at Crinan. What a river that would have made! As it is, the River Add forms a distinguished small salmon river of the west-coast spate type. It carries a good run of sea-trout and summer and autumn salmon and can fly-fish delightfully.

I cannot pass Crinan without pointing out that the canal that carries fishing boats and yachts from the inner waters of Loch Fyne to the outer waters of the Sound of Jura is itself a most pleasant little piece of trout fishing. I have found the canal lying gentle and warm on a May morning, reflecting the woods and even showing a pheasant or two on its banks, more like a slow English trout stream than a navigation canal. Trout rise well to wet fly here if the wind ripples the surface, and to dry in the idyllic conditions I describe in May. I found the fish to be of good size, several of twelve to fourteen ounces coming to the dry fly. I suspect the canal has its secret monsters, too, running to several pounds.

Loch Fyne itself has a little world of tributary rivers and a multitude of lochs in the hills behind. The Aray at Inveraray, the Castle water that one admires over the eighteenth-century bridge just before Inveraray, is a salmon-spate water with some excellent sport in a fining-down flood in summer and autumn. The Douglas, to the south, and the Shira to the north are good sea-trout and salmon waters. The public have access to these through the Argyll Estates office on payment of a reasonable daily rent. The River Fyne joins the sea-loch at its head, and provides some merry sea-trout and whitling fishing in summer and autumn, and salmon fishing of some note after summer spates. Many of the upper Fyne pools are deep and rocky and are wormed for their fish, but the lower parts of the river provide some good night fishing for sea-trout and much more open fly-fishing conditions. Here again the water can be rented, and local inquiries are likely to be fruitful. The estuary itself is a popular place for a sea-trout fishing holiday. Time and tide, however, need to be your allies here, for sea-trout come best to the fly at high tide and at dusk.

The south side of Loch Fyne is excellent country, but, apart from smallish waters that flow west (like the Kilfinan Water) and produce good sea-trout and the occasional salmon in summer, the main rivers of the district flow east or south. The dominating water system is the one centred on Loch Eck. This long narrow loch drains into the head of the Holy Loch by the River Eachaig, which, in proper ply in summer and autumn, can yield excellent catches of grilse and sea-trout, with many better salmon as well. Fish may, however, run through to Loch Eck, and anglers who have studied this loch and know where the lies are can often have good sport both on trolled baits and fly. Loch Eck often

yields fish remarkably early for the west coast, and late May salmon are not unusual, lying as a rule at the head of the loch. The loch is also noted for the size of some of its sea-trout. In autumn some huge ones of ten to twelve pounds run up the Cur to spawn, and these are sometimes taken in the Cur itself and occasionally in Loch Eck. This is autumn sport, and it is often well on towards the end of the season before the right running conditions are encountered.

Of the other Cowal waters that drain east and south, the Ruel of Glendaruel is the most prominent. It is a river with a lovely hill glen set in wild Highland country. Like many of its neighbours, it is a spate river, but in this west-coast area of Scotland it has a good showing of productive spates each summer and autumn. As one would expect, it is a salmon, grilse, and sea-trout river, with only the usual smallish population of Highland brown trout. The Ruel can be fished from at least one hotel in the area, the Glendaruel Hotel, and I have heard the fishings of this delightful little Highland river praised extensively.

Argyll has a very good list of small salmon waters. The Carradale in Kintyre fishes well; the Douglas, the Aray, the Shira (all, as I noted, clustered near Inveraray) have sport in summer, particularly the Aray. The Add carries a splendid run of fish and, water permitting, can fish really well. I have already described the Fyne and the Cur-Eck-Eachaig system. These represent only a few Argyll waters of the small salmon-river class. Throughout the county there are similar fishings, and some good sport to be had from smaller waters. Hill lochs abound in every area, and the furthest you may need to travel to a good day's loch fishing may be ten miles (I am thinking of Oban itself). Often you need only mount your trout rod and walk a short step to the water.

Before leaving the waters of Argyll, it might be worth while to look more carefully at two of them: the troutings of Loch Awe, and the salmon fishings of the Awe–Orchy system. First, Loch Awe – one of the largest, most popular, and at times most prolific trout waters of Scotland. Loch Awe is some fifty miles round, with extensive bays, inlets, shingle banks, and sandy spits. The western reaches of the loch from about Portinnisherrick to Ford on both banks have some of the best of the shallow water, but it lacks the character of the north-eastern end, which carries a scattering of tree-clad islands of striking beauty.

Three of the favourite trout-fishing centres of Loch Awe are Loch Awe Hotel, a mile or so beyond Dalmally on the Oban road; Ardbrecknish Hotel, eight miles down the south shore of the loch from Dalmally; and Port Sonachan Hotel, some nine or ten miles down the south shore. All these hotels, and others in the area, have boats on Loch Awe. There is a tradition that Loch Awe is the earliest trout loch of any note in Scotland. Lying, as it does, open to the mild west, it benefits from the warm influences of the Gulf Stream, the absence of frost and snow, and the gentle, wet mildness of the prevailing wind, all of which make for an easy start to the spring. I have seen records of tremendous bags in March out from Ardbrecknish and Port Sonachan. April often fishes well, too, and May finds trout still rising freely in the bays, often to dry fly rather than wet. Fishing early is, however, always something of a gamble. Weather can turn from a gentle spring to angry end-of-winter. Winds of March and April can shriek rather than fan. Yet Awe, year after year, provides trout for its Easter guests and for the innumerable anglers who make it the first club outing of their year.

It is quite remarkable that Awe has remained productive, because in recent years it has become rather over-fished. I have seen scores of parties fishing its waters on a spring Saturday, and have boiled at the crude way in which many of them thought to try. Loch Awe, more than any other loch I know, suffers from the legered-worm technique. However, it does not yet seem to have made too much of an impression. The size of Loch Awe may be the critical factor. This complaint does not imply that there are not also fishers in the best Scottish tradition, fly fishing from the banks and drifting the bays of the loch. A huge population of accomplished fly fishers returns spring after spring to Loch Awe, and it yields them fish. But the legering continues, and it can be annoying to anglers wading the bank waters, fly fishing as they go.

The size of Awe fish has in recent years run down from a half-pound average to about six ounces. The quality of fish, however, varies from place to place, and for some reason the very best trout are seldom taken in the usual fly-caught bag. I remember seeing the keeper on the Cladich worming the mouth of the river when it was in spate, and taking several trout of a pound and a half to two pounds. He trotted his worm with great skill, moving down the banks with it and letting the morsel bump over the stones. These good trout fought tremendously and gave great sport. I wish more of them would rise to our flies on the main loch.

Loch Awe has salmon, and the area round the entry of the Orchy is the most favoured. Fish are taken on troll mostly here, but it seems to me that local study and favourable conditions would bring good fly sport. Oddly enough, few charges are made for salmon fishing in the loch, although you need the permission of an owner or a tenant, such as the proprietor of a hotel.

At the head of Loch Awe, near Dalmally, there are perch and pike. They can be found also beside Kilchurn Castle, where a small reedy loch lies on the banks of Awe. Many of the pike in this little loch, called the Derclach Loch, are of a good size, and I have heard of fish in the 'teens of pounds.

The Awe–Orchy system is similar in its physical configuration to a number of other important Scottish salmon systems based on a short, heavy river that links a large loch with the sea, while at least one big head-river takes many of the salmon from this lower system into its pools. I have in mind the Ness system, the Shin system (before its recent change to a hydro régime), the Shiel system, and – by no means the last of the type in Scotland – Loch Lomond. If we compare the Ness system and the Awe system, we find some striking parallels. In both cases the best of the spring fishing is to be had in the upper tributary or tributaries of the loch, and not in the lower river – although, to be fair, in any river of passage like the Awe or Ness certain fish will be taken as they rest.

The Orchy is an earlier river than the Awe; the Garry is an earlier river than the Ness. The reason is that fish running into the larger river of the system in winter make for the colder waters of the feeder stream, and find their lies by perhaps as early as February. The Ness system is of course, as a whole, a true spring system, flowing east and taking fish into its waters in winter and very early spring, while the Awe is a west-coast system and not a true spring water at all. Yet the earliest of the Awe fish, running in March or even February (in small numbers), go straight through the loch to the Orchy and provide sport as far up-stream as Bridge of Orchy in March and April.

The bulk of the salmon sport in the Awe itself is summer fishing. It is a very remarkable river. On the one hand, it can be generous in summer, with multitudes of grilse and small summer fish of the eight- to ten-pounds class that provide sport of great character in the fast pools. On the other, the Awe has a run of large fish to make its name remem-bered. The Awe has produced its fifty-pounders and, more often, has broken and lost its fifty-pounders in the turbulent and fast pools strewn with great boulders.

In recent years, the Awe has become the centre of a remarkable kind of hydro-electric scheme. It is a scheme that depends not so much on the action of a head of water, falling through turbines from the river itself (although this conventional abstraction and fall-generation is still done to some extent at Inverawe), as on a storage technique. Water from Loch Awe, collected at a low barrage in the Pass of Brander, is pumped up to a storage reservoir on Cruachan. Off-peak electric power is used to raise the water to this storage height. Then, for the peak hours of next day, the water so stored is released to generate power.

Naturally the Awe has been affected by this scheme, but it is far from being as badly affected as, say, its smaller neighbour the Shin. The river is reduced in flow, but it is still impressive. One pool has been lost at the top where the barrage is – the famous disputed pool; but the river has kept its main characteristics. It is still subject to good flow in high water, it remains runnable for salmon in summer droughts (in fact, it always did this because of the vastness of Loch Awe), and it seems to be giving a good account of itself under the new situation.

The character of the old Awe, which presumably the new Awe will recall in spates at least, was formidable. It was a river of huge volume and great pace, and its bed was a mass of boulders and pot-holes. This character was reflected in some of the fishing techniques developed on the Awe, principally in that remarkable sport, worming the Awe. Anglers familiar with the bed of the pools realized that their flies were not searching the deeper and more difficult lies well, and the technique was developed of using a heavily leaded worm, or a group of worms, to search out pot-hole and difficult boulder lies that were under some surface turbulence but were themselves not turbulent. I have friends who tell the most hair-raising stories of worming the Awe. They speak of lines run out and tackle snapped; of heroic fights with fresh fish in conditions that took the angler stumbling and panting down through pool after pool of dangerous wading water. These are the sagas of salmon fishing, the very substance of its sport. Having waded and fly fished the Awe, I do not now blink at anything I am told about it. I have seen my own hook straightened out by a salmon in fast water, and have discovered just how hard landing a salmon from its waters can be. This character of being the *enfant terrible* of Scottish rivers the Awe shares with its similar (but now changed) Highland neighbour the Shin, where there is turbulence and pot-hole, power and hazard. The Shin, alas! is now, because of water-abstraction, a much more frail river than it was. The Awe is partly tamed, but to a significantly smaller degree than the Shin.

Argyll extends to embrace several of the islands, including Mull; but, acting in our own classification, we have taken the Hebrides as a world on its own. This is just as well, for Argyll would become unwieldy to describe if its riches, already great, were amplified by the jewels of the islands.

W.B.C.

Chapter Twelve

THE NORTH AND SOUTH ESKS

The burns that gather from the hills and form the North Esk river rise from the southern and eastern slopes of the same hills that provide the Aberdeenshire Dee with headwaters. The South Esk rises within a few miles of these North Esk headwaters, amid a cluster of peaks over 3,000 feet high. The two rivers run very nearly parallel, entering the sea within four miles of each other, the North Esk in a curious estuary among the sand-dunes three miles north of Montrose, and the South Esk by way of Montrose Basin.

On their courses, both North and South Esks begin in high heather and moor, but for most of their way run through delightful farming country, with well-wooded estates on their banks and rich meadows lying in the haughs. The North Esk may well take the prize for scenery in its upper courses. The splendid gorge at The Burn above Edzell remains vividly in one's mind. It is a series of deep pots cut into the reddish rock, of spouts and gushes of stream and what the fishers call 'loups'. These salmon leaping-places are always memorable, and none more so than those of the Burn gorge.

The South Esk runs through Glen Clova, not collecting many tributaries of note until it reaches what is in effect the first of the parkland estates at Cortachy Castle, where the Prosen joins the river. This meeting with the Prosen in the lands of the 'bonnie Earl o' Airlie' brings the river up to a fair size, which it retains for almost its entire length to its meeting with the sea at Montrose.

Both North and South Esks have good runs of spring salmon, and both rivers improved considerably in the course of the 'fifties and 'sixties. One of the principal causes of the improvement in the North Esk was the way in which spawning was opened up by the River Board; this achievement is associated with the name of Johnstons of Montrose, the netting people, and the late Mr Graham Smart, their manager. In an article in a salmon-netting journal, Mr Smart spoke of the tremendous increase in grilse that had followed the work on the obstructions of the upper river. There can be no doubt that recently both Esks have benefited from all that the netting interests have done

The Orchy provides fine sport after a heavy rain.

for conservation and development. It is a happy reversal of former times on the North Esk, when two difficult dams at Craigo (now virtually broken down) and Morphie robbed upper proprietors of many of their fish. There was at that time excessive river netting, and the killing of spring fish below these obstructions was little short of greedy exploitation. A happier and much more fruitful era may now have dawned for the Esks, and they are well on their way to being two of the best small spring-salmon rivers in Scotland. Further, the South Esk has splendid sea-trout fishing, and both have good grilse fishings. In short, these are two rivers with a marvellous range of sport.

The South Esk is, for much of its lower course, a slowish river with good flats for sea-trout fishing and with some excellent salmon pools. The most famous stretch for salmon fishing is the 'top beat' of Kinnaird, the Earl of Southesk's water. Here a dyke (though with a newly enlarged fish-pass in it) sufficiently impedes the course of the spring fish to make it one of the most productive early fisheries anywhere in Scotland. I have heard of fifty taken on the opening day, and in the first month totals ranging from 300 upwards. This is marvellous fishing and, not unnaturally, is expensive.

In contrast, the Cortachy fishings of the South Esk, including the Prosen pool but mainly concerned with the River Esk above the junction, are tremendous small-water salmon fishing. It is wonderful in late May and June, when the fish run up and will rise readily to small tube flies such as Stoat's Tail, Hairy Mary, or Thunder. This fishing may be done with trout rods. In the delightful little tree-lined pools of Cortachy, such a rod of nine feet six with a ten pound salmon on, plunging about in the falling waters after a spate, is sport indeed.

The fishings of the North Esk are not particularly easy to come by on a day-ticket basis, but there are certain beats of the river available for rent. Further, there is water available through Joseph Johnston & Sons Ltd, the netting firm who have angling facilities to offer as well. One regulation of this conservation-minded firm gives a free permit to fish the North Esk from Denmouth of Morphie to Kinnaber Bridge, but it is suspended while the salmon and sea-trout smolts are migrating downstream (in May). This is excellent sense, for the loss of a smolt successfully reared to this size over the hazards of two, perhaps three, years in the river is a far greater disaster than the loss of a hen spawner with her eggs unfertilized, even many hundreds of them.

Hotel fishings on the South Esk are best supplied by the House of Dun Hotel near Bridge of Dun. Day or weekly tickets are available through the Kirriemuir, Forfar, and Montrose angling clubs; further, beats may be rented at certain times from local estates – for example, the Dalhousie Estates office at Brechin. Trout fishing is usually easy to get, since most of the local anglers are keen salmon and sea-trout

The Ythan Estuary near Newburgh is noted for its excellent sea-trout.

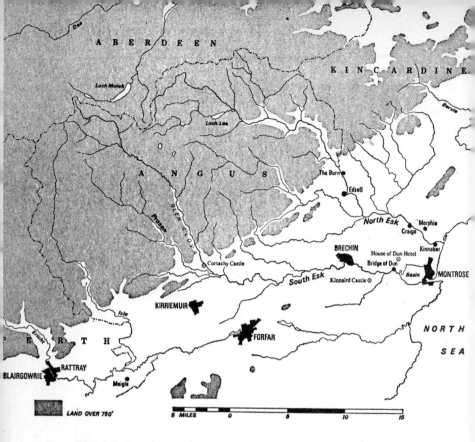

fishers. Many hotels can arrange free trout fishing on the river and on its tributaries.

The South Esk carries, rather like the Don, a run of big fish from mid-September onwards, and there are records of fish over thirty pounds that have fallen to anglers in the last weeks of the season. With such a good spring run also in the water, there is naturally a high proportion of stale fish in the middle and upper river. The lower river is, however, the best autumn fishing. This turns the South Esk into a kind of sandwich river. The best of the spring fishing is early – February to April or May, with the upper beats fishing well in May and June. The autumn fishing is at times outstanding, and the river becomes 'stiff with fish'. In between is an increasing run of grilse and sea-trout, which makes the filling of the sandwich.

To some extent the North Esk season also shows this sandwich form, but there is generally better autumn sport. In both North and South Esk there have been, in recent seasons, reports of overcrowded pools. Fish running into pools already well tenanted disturb the 'resident' salmon, and give that kind of frustrating day to the angler in which the air seems always to be full of leaping fish, but none will take his fly.

Every river sees this kind of thing in autumn, but midsummer conditions on the Esks sometimes produce it.

An outbreak of disease has marred the Esks in recent years. With several other Scottish rivers, they shared in the salmon-fishing blight called U.D.N. But the Esks have suffered salmon disease before. They have plenty of resources, and I am not being unduly optimistic in predicting a steady recovery from the outbreaks still with them during the winter of 1971.

W.B.C.

Chapter Thirteen

THE DEE

If I were to relate the first encounter I had with the Dee as a salmon river, it might help to explain why I think it is a salmon river flowing out of paradise.

I was invited to fish the Commonty water in mid-May, and I drove up from Edinburgh to Feughside Inn, where I was to stay. With my host and his wife, I drove over from Feughside after breakfast and stopped for a moment on the highest part of the road to take in the view of the Dee, winding down from Potarch Bridge through the Ballogie water, past Suie, and on to the Blackhall beat, with our own Commonty water on the right bank. The combination of wood, field, river, and the blue May sky with puffy white clouds was breathtaking.

We drove down to our beat, and I was invited to fish the Garden Pool opposite Woodend House, a most delightful streamy pool, running gin-clear over boulders, with a fine headstream and a purling middle and tail to the pool, strewn with boulders that formed perfect lies for salmon. The keeper gave me a No. 6 double Sweep of his own tying, and I began fishing down with my floating line bringing the fly steadily across the stream some twenty yards below me.

I was into a fish on my fourth cast, and – after a splendid fight, which was all the more enjoyable because the fish was so often visible in the clear water – the salmon was brought in, and I was able to tail it out. It weighed sixteen and a half pounds, a fine spring fish, big for the time of year. This was a superb start to Dee fishing. To grace such a start, the banks of Dee at that time were ablaze with the finest show of broom I have ever seen. The grass of the bank was strewn with wild flowers, incandescent against the dark green of the pines and the brighter greens of the riverside larches. If a river flows in paradise, it must surely be the Dee.

For much of its course the Dee has the character I describe at Commonty. It is clear, with fast streams and few of the idle pools we find on many Highland waters. Often it flows over whitish shingle beds, and the course is marked by pine-trees on the bank, haughs with broom bushes, and cropped grass and riverside paths that are well maintained.

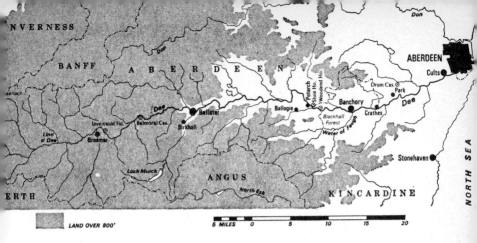

The pools have good huts, benches for anglers to lunch on, and (above all) good sport, for this is the salmon fly-fishing river *par excellence*.

It is a river born of the snows of Braeriach; at a picturesque spot, the Well o' Dee, the water gathers itself among the boulders and begins its first rushing course down the nine.y miles to the sea at Aberdeen. It falls nearly 3,000 feet from the Dee Wells to Braemar, for the river rises at a height of just over 4,000 feet in one of the highest corries in Scotland. Thus the highest part of Dee is a brawling mountain stream; but from Braemar down it becomes a brisk river for most of its course, forming some of the most fertile and attractive salmon fishings in Scotland.

One of the factors in the productivity of the Dee is its shallowness. It has been estimated to have an average depth of four feet and an average pace of three and a half miles per hour from Braemar to the sea. Naturally a river like this varies its pace, forming a few quiet pools such as those at Invercauld. The typical Dee salmon pool is formed over a flat or a wadable stream. So shallow are some of the best pools, that wading much above the knee may well take you over productive salmon lies, disturbing the fish.

It is almost certainly its shallow and streamy character that has made this river famous for its fly fishing. This is the home of the floating line for salmon, and it is the origin of 'greased-line' salmon fishing as we have come to know it in the 'thirties and later years of this century. One cannot think of greased-line fishing without recalling the names of A. H. E. Wood of Cairnton and his friend Anthony Crossley. The concept of fishing for salmon with the fly just under the surface has meant a remarkable advance in technique. On Dee, for instance, it has led to the use of small 'Dee tubes' – tiny wisps of Stoat's Tail or Hairy Mary flies tied with bucktail and fished on little plastic tubes running down in length from one inch (big for Dee) to a quarter of an inch. These tube flies – fished with No. 14 trebles in the smaller sizes – raise, hood, and hold salmon in a most sporting way when they are fished greased-line style. Often the salmon can be seen taking the fly. A back

117

breaks the water, or a snout emerges to engulf the morsel.

The spring fishings of Dee are, far and away, the main part of the year's sport. The river brings fish into its waters during the early spring months, and in a mild February provides springers of the eight- to ten-pound class up as far as Invercauld. The beats from Balmoral down to Ballater provide good stocks of springers in increasing numbers from February to May, when they reach their peak. They continue to fish for some weeks after this, and tail off as the summer heightens. July might be regarded as the end of the Dee salmon fishings, although the very lowest beats of the river, from Drum down to Cults, also provide some autumn sport with a limited number of heavier fish.

The beats below Banchory suffer a little in early spring from fish running on through to the upper reaches of the river. The Dee is a remarkably open river, with hardly an obstruction of note between the city and the Linn of Dee. Fish, finding the right water height and temperature, run fast and far on Dee, and the river seems to stock itself from about Invercauld down. However, the later spring fishings of April and May and into June provide compensation for the middle reaches, for as a rule they do exceedingly well in these months.

There are interesting variations in individual beats on Dee. For instance, Commonty water fishes better than Woodend, opposite, in high water and worse than Woodend in low water. Certain pools, for no very obvious reason, lend themselves to fly fishing from the left bank, but when fished from the right bank are comparatively poor. In terms of seasons, some beats may yield a fine result almost by chance in a late summer or autumn fishing – for instance, the famous catch of 200 fish in an autumn fishing at Crathes, near Banchory, which Calderwood mentions. But all in all the Dee is the most consistent river I know, and has more holding lies strewn over its entire length than any other water; it is also more responsive to fly fishing than any other Scottish river. This adds up to a sporting salmon river of the greatest distinction.

One of the reasons why the Dee is of such note is that it has proprietors who take the greatest interest in their fishing, and spare neither effort nor expense to keep their river in good heart. In the past they have bought off nets, instituted hatchery programmes, and (with the help of the A.C.A.) fought and won pollution cases against local authorities. It is a water under the strictest preservation, with riverside estates along its entire length. One of the most famous of these is Balmoral, owned by the Queen. The royal fishings extend from below the Old Bridge of Dee at Invercauld down to Birkhall, with some excellent spring salmon fishings over the stretch. Beautiful estates like Park and Drum lie between Banchory and Cults, and a score more grace the banks elsewhere. Some hotels have fishings on the Dee; these are usually taken as lets available from year to year. A certain amount of local research, preferably done by oneself, can often yield a good beat for the following season. It is fairly easy to get fishings after the end of May, and, while many would think the best catches finished by then, others would be as delighted to take a brace of salmon on fly in a summer day as the six in a day's angling that he would have taken in April and May.

An interesting situation exists on the Dee over its sea-trout runs. There is a good run of smallish sea-trout into the river from the end of May onwards, and anglers often find good evening sport with these fish, reaching about three and a half pounds. The salmon-fishing interests of the river do not like the sea-trout, partly because there is undoubted competition for food between sea-trout fry and salmon fry, and partly because there is every chance that sea-trout feed extensively on salmon ova in the spawning season. Yet the sea-trout are splendid angler's fish, and it is sad to think that sometimes they are regarded almost as vermin on a river like the Dee.

One way of reducing the numbers might be to fish them hard. Think of detailing a task force to fish for the sea-trout of Dee; doing, say, a series of 'night shifts' on the job! I know that this is rather a ridiculous idea, for angling never reduces sea-trout very far. But the sea-trout is such a desirable angling quarry that I find it hard to believe that sea-trout fishing goes a-begging on Dee, or that there is a real antagonism towards the fish by the salmon anglers.

The Dee has been said to be the second most famous water in Scotland (perhaps with the Spey first) and the best fly-fishing salmon river. In a whole year the Dee may yield to rods and nets more than 15,000 salmon. This figure is based on the assessment for 1920 given by Calderwood. It is hard to see whether this is now very far below the mark for the early 'seventies or fairly close to it. Certainly the river is no less productive than it was, for it has during many years had excellent management, purer water, and a good hatchery programme. In setting, the Dee is unforgettable, and in fishing character excellent. Let us salute those who have added nurture to nature in this way and provided us with a salmon river of such memorably high quality.

W.B.C.

Chapter Fourteen

THE DON AND THE NORTH-EAST

The Lecht Road from Tomintoul to Cock Bridge is one of the best-known stretches of public highway in Scotland. From November to the end of April (and occasionally later) it is liable to be blocked by snow. After the spectacular descent into Bridge of Brown, when one is driving to the Don from Speyside, the road rolls up through Tomintoul, over the windy moors of the Ladder Hills with the Lecht as the high pass between two nearby summits. At this point the road is one of the highest in Britain, 2,090 feet above sea-level. From this exhilarating height it begins its descent into Strathdon.

The descent is exciting, not so much because of its gradients as because of the dramatic changes in landscape that Strathdon brings after the open hills of the Lecht. You are still 1,500 feet up when you first see the Don at Cock Bridge, and even at this high point not five miles from its source the river has a striking character. It runs streamy and clear and announces itself to every angling eye as a trout stream of merit.

The stripling Don gathers waters from many hill burns between Cock Bridge and the village of Strathdon, including the substantial Ernan and Nochty waters, and, clinging hard by the main road for many miles, it gives the traveller tantalizing glimpses of stream and pool and long dimpled flats in which, on May evenings, trout rise continuously. By Kildrummy Castle – now a very attractive country hotel – the Don is a fair-sized river, with a share of the salmon runs. Kildrummy is probably the upper limit for salmon fished in proper salmon pools, although there are places above this where one might, in a favourable year, take fish – for example, at Glenkindie and Glenbuchat. By Alford, however, the river is a very attractive spring salmon water and a most excellent trout river, with no equal that I can suggest in the whole of Scotland.

I have a very clear picture of the fatness of Donside. One April I was driving down to fish at Alford. The snow on the Lecht had been as high as the car windows, forming a great white wall where the snow-ploughs had cleared the way. Seven miles on, in a rushy field in Strath-

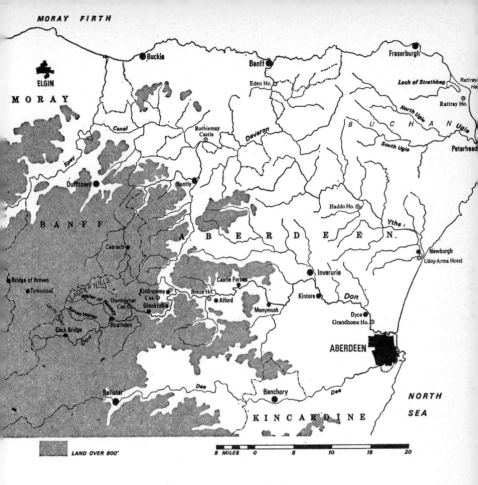

don, I saw about fourteen cock pheasants feeding in the evening sun, and they glowed like burnished gold. Donside took on the character of El Dorado. On the following day I found how productive was the Breda House water of the Don above Alford, for four brace of excellent trout came to the net, half of them over the pound mark. They were really good sport, nice risers to the fly, good fighters and handsome fish.

The stretch of the Don below Alford, where it forms a great northern loop, is perhaps its finest. This is Castle Forbes water, and there is splendid trout fishing, and spring and autumn salmon fishing in streamy water with attractive pools. The banks are, for the most part, open and offer easy casting.

The salmon of the Don divide themselves into spring and autumn fishing. Springers run the lower reaches in March, and may also be taken as high as Alford by the end of the month, although this is rare. It is much more likely to be April or May before the spring fish at Alford appear in any dependable numbers. The spring run of Don is

not vast, but it is significant. I have heard of four and five to a rod in a
day. This, however, is really something of a wonder in the middle and
upper reaches of the river.

The autumn run salmon of the Don are more plentiful, and are often
much larger. Calderwood tells the story of an angler who struggled with
a big fish at Grandhome, and at last managed to get it out – forty-one
and a half pounds. Another angler below him was playing a good fish
at the same time, and, having got his fish out, the first angler went
down to gaff out the other salmon for the man downstream. The second
fish weighed forty-three pounds!

In many years the grilse run on Don brings enormous numbers of
fish to the lower river. Unfortunately they are, all too often, slaughtered
by the nets. Apparently the Don has in the past had bumper years for
grilse, and they have then suffered the same fate. One year on record
showed 5,000 grilse netted in July alone.

The lower Don has a very different character from the middle and
upper river. At Monymusk, Inverurie, and Kintore the river slows
down considerably. It flows through rich farm land, and in places
shows ox-bow lakes, luxuriant weed-growth, and some of the fattest of
trout rising to flies. The angling club stretches at Inverurie and Kintore,
good both for salmon and trout, are comparatively heavily fished, but
still seem to yield well as beats for spring and autumn salmon.

The lowest reaches of the Don for years suffered considerably from
industrial works along its banks. The river has had weirs and other
obstructions, and salmon have in the past had tremendous difficulty in
running upstream. Further, there was foul pollution of the water below
Dyce. Trout that managed to survive were tainted, and salmon shunned
the polluted water, yielding less and less sport. It was intolerable that a
river of this character should be so misused, and the A.C.A. and angling
proprietors recently brought the matter of pollution to a head. Now
more than a million pounds has been spent on sewage plants, and the
Don should surely improve as a salmon water.

The Don has very few sea-trout. Such fish as do run the lower river
nearly all find their way out of the main stream into tributaries. For
instance, only one sea-trout has been recorded at Alford in fifty years,
and it was regarded as a curiosity. Why sea-trout are so scarce in the
Don is not clear. Perhaps the prominence of the river as a trout stream
has a link with its lack of prominence as a stream for migratory trout.
There certainly would be fierce redd competition, but this alone would
not account for the low sea-trout stocks.

It is also very interesting that the Don and the Dee more or less share
the same coastal waters, yet the Don has an autumn run of fish while
the Dee does not. One major proprietor on the Dee maintains that he
puts his rods away finally in late July. At that time the Don is in the

doldrums waiting for its grilse, and for its best runs of the season, with fifteen- to twenty-pound fish (and heavier) entering the river from August onwards. Salmon run into the Don until the end of October, when the fishing stops, yet the Dee apparently does not take any significant run of fish at this time. This is, among other things, a remarkable proof of the specific homing instincts of salmon. Don fish never appear, by an error of navigation, in the estuary of the Dee. They have their own characteristics, and late running is one of them.

The Don I remember, and shall go many times again to fish for its trout, is a lovely clean river. It is not the canal-like lower stretch; it is the river – half Highland, half pasture-land – of the Castle Forbes, Alford, and Kildrummy beats. There I have seen hatches of fly where trout in April and May fed excitedly on Olives, Iron Blues, and March Browns. There I have had both dry- and wet-fly fishing for trout that in Scotland are unexcelled. I wish Scotland had more trout rivers like this. Far too often the Scottish river has either a scattering of good trout that rapidly become fished out, or a vast population of small fish that snatch naïvely at the flies.

The fertile north-eastern part of Aberdeenshire, and the rich lands of the Moray–Buchan area north of this, not only rear some of the best cattle in Britain, but provide in this little-visited area a wealth of river and stream trouting with sport of a very high order. But there is more than trouting available. The Ythan and the Ugie both carry runs of notable sea-trout. The Ythan estuary, one of the best fishings in Scotland, is without doubt among the very best sea-trout fisheries of the east coast. The Deveron is a splendid stream for all three game fish.

The Ythan falls about 800 feet from its source to the sea, over some twenty-six miles of course. For most of this way the river flows through rich and beautiful farming country, with some pleasant riverside stands of trees. Its middle reaches cross the beautifully wooded policies of Haddo House, a charming estate with extensive park land, ornamental lakes, and a deer park. Haddo House is famous for its connection with the arts. Its present owners, the Earl and Countess of Haddo, are among Scotland's most prominent patrons of music and drama. Each year there are productions of opera and drama, and many musical recitals.

The Ythan harbours a few pike in its lower reaches, but these seem to have little effect on the run of excellent sea-trout that the river brings in from the sea each season. The estuary is four miles long and is uniquely formed, with a sand-bar at the seaward end and what in effect is a rich tidal lagoon between Newburgh and the open sea. In this long stretch, sea-trout and finnock feed and are excellent sport for rods fishing from a boat or by wading. The fish themselves can run large – up to six or seven pounds; but a bag of five two-pounders would please all but the most ambitious fishermen.

Spinning and fly fishing are both followed on the Ythan estuary, and, since the fly used is often of the 'demon' or 'terror' type, the sport clearly centres on trying to imitate the sand-eels and small fish that swarm in the shallow tidal water. Most of the fishing of the estuary is done from the Udny Arms Hotel, and there are anglers from Edinburgh and elsewhere who return many times to fish the water. It is a specialized form of sea-trout fishing dependent on various factors, including tide, state of light, and the height of the river itself. Often in a period of river drought the sea-trout of long estuaries like this provide splendid sport, when tenants of river beats find their fishings quite useless.

Many of the smaller burns that feed the Ythan take good runs of sea-trout and finnock from the parent stream, and, towards the end of the summer and into the autumn, some very small waters are highly stocked with sea-trout. These can provide good sport, often at dusk or into the dark. Fly fishing with trout tackle gives the best sporting return for this style of fishing.

The Ythan also has a good summer run of salmon, and, although these fish are to be taken in many of the association and private beats of the river, few people think of the Ythan as a salmon stream at all. Its sea-trout provide sport of a more reliable and, some argue, a much more exciting kind. For salmon, the Ythan is considered an autumn water rather than a spring one, but in recent years there has been a distinct improvement in the spring runs, and March to May now gives the angler a fair chance of sport. The best of the sea-trout fishing begins in June and continues right through until the end of September, although there are some fresh fish running the river as late as October.

The Ugie, entering the sea just north of Peterhead, is a splendid little trout and sea-trout stream with some salmon. The water is slow-flowing for much of its lower reaches, and this provides some excellent evening and night fly-fishing. Beats on the Ugie are usually rented by the season, but there is some association water near Peterhead, and, in the upper reaches, some excellent trout and sea-trout water is available on permits purchased in Peterhead through the local tackle-dealers. The Strichen Water, often called the North Ugie, is a trout and salmon water, and, although it is often possible to get permission to fish trout here, the salmon fishing is usually reserved by the proprietor. Local conditions, however, change from season to season, and I would strongly urge visiting anglers to inquire at the usual places about fishing – tackle shops, local hotels, and local estate offices. Often fishings are available that no previous list could possibly predict; for example, let's not fully taken up and the inevitable cancellations.

This is not a region noted for lochs. Indeed, it earns its title of the most lochless in Scotland; its still waters are fewer even than those of the Nith valley. There is, however, one water worth noting: the Loch of Strathbeg. This, about a mile long, is close to the sea, north of Rattray Head. It is a low-lying but exposed water that can produce some very good brown-trout fishing. It is at its best from May to the end of June, but sport runs through the summer to the end of September. Access is via local hotels at Rattray or the local estate.

The River Deveron, flowing north into the North Sea at Banff, is one of the rivers of Scotland that have been brought back from a poor state caused by pollution, netting, and cruive fishing; it is now one of the finest salmon and sea-trout fisheries in Scotland. Only in 1966 it was, quite remarkably, saved at the last gasp from a water-abstraction plan for building a reservoir at the Cabrach on the upper reaches, to supply Aberdeen County with water. Objections were raised, and a public inquiry was set up, the findings of which came out against the proposed plan. The Secretary of State overturned the reporter's recommendations, and it looked as if this high-handed action would settle the river's fate and reduce its flow considerably; but Parliament rejected the bill. For the time being, the Deveron proprietors and anglers have (by the skin of their teeth) won their fight against bureaucracy, and the Deveron continues to be a prolific stream for all three game fish.

During the inquiry, the river was described as a 'first-class second-class salmon river'. That is to say, the river is no rival for the Spey, Dee, or Tay, but – short of these élite waters – is top of its class.

The summer and autumn runs of salmon on the Deveron bring in some heavy fish. The late-run fish, coming in during late August, September, and October, include some salmon of twenty to thirty pounds. There are records of a fifty-six pounder from the river at Eden pool, and fish in the forties have been taken from the autumn run Springers run from eight to ten pounds, with larger fish occasionally.

The sea-trout of Deveron offer magnificent sport in June, July, and August, particularly in the Huntly and Rothiemay areas. Dusk and dark-night fishing with fly is the best. Some Deveron sea-trout are large, and six- to eight-pounders are taken in reasonable numbers every year, almost all during night fishing.

As a trout stream, the Deveron is a fair rival of the prolific River Don. In April and May, when the trouting is at its best, beautifully formed fish of a pound and a half to two pounds are not at all uncommon. They are well-marked, strong-boned, and hard-fighting trout, and provide some of the best fly fishing an angler could expect in any Scottish game river. Strangely enough, the Deveron is not regarded as 'on the normal beat' of tourist anglers in Scotland. It is tucked away in its own delightful corner of the country, and the main stream of tourists goes direct from Perth to Inverness. I should not like to see a river like this piled with visitors, but it should attract the keen sportsman more often than it seems to do.   W.B.C.

Chapter Fifteen

THE SPEY AND THE FINDHORN

When I write about the Spey, my heart bounds with enthusiasm, and it would be natural for this chapter to contain more superlatives than any other. The Spey is beautiful – a Highland stream pouring down a valley of the most impressive scenery in Scotland. The Spey is productive, with some of Scotland's most exciting spring and summer salmon fishing. Further, the Spey is long and varied – in some ways much more varied than you could expect any river to be. At one point it moves as slowly as a canal; at another, it forms a water like Loch Insh; from Grantown down it opens out to give fast, rocky streams for miles on end; in its middle and lower reaches it forms pools as promising as anything in the salmon-fishing world.

I love the description of the Loch Insh country given by Grimble in 1899. He described travelling north on what was then the Highland Railway: '[The river] expands into Loch Insh, that beautiful sheet of water some two miles in length, by the side of which the Highland Railway runs to Inverness, offering the sportsman an ideal panorama of hills, valleys, woods and waters rarely viewed from the window of a railway carriage. There are stags on the hills, grouse on the moors, salmon and trout in the loch, roe and pheasants in the covers, partridges in the fields, and duck and snipe in plenty in the marshy, reedy shores of Loch Insh'. In later days, when the railway company was the London, Midland, and Scottish, I used as a boy to travel north to Highland family holidays, and Loch Insh looked just as exciting as that. I don't think I ever actually saw a stag there, but grouse, partridge, and duck I certainly did see, together with what seemed to be millions of rabbits. Grimble went on to add that the salmon and trout of Loch Insh were very dour, and that it was rare to hear of anyone who had caught any there. Tenants of the sporting estates, he commented, had to net their fish.

Loch Insh is one of the punctuation-points on the course of the Spey. It lies sixty miles from the estuary and forty miles below the source. To a large extent it also marks the top limit of sea-trout fishing and of winter finnock fishing, and the top beat of any importance as a salmon

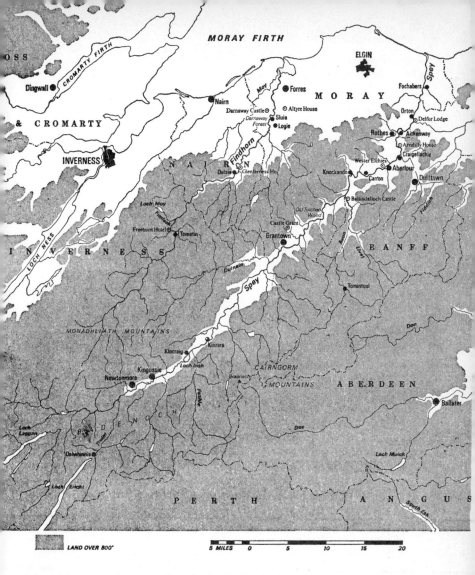

MORAY FIRTH

ELGIN

Dingwall

Fochabers

OSS

CROMARTY FIRTH

Spey

Nairn

Forres

M O R A Y

Orton

Delfur Lodge

& C R O M A R T Y

Darnaway Castle

Altyre House

Sluie

Logie

Rothes

Aitkenway

Craigellachie

INVERNESS

N A I R N

Darnaway Forest

Arndilly House

Dulsie

Glenferness Ho.

Wester Elchies

Aberlour

Dufftown

Knockando

Carron

Ballindalloch Castle

Loch Moy

Old Tulchen Wood

Fiddich

Findhorn

Castle Grant

Freeburn Hotel

Tomatin

Findhorn

Grantown

B A N F F

I N V E R N E S S

Dulnain

Spey

Tomintoul

Avon

Livet

LOCH NESS

MONADHLIATH MOUNTAINS

Don

Kincraig

Kinrara

Kingussie

Loch Insh

Newtonmore

C A I R N G O R M

MOUNTAINS

A B E R D E E N

Braeriach

Feshie

Loch Laggan

B A D E N O C H

Dee

Ballater

Dalwhinnie

Loch Muick

Loch Ericht

P E R T H

A N G U S

South Esk

▨ LAND OVER 800'

5 MILES 0 5 10 15 20

fishery; in a sporting as well as a physical way, it marks a change in the character and the fishing value of the river.

From its high source in Badenoch, rising in a small loch not far from the Roy, which drains west and north into the Lochy, the Spey runs as a brawling hill stream for many miles. At this height it is no more than a thin Highland trout water, but one with some good trout in its more sheltered pools. It does not yet flow through any lochs, nor is it, to any substantial degree, fed by lochs, although among the smaller hill tributaries there are some lochans worth noting. Further, apart from the Truim, which joins the Spey above Newtonmore, there are only minor

127

burns swelling its volume above Loch Insh. Indeed, it is interesting to reflect that the Spey has very few tributaries of any size throughout its entire length. The Avon and the Dulnain are the two largest, and to these might be added the Feshie and the Fiddich. But Spey has no Tummel, no Teviot, to change its character suddenly. It is striking as a river with a very long watercourse (100 miles), a very large drainage area (1,097 square miles), and a powerful flow of water, yet for the most part it draws its volume from small hill-streams.

The Truim – a shingly, clear stream – runs hard by the road from Dalwhinnie to the point above Newtonmore at which it merges with the Spey itself. It is a curious little tributary with a pronounced spate character. I would pass it by as a spawning stream for Spey salmon, hardly legitimate for any serious Spey angling, and for trout no better than a thin spate stream anywhere in the Highlands. Yet a remarkable little book was written about the Truim. John Inglis Hall, in *A Highland Stream*, spoke lovingly of its trout fishings. He described how trout of over two pounds had been taken; he tantalized the reader by waxing eloquent over this seemingly unimportant river. I have often thought about his descriptions as I have driven past the Truim, and to this day I wonder at them. I don't expect I shall ever manage to stop the car and try for a trout myself, for I am inevitably travelling fast northwards to the Spey itself or rivers beyond. Further, there seems of late to be rather a large number of trout anglers fishing the Truim whenever I pass. Perhaps they have read of its fame, too.

The upper Spey provides magnificent spawning gravel for salmon. But the whole Spey system is extraordinarily rich in fine spawning. The fish that do forge up to the high waters would perhaps find just as attractive spawning in the Fiddich, or the Avon, or its tributary the Livet. In this high reach of Spey some salmon must spawn eighty or ninety miles from the sea. Only in Tay or Tweed could this be equalled in Scotland.

The stripling Spey, with its gravelly and well-scoured Highland valley, changes its character between Newtonmore and Kincraig. The pace slows, and the river begins to meander; it floods the mossy drains that join it; it soaks square mile after square mile of marsh. Here the Spey is a canal-like river quite different from the world-famous salmon river we are to find at Grantown and lower. Here, in a wildfowl paradise, the waters of the river join Loch Insh and make that feature of the scenery which so captivated Grimble – and Thornton many years before, and multitudes many years later. This is a pikey area, and I have myself seen pike taken on a trout fly in Loch Insh on a summer evening. Some efforts to reduce the pike population of Insh have been made, and there is some sign that the balance is now in favour of the trout and, more important, of the smolts that migrate through this loch on their difficult way down to the Moray Firth. Trout are fished (not always successfully) on Loch Insh, and there is some trolling for salmon in the later spring months of the year. A trolled bait for a 'fish' often picks up a pike or two, or a kelt rather than a fresh fish.

At the north end of Loch Insh there is a remarkable little knoll. This is the 'island' that gives the loch its name. Ironically, it is an island only in times of very high flood. I have never seen it cut off, but clearly in times past it was island-like enough to merit the name 'Insh'. (There is, however, another island in the loch immediately behind the knoll.) Known as Ion Enonan or the Isle of Adamnan, the knoll is one of the most important archaeological sites in Scotland. Here, about A.D. 690, the church of Adamnan was dedicated by St Columba on one of his visits to the Picts. Adamnan was Columba's biographer, and he was later canonized. This is thought to be the oldest ecclesiastical site on the mainland of Scotland. It is certainly the oldest in the Highlands. Church has been built on church on Adamnan's site, and today it bears the recently restored parish church of Insh, beautifully set among trees, looking north-east to the Cairngorms.

The Spey becomes a river again below Adamnan's Isle, but it is still sluggish. The Feshie, the tributary that joins the Spey a short distance below the loch, has in past years brought down a great weight of detritus from the hills, and it has choked the Spey course. This is said by Calderwood to be why Loch Insh is there. I wonder whether this is the whole cause? I would suggest that glaciation almost certainly scoured out debris from the upper valley; this debris it then deposited, inundating the Spey drainage as a result. There are some splendid pools on the Kinrara stretch of the river below Loch Insh, but this whole portion of the Spey, and indeed the score or so of miles from Loch Insh to Grantown, is generally regarded as poor salmon water.

Calderwood made some interesting remarks on this state of affairs. He claimed that the tenants had accepted the dearth and as a result had not bothered to fish. With 20,000 acres of splendid shooting, he argued, people were not too worried about a dearth of salmon. I have fished Kinrara water for trout a good many times; and – before marvellous-looking pools like the Duchess, and others on the stretch – I have stood and wondered why this part of Spey had no spring salmon fishing. The answer may have been in my own hand: my trout rod. The Spey at Kinrara can provide good trouting, and it is possible that this has distracted anglers from plugging away with a spinning-rod for springers, or trying a greased line in May for the salmon that they know are by then upstream in numbers.

The notable salmon fishings of the Spey are generally taken as beginning at Grantown. Certainly it is here that the Spey takes on its dominant character of a streamy river with a gravelly, boulder-strewn bed. The association water at Grantown, which includes the Dulnain river, the tributary that joins the Spey on the left bank above Grantown, offers some of the best ticket fishing in Scotland. This water fishes well with wooden devons in late April and May, and gives some lovely fly sport from about the beginning of May to the end of June. Then there is a pause, and the grilse and sea-trout arrive. Grantown can be a most favoured summer water, inexpensive and yet of high quality.

The Spey below Grantown is reputed to be very fast, and those who have waded its waters there agree. The river tears at your legs, trundles you down on sliding gravel and, at times, fills your wading trousers with the coldest spring water imaginable. It is an axiom on Spey that where it runs hard the salmon are best caught.

The Castle Grant and Tulchan waters on Spey below Grantown are productive waters, each with many well-known casts and pools. Notice that on Spey 'casts' need not be 'pools'. Many of the best stretches are long, fast flats with lies behind stones. Some of the finest fly fishing of the river, reminiscent of the Dee, is in open, streamy water with lies rather than pools. It is on this streamy water that some of the characteristic Spey fishing techniques have grown up. Spey is a wonderful fly-fishing water, and it is ideally suited to greased-line fishing, or floating-line fishing as it is usually practised today with permanently floating modern fly lines. Salmon come up magnificently to the fly near the surface, and I have seen nothing nicer than a Spey back breaking the surface as the fly was scooped in from its high water fishing set. In the fast water the fish fight well and give a very sporting account of themselves.

The speycast is of course a branded export of the Spey, nearly as famous as the whisky distilled on its banks. Basically, the speycast is a fly cast in which the line does not travel behind the angler, but is switched upstream across in front of the caster and plucked off the surface of the river with a great flowing loop of line as the forward cast is made. This can take out thirty yards of line, or more. To see some of the Spey ghillies doing this is a delight. One of them finally took me in hand and succeeded in teaching me the rhythm of the cast. Since then I have found it tremendously satisfying, and I am given to using it whether or not the bank behind demands it in the way of overhanging trees or bushes.

The Spey has also, by its delightful streamy fishing, produced a method of spinning that is as sporting a method of bait fishing as there is anywhere. The Spey devon is a light wooden shell anything from an inch and a half to three inches long, but usually about two inches, and it is fished with a spiral lead up the trace, perhaps two feet above the devon. This produces a light and sensitive bait than can fan and flutter over rocky lies, rising and falling with the vagaries of the current. The best Spey fishers use rods of nine or nine and a half feet, with multipliers, and they fish their devons round below them very much as they would fish a fly round. Sometimes one would think the handle of the reel was only for final retrieval, after the stream had fished the bait round so well. Spey spinners mend their lines like fly fishers, and often fish baits well up in the water with good results. On Spey heavier baits merely snag the bottom.

The best of the middle fishings of the Spey are probably from Ballindalloch, where the Avon joins, to Aberlour. The Ballindalloch fishings – beats like Carron, Knockando, Aberlour, and Wester Elchies – offer some of the most perfect salmon-fishing streams in Scotland. In April and May the spring fishings can be as rewarding as any spring beats in Scotland. Interestingly, the yield of the Spey has increased radically in the last few decades. The fact that Calderwood, in 1921, quotes Grimble's figures with approval suggests that similar returns were expected in the 'teens and 'twenties of the century. In a good year around the beginning of the century, Ballindalloch might take 100 fish; Knockando, downstream, might take eighty or ninety; Wester Elchies, on the left bank above Aberlour, might take 150; and Aitkenway, just above Delfur, below Rothes, might take 100, although there were surges occasionally to give Aitkenway better than 200 in a season. These last figures were offered by Sir George Macpherson Grant of Ballindalloch, when he was giving evidence before Lord Elgin's Commission in 1900. Today it would not be unusual for each of these waters to take this number of fish by the end of April, and to treble them by the end of August. Let me quote one hard figure to demonstrate how greatly the Spey rod fishings have improved in recent years. The Glebe pool at Aberlour is fished by the local angling club. It is heavily fished, but it is not really what one would call by Spey standards a very good pool. In 1962 the local club took 550 spring salmon from this pool alone before the middle of June. In that year some of the Spey ghillies took better than 100 salmon on their own rods in the spring fishings, and records toppled everywhere.

There is some evidence in recent years, say from 1963 onwards, that the Spey is adding a very much increased run of summer fish, both grilse and salmon, to its existing spring run. Some say the river is doing this at the expense of its spring runs. Time alone can prove whether it is so, but the increase in June and July sport (and in some cases August sport) cannot be denied. Further, sea-trout fishing from about Carron down has been wonderful in some seasons of the 'fifties and 'sixties. Fishing tenancy patterns may well alter in the long run as a result of any changed pattern of salmon runs.

The Avon (pronounced 'A'an') is a remarkable tributary of the Spey.

It is by far the clearest river known to me in Scotland. It really lives up to the description 'gin-clear'. It is a cold, boulder-strewn water with a good head of salmon, grilse, and sea-trout from about May onwards. Sport is had with the Avon salmon right up into the hills at Tomintoul. This is a charming river, difficult to fish, but beautiful in stream, on bank, and in setting.

The Spey, after its fatter middle beats, runs streamy and open from Aberlour to Craigellachie with some quite good holding water. This is in part excellent hotel water fished from Craigellachie, and it is splendid in April when, with luck, running fish may wait long enough in your streams to take your bait or fly. Below Craigellachie, however, another very fine section of the river is encountered. Arndilly, Rothes, Delfur – these are names to conjure with. Some of these beats offer the most perfect fly fishing imaginable. Delfur will often take twenty fish in a day in April or May. Rothes can do similarly, depending on how the fish run and where they stop for a breather. Below this lie Orton and Fochabers waters, with the Brae beats just above the tidal reaches of the river. All of this is tremendous spring fishing, with bumper opening bags in some years – I have heard of an opening day of seventy salmon, and individual bags in a day of well into the 'teens.

Let me draw one slightly darker strand into this tapestry. Salmon disease broke out on the Spey in 1967 and ravaged the whole river in the autumn. Spey – like Tweed, the Esks, the Dee, and other waters in Scotland – lost numbers of its spawning fish, and there have been some uneasy comments about the effects on the stock. Fish have, however, been spawning regardless of the U.D.N. infection still with us in 1971, and there is every chance that this will produce immune salmon. I fervently hope so. Meanwhile, people really keen on the Spey are apt to magnify the importance of this disease. It is a natural setback; it is not a natural disaster. Look through the records of every Scottish salmon river, and you will find entries of despair every so often because of salmon diseases like furunculosis or diseases that look exceedingly like U.D.N. Let history comfort us. What we survived before we can survive again.

The tremendous improvement in Spey fishing in past decades is the result of enlightened restrictions, a tolerable netting policy, and above all a splendid advance in the treatment of distillery effluent. The proprietors of the Spey and the A.C.A. found the distillers cooperative, and new techniques of dealing with the infamous 'pot ale' of the distilleries were developed. Now, in addition to sending a nearly pure effluent into the river, the disposal process produces a valuable fertilizer for farms in the Spey valley. A film produced by the distillers (*Watch on the Spey*), and shown by the A.C.A. to many groups of anglers, makes clear the significance of the new disposal processes. The industry is to be congratulated on showing others what effort and care can do. I wish some of the Speyside burghs had acted as decisively on their effluent disposal problem. Burghs like Aberlour and Dufftown spent at least a decade promising to deal with their dreadful sewage pollution of the Spey, and only now is a sewage plant under construction.

A final word about the Spey as a trout stream. It can be so good that it has made me stop salmon fishing to try for the great yellow trout that were sucking down Olives on a spring day. These trout, plus the extraordinary stocks of wintering finnock that the Spey holds, can give great sport around Easter. I would suggest that trout fishers have fun with the finnock, but that they do not kill more than a respectable breakfast-taking of the fish, for these are the grilse of the sea-trout. If we want Spey to continue to dazzle us as a summer sea-trout river, we must protect the wintering finnock. But by all means let your sons enjoy the finnock in the warm middle of an April day when you are trying a greased line for a salmon. Perhaps Grantown is the best reach for finnock on the river at this time. The association water also contains some splendid trout, and the twenty miles of poorish salmon waters above Grantown have some nice sport to give a good fly fisher for trout, particularly a good dry-fly fisher.

The Findhorn is a picturesque smaller salmon river, running from the Monadhliath Mountains almost parallel to the Spey, and passing under the main Perth to Inverness road where it traverses one of the most hideous concrete bridges that man ever devised, just south of Tomatin. The upper part of the Findhorn is held in a broad Highland valley with great areas of shingle, but with rocky holding pools in places. There is some nice holding water above Tomatin for the salmon that reach this distance. The Findhorn, however, is famous for the lovely reaches of rocky Highland river scenery that characterize its middle reaches. Some of the pools -- such as the famous Sluie pool, which used to mark the uppermost limit of salmon fishing – are spectacular gorge pools with swirling dark waters. Fishing the gorge pools of Findhorn has given rise to a school of speycasters that, I am certain, outclass many of the speycasters of the home water, the Spey itself. In some of the pools described to me by proprietors and keepers, the angler has to stand some considerable way above the water, yet has to contend with a cliff sheer behind him. This height actually makes speycasting (or good roll casting) easier, but many of the cliffy pools demand impeccable speycasting, with better than twenty yards going out over the river.

The middle reaches of the Findhorn give some tremendously scenic prospects. From the beginning of the canyon at Dulsie Bridge, just above Glenferness House, to the junction of the Funlack Burn, the left bank tributary flowing from Loch Moy, is twenty-four miles. No other Scottish river has such an unforgettable stretch of gorge. Charles St John, the Edwardian writer on the Highland sporting scene, said this of the view: 'Hemmed in by the same kinds of birch-grown banks and precipitous rocks, every angle of the Findhorn river presents a new view and new beauty ... At Logie the view of the course of the river, and the distance seen far up the glen till it is gradually lost in a succession of purple mountains, is worth a halt of some time to enjoy'.

This spectacular scenery in the middle river does not, however, detract from the lower-course scenery of Darnaway and further down. Not only are the Darnaway banks timbered in a most beautiful way, but the river, opening out in the gravelly pools of Altyre, takes on a sweeter Highland character, until it finds its meeting with the Moray Firth in a veritable Sahara of sand-dunes on one of the most interesting parts of the Moray coast.

The salmon of the Findhorn are, largely speaking, summer and autumn fish, although in recent years there has been a distinct promise that the earlier fishings – in April and May – would improve. The summer sport, however, can be tremendous. I have seen some wonderful sport with grilse in the lower waters of the river in July, and I have had some encounters with really solid sea-trout in the same part of the season. The autumn fishings are often remarkable, with good numbers of fresh fish available in all the river's reaches, right up into the hills above the glen.

Trout in the Findhorn have been something of an undeveloped potential. The Freeburn Hotel beat, near Tomatin, has some very good trout in it, and in late April and May some fast sport is to be had there. The pollution of the water at this point from at least one famous distillery has been eliminated in recent years by the installation of a large new effluent plant at Tomatin. This can spell nothing but good for the Findhorn. To begin with, it might make the river easier to wade, for the Freeburn Hotel rocks on at least one pool were once like oiled cobbles because of the distillery effluent. Those days, however, seem to be over.

The Findhorn has something of a spate character, as you would expect from a Highland river coming off the hard rocks of the Monadhliath. It rises fast and falls fast. This has one good and one bad effect, both well known to anglers. The good effect is that the river has freshets that move salmon upstream and animate the 'residents' already in your pools. The bad effect is that the river can fall to a gravel-bed in times of drought and provide little sport. High- and low-water conditions are part of the angling scene everywhere, and one must not make too much of them in any one case. Findhorn in spate is a wonderful sight in the gorge, and even better is Findhorn falling and looking as brown as porter, promising memorable fly sport. Above all, Findhorn is a river of nice size. It is not so large that it cannot be waded and easily covered – where wading is possible – by moderate casting (the Altyre stretches are typical in this), and it is not too small to provide 'big-river' salmon pools that give adequate lies and the chance of first-class sport with room for the salmon to fight. In a word, Findhorn is an experience on its own. It is not an apology for the Spey. Findhorn is unique. I wish it were not, for then Scotland would have more than one such breathtaking river to enjoy.

W.B.C.

Chapter Sixteen

INVERNESS-SHIRE

One of the most impressive physical features of the Highlands is Glen More, the great fault cutting decisively across them from Inverness to Fort William. This valley almost makes the northern Highlands a separate island, for only a few hundred feet of land prevent the North Sea from flooding through to the western seas of Loch Linnhe and the Atlantic Ocean. Man has done what Nature just failed to do. He has joined the oceans, linking the three large lochs of the great glen – Loch Ness, Loch Oich, and Loch Lochy – by three sections of canal, usually all called the Caledonian Canal. To the south of this great glen lie the Monadhliath Mountains, that mass of almost trackless highland with something like forty tops over 2,000 feet and many over 3,000.

The Monadhliath is an exciting, but more or less gentle, prospect from Speyside. There, in the glens above Kincraig and Kingussie, the burns that feed the Spey flow east. But the side of the Monadhliath facing lochs Ness, Oich, and Lochy presents, for much of its length, a steep, high scarp cut into at only a few places by rather small glens. Most of the waters draining into Loch Oich and Loch Ness – for example, the Garry, the Moriston, and the Enrick – flow from the northern side of the great glen. The rivers feeding in from the south include the smallish River Foyers and the Farigaig.

Of the three lochs of the great glen, Loch Ness is by far the largest. Its waters and the waters of the smallest of the trio, Loch Oich, drain north-east to Inverness and the Moray Firth. Loch Lochy drains west by the excellent River Lochy to the waters of Loch Linnhe and the Atlantic. Just below Loch Lochy, the south wall of the great glen is broken by the Spean river, the only significant southern tributary of the system between Inverness and the estuary of the Lochy. The glen of this river seems to cut off a massive island of mountains from the bulk of the Monadhliath, and in this 'island' lies Ben Nevis, the highest British mountain (4,406 feet), two other peaks over 4,000 feet, and half a dozen tops of better than 3,500 feet. The little Water of Nevis cuts back gallantly into this mass of ancient rock, and provides a route round the western and south-western sides of Ben Nevis, as well as some mixed

The Spey near Grantown offers restful scenery as well as sporting fish.
OVERLEAF *Brown trout, salmon, and sea-trout are caught in River Shiel.*

game fishing in its pools and streams in that spectacular glen.

This area, Glen More, gives us a 'spine' for the description of the fishing of Inverness-shire. Working back from Inverness, the old fortress town standing on both sides of the Ness river at the estuary, the first and most interesting water is the Ness itself. This is like several remarkable rivers elsewhere in Scotland by being a short, heavy river draining a large loch system, the tributaries of which are themselves salmon rivers of note. But in this company the Ness is king, for not only does it drain a larger quantity of water from a more extensive hinterland than any other loch and river system in Scotland, but it is also one of Scotland's principal early spring waters with a great reputation. Over 700 square miles of Highland territory drain into Loch Ness. Further, it is a remarkably deep loch, second only to the smaller Loch Morar, but in its averages far deeper than anything else in Scotland. Loch Ness has a maximum depth of 754 feet, but a mean depth of 443 feet. Thus over a cubic mile of water lies in Ness. Loch Lomond is, by surface area, a little larger – twenty-seven and a half square miles as opposed to twenty-one and three-quarter square miles; but Loch Ness has more than twice the volume of Lomond. This huge quantity of water feeds the six-mile Ness river, giving, with its drop of fifty-two feet, a fine streamy river, powerful and clear.

Salmon run the Ness exceptionally early (or is it late?), for the fish that one catches in Loch Oich and in the Garry river on the opening day of the season in February are often coloured fish of some weeks', or even months', standing. In the old days, the rod fishings of the Ness opened for the 'spring fishings' on the 14th November and, according to nineteenth-century records, gave their maximum yield in December and January. These were spring fish, or – if you care for the name – winter fish, for they would run the Garry as the spring temperature rose and find their way through Loch Garry to the Kingie and the upper Garry and there spawn in the following autumn; that is, at least nine months after entering fresh water.

The modern arrangement on the Ness is that rod fishing begins on the 15th January, and, among the kelts, some springers are caught. Almost certainly the main spring runs have already passed through the Ness by the opening day of the rod season. The temperatures of the Ness, which have been studied by inspectors of salmon fisheries and others several times, show that the Ness has a significantly higher winter temperature than the Garry; thus fish run fast through the lower river and make their way to upper Loch Oich, where they lie waiting for the April and May temperatures of the Garry to rise and make their passage to the waters above attractive.

Salmon run the Ness constantly, even if the bulk of the springers do so during the close season. Fish of ten to fifteen pounds are taken on the

Anglers come ashore from Loch Ruthven.
PREVIOUS PAGE *An angler tries for sea-trout as the tide ebbs from the Sea Pool of River Shiel.*

LAND OVER 1000'

5 MILES   0   5   10   15   20

Inverness town waters and on the beats above the town right through the season. The autumn fishings are often very good in the Ness, and often low water in summer helps the river to hold a good head of fish, including excellent sea-trout and herling runs. The angler who wants to get the best out of Ness fishing would be advised to wade deeply. It is a heavy, streamy water, but there is no doubt that, as with Tweed and Tay, the angler who can manoeuvre into a casting position and

cover the salmon lies with his flies from a more attractive angle is the one who will kill the most fish. This is particularly true of the fly-only fishings that the Ness enjoys when the water falls below a certain mark. I have taken pleasure watching the excellent fly casting that locals demonstrate with their long, spliced greenheart and spliced cane rods. Many of them are marvellous fishers, and they show that, on rivers where spinning is kept firmly in its place, the art of fly fishing is fostered and good takes of salmon result.

Permits to fish the Ness are available through the local Tourist Board offices and also through local tackle-dealers. I have always found the Inverness tackle-dealers exceedingly helpful, and they can recommend many a good beat. A visitor would be well advised to ask locally about fishing permits and rents, for they are clearly local matters, and they are well handled by the people concerned.

The salmon of Loch Ness come very close to rivalling the salmon of Loch Tay, and there is no doubt that since the Second World War a considerable study has been made of the lies of fish in the loch, with worthwhile results. The sport, as on Loch Tay, is almost all trolling, and is of the four-inch sprat, phantom, or toby variety. Indeed, Loch Ness may be one of the last phantom minnow strongholds in Scotland. This trolling lure, which had a tremendous vogue in the earlier years of this century, has largely died out elsewhere in favour of the sprat, and this in turn is rapidly dying out and being replaced by the long, attractive Swedish spoon called the toby. Naturally, trolling on a loch over twenty-five miles long is very much a question of local knowledge, and the local hotels nearly all insist, for safety and for results, that an angler should hire a local ghillie. Loch Ness is like a stretch of the sea. The valley, with its steep sides, can funnel winds down to give remarkably sudden storms, and there is no doubt that a local boatman can sometimes be of the greatest help.

The Moriston river joins Loch Ness about four miles from Fort Augustus on the northern shore. It is a spring river, but not with the distinction of the Garry. Beats on the lower Moriston fish first, but in recent years the hydro-electric activities on this river seem to have considerably affected the fish. The fluctuation of the water-level, caused by water abstraction and diversion, makes fish move erratically. It is said that the late afternoon is best, when the water-level rises again after being low all day. I have had no personal experience of this, but it sounds like a most unpleasant business, irritating to the angler and unproductive.

The trout fishings of the Moriston in recent years have been at times outstanding. The fish, which come to both fly and spinner, particularly after small floods, have been taken to weights of two and three pounds, and I know one Inverness fisher who thinks there is no finer trout sport in the Highlands than Moriston. Some anglers have taken to returning all fish under one pound, such is their confidence in the water.

The river from Torgyle Bridge has a pleasant, streamy, open character with reasonable access from the road; the part from the bridge down to the dam at Dundreggan is more treed and for the fly fisher would demand some care in casting. Local hotels and the Glenmoriston Estates office have tickets for various parts of the river, and a visitor should find out from his hotel, or some other local source, where to apply his skills.

There are two areas of loch fishing not far from Inverness that reflect the variety of trout fishing in the county. The first is the area of hill-loch fishings made available by the Glenmoriston Estates and usually known as the Glenmoriston hill-lochs, or the Levishie lochs. These waters form a group, many within walking distance of each other, and those who like walking and fishing will find their pleasure here. The lochs lie above the Invermoriston–Cluanie road, roughly twenty-five to twenty-eight miles from Inverness. There are seventeen waters in all. An estate road leads up to a point on the hills from which groups of waters may be fished. You should ask locally about this access road, for, although the hills themselves are not so much craggy as gently rolling, you should not feel it necessary to walk the whole way from the main road to the fishings. The estate office will either give you a leaflet map or point out the way on your own map.

The largest loch, Loch a' Chrathaich, is stocked each year with two-year-old trout. Headpond is a small artificial loch of the group, well worth a cast, and Loch ma Stac, a fairly good walk off the track, is said to be well worth the effort of getting to it. It has some really big trout. The estate has at least one boat on Stac for trout fishers. I have not named many of the lochs, but, remembering that there is a very wide variety of fishing, from tiddler trout to very large browns, a visitor would do well to get local advice, say from the estate office in Glenmoriston when he is booking his permit.

It is a wonderful area for vistas, especially from the hill-loch area. On a good day the whole range of mountains from Kintail to Ben Nevis and round to the Monadhliath can be seen. Add to this the possibility of varying one's activities, on a short stay, between salmon or trout fishing on the Moriston river and hill walking or fishing the Levishie lochs, and this will be seen to be a very agreeable centre, inexpensive and yet summing up a great deal of what is good in Scottish fishing.

The second area of loch fishings in Inverness-shire that must be mentioned includes the waters lying in the hills to the south of Loch Ness. These are often referred to as the Whitebridge lochs, and they are in sharp contrast with the hill-lochs of the north side of Ness, for a great many of the Whitebridge waters are accessible by good roads. There are eight major lochs in the group, and among them is Loch Ruthven, a water that can give excellent account of itself in spring and early summer. Others include Loch Killin, set at the head of the Feehlin river, a part of the Foyers system. Killin is like many a Highland loch in that it has two distinct classes of trout. The smaller fish, quarter-pounders or perhaps better, keep one's flies in action fairly regularly, but the larger class, which may run to five or more pounds, occasionally move to the angler's flies and give him the experience of a lifetime.

A trout fisher should tour this area savouring its quality, which is typical of free, open Highland fishing. This is wonderful hill country, but not so remote as to make you feel cut off from the comfort of good hotels and the convenience of roads. Inverness is near by for shopping, and Loch Ness, with its excellent lochscapes and views to the hills beyond, is as uplifting an environment as anyone could wish for.

At the head of Glen Moriston lie two large trout lakes, Loyne and Cluanie. Both are in magnificent hill country, but it is Cluanie that excels as a trout water. This is yet another Highland loch whose level has been raised recently; the subsequent fishings have been very good, and occasionally spectacular. Large trout of the three-pound class are regularly taken on both dapped fly and wet fly. Cluanie is a big-fish water, and this means that careful study and long acquaintance repay the time and trouble involved.

The Inverness-shire Garry, running from a source within four miles of the sea at Loch Nevis on the west coast, where the headwaters are called the Kingie, flows down through tremendous hill country in Glen Kingie, and, in its other branch from the burns above Loch Hourn, through the impounded Loch Quoich to the Gearr Garry river. Both fill Loch Garry itself, a water well known for its excellent trout fishing, with a particular reputation for what we used to call *ferox*, the great loch trout of the Highlands. At present Loch Garry holds the accepted British rod-caught trout record – just over eighteen pounds. Some people are rather cynical about the smallness of the 'official' record trout, for many larger trout have been taken in Scotland, but usually the evidence for these fish was minimal, and the British (Rod-Caught) Fish Committee decided to start again in the 'fifties.

Both Loch Garry and Loch Quoich, above it in the hills, are now impounded lochs, part of the hydro-electric scheme for the whole upper Garry system centred on a generating station at Invergarry. We shall have more to say about the effect on the salmon that this particular scheme has had, but for the present let us merely think of one blessing that the raising of Quoich and Garry has brought. Lochs in the Highlands often suffer from shortage of body-building foods. When a loch is flooded, and the waters cover what was formerly loch-side fields, there is added to the bed of the loch some splendid food-bearing water. First there is the bounty of earthworms; then aquatic flies, finding good shallow water with a splendid bed for hatching eggs, set up flourishing colonies of underwater larvae. The fishing of a newly flooded loch is usually superb for several years after the loch level is raised, but there comes a balancing out of resources, and most spectacular lochs tend to go back somewhat.

Quoich is a perfect example of how this happens. In the late 'fifties and early 'sixties it was a superb fishery, with boatloads of trout running to two pounds each, and many fish dramatically larger. One Glasgow angler – Mr C. C. Mann, the tackle-dealer – took a trout of nine and a half pounds during this period of bounty. Others had memorable fishings, if hardly in the same weight class. But by the mid-'sixties Loch Quoich was showing much poorer bags. The fish were thin and tending to be worm-ridden. The weight was down over-all, and the sport was distinctly on the wane. Often, of course, lochs become stabilized after this period of swinging from fat to lean. It is to be hoped that Quoich will be stabilized with good large trout, and not with hordes of lean, small fish.

Some parts of Loch Garry, on the other hand, seem to have risen to a new peak of trouting under its flooded conditions and are not showing signs of going back at all. This is particularly true of Inchlaggan, between Poulary and Garry proper. It was always a good trouting area. The upper Garry and the Kingie both had splendid trout before the hydro régime came along, and under the new levels, with the river between Loch Poulary, Inchlaggan, and Loch Garry below flooded to form a splendid trout-feeding area, the trout fishing has improved considerably. It was at Inchlaggan that the record trout of eighteen and a quarter pounds was taken, on a fly, in 1965. It can be great fun in May, giving bags of three-quarter-pounders and better, and the fish themselves are wild and free-rising – sporting Highland trout. Centres for fishing in this area include Tomdoun Hotel and an enterprising anglers' hotel at Garry Gualach, as well as Invergarry Hotel some miles downstream.

The salmon that run in the winter and early spring from the Moray Firth do so for the most part through Loch Ness and the River Oich into Loch Oich, where they wait until the temperature of the River Garry is sufficiently high (most anglers agree that 40°F. is the critical line); they run up into the pools of the Garry and through the fish-pass into Loch Garry beyond. The hydro scheme has changed the Garry considerably. The water abstracted from the raised Loch Garry is fed down through turbines at Invergarry, thus short-circuiting the river for the whole of its course, save for the last, long pool where the river enters the loch. This has had two effects. First, fish that would normally have waited in some numbers in the Garry itself do not now do so, and the actual river pools have fallen back in yield, but the effect on the long pool where the river joins the loch has been beneficial. The springers seem to lie there in very healthy numbers. Some good execution can be done in April and May with spinners, but the excellent fly fishing of the middle pools of the Garry river seems now to be in decline. The excellent hatchery work being done in the Hydro Board's Invergarry hatchery may well help this situation, but the feeling among anglers who knew this river well before the coming of the Hydro Board is that things are but a pale shadow of their former selves. This comment does not mean that there is no longer sport to be had on the lower Garry. Rather does it mean that what was once a most striking salmon fly-fishing river has significantly changed its character and its yield. I would still very much enjoy the last fortnight of April or the first fortnight of May on the Garry. Even under its new régime, it is a lovely water set in well-tended beats and fished from a well-run anglers' hotel.

The fishings on the River Garry are usually arranged so that a boat on Loch Oich is available if the river is out of condition, and trolling or loch fly fishing for salmon may be done. The salmon fishing in Loch Oich can be very good indeed; and from the earliest part of the season, through February and March, the springers that have worked their way through Loch Ness are taken. Loch Oich also has some splendid trout in it, and, although they have sometimes gained the reputation of being hard to take, the fish that do come to the net are usually large. This is really true of the whole of Glen More. Loch Ness trout are good if you know where and when to get them; Loch Oich fish are often well over a pound; and Loch Lochy trout, almost uncatchable for the summer months, can in May or June come splendidly to the fly and be excellent sport.

Loch Oich and the Garry belong eventually to the Moray Firth, but the third loch of the great glen, Loch Lochy, belongs to the Atlantic. Out of the loch flows the River Lochy, an excellent smaller salmon river – and by saying 'smaller' I do not mean to disparage its sport in any way. It can give most memorable summer sport, with salmon and excellent runs of sea-trout. Further, it is a river with a clear management policy for the letting of beats, and in this arrangement the fishings of local people and of ticket-buying visitors are not forgotten.

The Lochy is joined almost at its exit from the loch by its major tributary, the Spean, and on this Highland spate river and its tributary – the delightful, wild Roy – some interesting salmon fishing is available. The Spean is affected by the dam arrangements at Loch Laggan, where there is a scheme for water power for a local factory at Fort William. It has a compensation flow, and my recollection of Loch Laggan is that in June and July it is usually very low; but, given a period of constant wet weather, it can flood and overflow and give the Spean some enormous spates. With the Spean, as with so many rivers of controlled flow, it is largely starved of floods, and certainly of sustained high water, but is subject to tremendous inundations when the dam above overflows.

The Roy is a natural river, and it has salmon pools in its scenic course down through the spectacular glen it has carved for itself. It too is a spate stream, and its smaller rocky pools have sport to offer for salmon. It is good fly water, and may well give some nice summer sport after the fish have run the Spean. Local people will know when the salmon are up, and visitors do well to ask for advice from members of the angling club. The river is said to be in its best ply immediately after a spate; that is, when the water is still high but falling.

The high reservoirs of the Lochy system include, as we have noted, the waters of Loch Lochy itself, but to the north-west above Lochy lies Arkaig, one of the long lochs of the northern Highlands lying in the characteristic north-west to south-east configuration. Salmon from the Lochy prefer to run to Arkaig rather than to lie in Loch Lochy, but only a few Arkaig salmon are taken each year. It is as a trout loch that Arkaig has made its name, and more so in recent years since hydro-electric impounding at Mucomir has prevented many salmon from ascending. It should, however, be mentioned that the Mucomir pool on the Lochy has produced some magnificent fishings as a result of the dam, and it would be perfectly reasonable to argue that you can't catch your salmon (or your sea-trout, for they are very plentiful here) and have them in Arkaig too.

Arkaig is, like Cluanie, one of the big trout waters of the Highlands. At times it yields trout of the two- to three-pound order, and it has attracted a good many anglers of the dapping fraternity recently; so has Cluanie. Trolling is permitted, I think unfortunately, but some wonderful fly fishing is still possible in a most beautiful loch set among high hills with steeply plunging sides and long views to the north-west where the hill waters, the Pean and the Dessarry, cut their glens back almost to the steep shores of the salt Loch Nevis on the one hand and the freshwater Loch Morar on the other.

To the west of Fort William, over the Corran ferry, lies a most attractive part of the Highlands, Ardgour and Moidart. The association of this area with the Jacobite movement is well marked by the Glenfinnan monument, which indicates the rallying-point of the clans to the support of Prince Charlie in 1745. Ardgour merges into Sunart and Ardnamurchan, while south of Loch Sunart, the beautiful sea-loch, lies Morvern, facing Mull. Until 1966 this region was a *cul de sac*, and only those who 'had business in the area' drove their cars into it. A new road – a most excellent one, with views of great beauty taking in Eigg and the small isles – was opened between Kinlochmoidart and Lochailort; it has become possible to drive round part of the area at least, and this has undoubtedly brought it nearer to civilization. This area is technically Argyll, but it falls on the angling map into the Fort William area, and we have treated it as being psychologically part of Inverness-shire.

The fishing that dominates this area is Loch Shiel – that long and very beautiful sea-trout and salmon loch that lies between Ardgour and Moidart like a ten-mile moat. Shiel pours its clear waters down to the loveliest of sea-lochs by the short River Shiel, three miles of extraordinary water, highly preserved, highly cherished by those who fish it, and the scene of many of my most vivid fishing memories. For me it is a river of summer nights with quiet, warm skies and impressive skylines that – as you fish from Grassy Point and Cliff to Garrison Pool – vary between silhouettes of cliffs and treetops to far-off views of the Sgurr of Eigg etched against a glowing June sunset. It is above all a river in which one has memories of sea-trout, big sea-trout, and of battles in the dark.

For many anglers, Loch Shiel also is a place of skylines and memories of sea-trout, though there it is more likely that daylight scenery and dapping will form the pattern. The loch takes an excellent run of sea-trout from about the end of June onwards, and throughout the summer gradually fills up with fish to provide excellent drifting wet-fly and dapping sport. As with any loch, you should know it well, or take out a ghillie or a friend who can guide you to the best drifts. If in complete doubt, look for the bays and for water roughly ten feet deep, and drift and dap that. Let the sea-trout be your best guides; watch for leaping fish and, of course, for rises to your flies. Sea-trout, especially fresh ones, are spectacular, lunging and leaping and rolling about on the loch surface.

If the Shiel is a short river pouring out of a long loch, the neighbouring water, the Moidart, is a charming long river, pouring out of a short loch. The whole Moidart system is really a Highland river in miniature. The river itself, part of which may be taken by the day, is a rocky stream with some nice pools in it where sea-trout lie. The interesting thing about the Moidart is that its sea-trout are by no means small. If you can catch them, they may run to ten pounds or more. But be warned: this is a spate stream, and its fishings are wholly dependent on water and tides.

In the hills above Kinlochmoidart lie some lively hill trout lochs with good trout in them, and at least one of the Kinlochmoidart estates gives day tickets to fish them. On top one has a superb view of the Moidart glen, and over the hills southwards to Loch Shiel. It is heady plateau country above the ringing plains of Moidart, and up there I have had as fine a day's trouting as I have ever had.

One other small area comprises the fishings of the little River Aline and Loch Arienas in Morvern. The river is of the spate type, and it brings some good sea-trout and smallish summer salmon into its pools from June onwards. These provide some nice fly fishing in Arienas, especially in late August and September. The sea-trout here are not large, but they are pleasant sporting fish of the two-pound order, not to be sniffed at anywhere. The area is delightful, and the light and salt wind off the Sound of Mull is bracing.

The new road from Kinlochmoidart to Lochailort links Shiel and Moidart with another notable sea-trout fishing area in western Inverness-shire, that of the River Ailort and Loch Eilt. Travellers by rail from Fort William to Mallaig will remember the sight of Loch Eilt, the long sea-trout loch with tall pine trees on its islands, remnants of the old forest that might well have clad the whole of Scotland but for the arrival of the sheep. These islands of Eilt adorn a water with sea-trout of the highest quality and including some of the largest of their kind. One of my friends has had from Eilt a sea-trout just short of eighteen pounds, and I have seen records of many more well over ten pounds.

Not far round from Eilt and the little River Ailort is Loch Morar, the deepest loch in Scotland. It is yet another system of a long loch and a short river such as we have seen throughout Scotland. The shortness of the River Morar is astonishing – less than half a mile. There is a splendid sea-pool, and there are one or two other dreamlike stretches of water, but all too little of this is for the angler. The sea-trout and salmon run rapidly through into Loch Morar, and there they take a little more skill to find and catch than they might have done in the pools of a Highland river. The salmon are mostly trolled out of Morar, and your ghillie will tell you where the best fish lie. The sea-trout come well to the dap or to the wet fly, and the bays where the shelved bed gives shallow water are undoubtedly the best. A favourite drift is at the head of the loch, where several hill-burns feed the water, but it is a long sail in even the best of weather to this fishing ten miles off.

I shall say no more about the fishings of this western Inverness-shire region, not because they are all named in this short chapter, nor because they are not worth mentioning, but rather because I have characterized them in the waters I select.

Let us return to a river that flows east: the Beauly. It enters the sea only a few miles north-west of Inverness, the county town from which we began our survey. There, at the head of the Firth that bears its name, the Beauly flows into a seaweedy, sea-trouty arm of the Moray Firth; anglers spinning or fly fishing the tide here often take bags of sea-trout and finnock, and in recent years the firth has become popular. The popularity of the sea-trout fishings of the Beauly Firth, and their proximity to the main road and to Inverness itself, seem to have caused a minor famine in sea-trout during recent years. In the mid-'sixties the lower Beauly, and the tidal waters themselves, were poor for two seasons running, and this is almost certainly a case where the sins of one angling season have been visited on the anglers of another. If one kills pullets, one cannot have grown fowls; if one slaughters finnock, one cannot have grown sea-trout.

The Beauly itself is dammed at Kilmorack a few miles up from its tidal reaches. Here there is a Borland fish-pass, and salmon do pass up through in some numbers – well over 10,000 salmon and grilse in a good year. These fish run up into what used to be a most spectacular gorge between Aigas and Kilmorack, a gorge with sheer sides and fast, virtually unfishable water. The controlled flow between Aigas dam and Kilmorack is not really a loss to angling, although it may be a loss to natural scenery.

The Beauly receives one of its main tributary waters a few miles above Aigas. At Erchless the Farrar joins the Glass to make the Beauly proper. Glen Strathfarrar is an attractive, well-forested valley through which the Glass runs – now, alas! with a controlled flow. The river itself gathers most of its water from Loch Monar, which lies high and remote over the boundary between Inverness-shire and Ross-shire, and within a few miles (as the corbie flies) of Loch Carron with its douce lower glen. Loch Monar is also dammed, and this has raised its levels somewhat. Being a steep-sided loch, it offers less shallow feeding by this flooding than other waters with raised levels offer, but it does have some nice trout-fishing water at its head, which a far-travelling fisher might appreciate. However, it is a remote, houseless area, and a long haul from the nearest hotel.

The Glass forms the best of the Beauly salmon fishings and provides sport with fish from June onwards. Later in the summer the fishers from Glen Affric Hotel have some excellent sport on this river in the neighbourhood of Cannich. It can be delightful water to fish, streamy and clear, and set in wonderful strath scenery. It is at Cannich that the river again divides and changes its name. The Glass above Fasnakyle (the highest point for salmon fishing) becomes the Affric and the Amhuinn Deabhag. Of these the Affric is the more famous water. In the glen of the Affric, and in the magnificent scenery of the loch, Inverness-shire has some of its finest scenery. Loch Affric has also been affected in level by hydro-electric work, but it remains a charming place, and as a trout loch still provides good trouting with a smaller class of fish – family trouting of a high order in an area to which tourists return many times for their holidays.

The second main stream at Cannich, joining the Glass from a glen further to the north than Affric, is the glen of the Cannich river. This reflects the geography of the whole area – of Strathfarrar and Loch Monar above, of Affric and Loch Affric below, and of Moriston and Cluanie still further south. The Cannich drains Loch Mullardoch, a water famous for its excellent trouting, with well-marked trout of the pound average. Here again, like its neighbouring large lochs, Mullardoch lies partly in Inverness-shire and partly in Ross. Its headstreams practically shake hands with the burns that form the Elchaig, whose waters flow into the western sea at that beautiful point where Loch Duich becomes Loch Alsh, one of the channels between Skye and the mainland.

This superb region comprising Glass, Farrar, Cannich, and Affric is one of the wildest parts of Scotland. It is liberally supplied with hills over 3,000 feet high, having several peaks like Carn Eige (3,880), Tom a Choinich (3,646), and Toll Creagach (3,455), which range themselves out in a marvellous line south of Mullardoch and north of Affric. This is a world of big hills, contrasting in kind with the highlands of smaller hills in Wester Ross. Massive, and deeply satisfying scenically, it might be called the backbone of Inverness-shire, linked rather with the east than with the west. The streams of that remote glen, Sithidh, which start in a tiny loch high on the slopes of a 3,771-foot mountain, eventually flow through the rich estuary lands of the Beauly sixty miles away. But that tiny loch is only a tenth of that distance from the houses of Morvich, on Loch Duich, where the Five Sisters of Kintail – those marvellous tops – look down on the estuary of the Shiel of Glen Shiel.

W.B.C.

Chapter Seventeen

ROSS AND CROMARTY

To conquer Ross and Cromarty, in the descriptive sense, one must follow classic advice: divide it. In a gross sense this is easy, for Easter Ross – that fertile coastal strip running from the county boundary on the Beauly Firth right through to the Dornoch Firth (with one possible exception above Dingwall, where it narrows almost to a road-width) – is as different from Wester Ross as field is from fjord. Wester Ross is extensively Highland and, except in the straths, largely infertile. It is strewn with little lochs in the hills, and the larger valleys are almost all occupied by larger lochs like Maree, Fionn, and Fannich. But a division into such grossly different areas still leaves each part with a very wide variety of fishings to be described, for both Easter and Wester Ross are prolific angling areas. From all these I shall select certain areas of special angling focus.

EASTER ROSS

On the main road north after the straight into Muir of Ord (that choice point of routes, where you either go on to Dingwall and the north or turn west to Garve and the whole tumultuous range of Wester Ross), you cross the Conon river. As an inveterate looker over parapets, I was always disappointed that the old Conon bridge was so narrow, so crowded, and so dangerous with traffic that I could not linger to stare down into the waters. Now it has been replaced and I shall manage to hang over its parapet and dream about the headwaters, the lochs, the tributaries, and above all the fish of the system. The Conon system is in many ways ideal for dreaming about, for its waters embrace a magnificent tract of country and a great range of fishings of a sort that no trout, sea-trout, or salmon angler could resist.

The full complement of the waters of the Conon are reached only in its last few miles, where the Orrin, the lowest of the tributaries, joins it. Even then it suffers from a distributary just above Cononbridge. This lower part of the river has some fame as a salmon beat in summer, and in the recent past had also good spring fishings, but anglers have noted a decline in the spring fishings of the river as a whole. Valiant efforts are being made by the North of Scotland Hydro-Electric Board to redress this balance, and, by careful breeding of salmon, to produce a spring-returning Conon stock of some size. It is too soon to say whether this policy has yet proved successful. At least it is a positive policy, backed by a large hatchery at Contin, where salmon research and hatchery are carried on in excellent conditions.

From mid-May onwards, the Conon is one of the most striking rivers in the north. The grilse run in some of the summers of the 'sixties has been remarkable, and tremendous takes of fish have resulted. It is not an autumn water in the real sense, although numerous fish are available in the pools. A river filled with summer fish ready to spawn can be frustrating, for often the coloured fish splash a great deal but do not take. In certain conditions of water, however, autumn fish on Conon can keep a rod bending for hour after hour of a full fishing day.

Conon has a good run of sea-trout, taken in the river in the usual June to September season. But there is considerable sport to be had with finnock that winter in the Conon and are taken in spring on the lower beats, or even in the tidal reaches or the salt water of the Cromarty Firth itself. This can be fast and furious sport in March and April, and there are occasional reports of really big bags of these little silvery fish, so good for eating. I confess to being very worried by the tradition of taking big bags of finnock in rivers like the Conon. These are not only the growing sea-trout of the river; they are the young fish that have successfully passed through the spawning-beds, the hatching, the parr years, and the first stages of sea-feeding. They are the actual stock that forms the sea-trout of three months later, and in subsequent seasons they will return as fish of anything up to and exceeding ten pounds. To kill eight-ounce fish in a sporting way is fine, provided you do not take too big a harvest.

The Conon is joined on its left bank by a very important tributary about five miles up from its estuary in the Cromarty Firth, the Black-water. This stream attracts a very good run of late spring and summer fish, and, given right amounts of rain to keep its rather depleted levels up, it can produce some marvellous baskets of fish in May, June, and July. The sport does not improve after that, although, in a later summer, the main runs may not be in the pools until August. A very early fish in the Blackwater might be March, but I would take the first part of May as the time for the best sport to begin.

The Blackwater is depleted in flow; indeed, along its reaches below the Glascarnoch and Vaich dams it is often severely so. There is a compensation agreement, but most anglers seem to feel that this is too low for good salmon fishing, and it is certainly not good enough to make salmon run in any freedom. The local spates that the Scottish summer

brings are thus of the greatest importance. The angler on Blackwater today is as dependent on floods as other anglers are on spate rivers. The 'compensation-water' angler, however, loses on the aftermath of natural floods, because the continuing 'run-off' after a flood needs the natural flow of lochs, with hill-burns draining the great sponge of moorland bog and a general flow reduction of the surface water. Under a hydroelectric régime, rivers like Blackwater lose both their natural levels and the character of sustained floods. But they gain a guaranteed minimum flow, and where this is adequate they may make a great deal of sporting capital out of being fishable when nature would have had them bone-dry. In the case of the Perthshire Garry, for instance, where there is no compensation, we have a dry bed; in the case of the Blackwater, we have a flow regarded as somewhat low for good fishing. Let us, however, be thankful that we have even that flow. In some other countries, hydroelectric work has ignored fishing interests and ruined many rivers, and the authorities have finally been forced to see their mistake and spend considerable sums in trying (often vainly) to restore the fishings. I think principally of Finland.

Loch Garve lies on the Blackwater course, and it is a water that anglers should note, for in recent years it has improved its reputation considerably as a trout water, and some splendid baskets have come off it in spring and early summer. Fish of up to six pounds have been caught in this water in recent seasons, and, although spinning and fly fishing are both allowed, Garve is a loch well worth drifting with fly. The local hotel is a good centre, and its proprietor will give advice on the best locations.

I must confess to not liking the look of Loch Glascarnoch at all. With its great dam, it is stark and virtually without the varied, attractive bays you want on a good trout loch. Yet Glascarnoch is one of the big trout lochs of the area. It may not quite rank with Cluanie and Mullardoch, but it does have some remarkable trout. The average is said to be about a pound and a half, but much bigger fish are taken there every year. If I were to choose a time to fish for these trout, I would specify late May or early June. This coincides with the first-blush feeding period after the winter (later in the hills than in lower lochs), and trout fishing can be excellent while this comparatively free-rising period lasts. It is, however, only a comparatively free period, for Glascarnoch trout are as dour as their surroundings. The specimen-hunter may find it his ideal loch. There is a hotel on the banks of Glascarnoch, the Aultguish, that handles fishers and their needs. An outboard motor should be brought, for the local fishers say that the best bays are the ones on the far northern shore.

In the Strathgarve area there are hill fishings that local hotels at Garve control. It is fishing for the hill-walker, and it is, in compensation, generally better than we should expect hill fishings to be, for lochs like Loch an Tuirc can give the angler fish of three-quarters of a pound and sometimes more.

The Conon river also has several anglers' lochs associated with it. Loch Achonachie, for instance, has both salmon and trout. Here you would look for a late spring salmon – from the middle of May onwards, say; but as the summer goes on the stock of fish increases (although the catches do not necessarily rise), and both trolling and fly fishing are available for anglers to try. The brown trout, as in so many waters in this area where levels have been raised, are of two classes – the run-of-the-mill and the monsters. The ordinary fly-caught trout of Achonachie runs to about a pound, but the larger brethren, caught on ordinary flies, have reached three and four pounds. The best season for trout in this part of the world is during June, July, and (if you are lucky and escape thundery conditions) August.

A local club also controls the salmon fishing in the loch above Torr Achilty hydro dam, and visitors' tickets are obtainable. These are in considerable demand, and visitors should book where possible.

Loch Meig, on the waters of the River Meig, a tributary of the Conon, is regarded as the best of the local trout-fishing lochs. It is set in beautifully wooded hill country and, as a long strath loch with steep sides, gives marvellous drifts in Highland scenery. It is fly only, and produces baskets of trout of a pound average (which represents an admirable trout, I should remind anglers) and many larger fish up to those of the four-pound order reported in recent years. Fish Meig in June or July, but early rather than late.

These waters on the Conon system are in many ways a world to themselves, for the angler who fishes the trout of the hill-waters and the new reservoirs is not likely to be the tenant of a good beat of the Blackwater or the Conon. That fishing suits a different taste, and a different pocket.

The small spate river Alness, which you see in its hill course on the road north after you have branched left from the Dingwall–Tain road to go over Struie, is a sea-trout and salmon river that gives some excellent sport. The tidal reaches of the Alness are fished for finnock and the odd springer, and, given good water conditions, salmon can run like those of the Conon. This is not a principal spring water. The main part of the river is in private hands, and some of its summer and autumn spate fishings can be very good. I have heard local people tell tales of the Alness that make it sound like the autumn river *par excellence*, with very large fish taking the fly or worm in small pools and creating high excitement. These almost certainly are embroidered tales, but there is body in their material. I expect that good sport dependent on water conditions is available to the lucky tenants of this charming, boulder-strewn stream, which cuts such an attractive course in the Easter Ross hills.

Ross and Cromarty has two river Carrons and at least two Blackwaters. The Carron that flows north-east into the Dornoch Firth is a most attractive salmon water, with a good run of sea-trout and some excellent brown-trout fishing in its upper waters above the spectacular Glencalvie falls. The Black Water that joins the Carron some eight miles up its course is a beautiful little hill-stream of the sort so common in Scotland, a combination of still, 'dead' waters – which can be fished almost like lochs for their salmon and sea-trout – and rocky pools with salmon lying in streamy water. I have the happiest memories of fishing the Black Water at Croick, where, before it was opened up in the mid-'sixties, there was a rock barrier across the river, making a series of pools below in which many salmon and sea-trout lay. The night fishing for sea-trout behind the Manse of Croick was excellent in July, and when the water rose salmon fishing was, at times, great fun. In spates, worming was sometimes undertaken, and fish came easily while the 'mad' spate conditions prevailed.

Night fishing a water like this is delicate work. First, as the sun goes down and the light fades to a lingering gloaming, the sea-trout begin to move in the tails of the pools making a wave-pattern of archers' bows. To cast a fly too early is to terrify the fish, but after twenty minutes or so, when the gloom deepens, careful fly fishing of the tails of the pools and of the lies above them produces some exciting rises. These Black Water fish are two- and three-pounders at best, but on a trout rod at night, in heathery Highland country, this is fishing that I relish. It can be remembered for the way the senses are involved – by the perfume of blossom and foliage in the moist dusk; the sounds of bird and beast moving beside you; and the tiny signals of sight as a sea-trout rises, creating a silver line over the surface where your flies are fishing. Often it becomes an experience of some sixth sense when, for a reason not altogether clear to yourself, you tighten and find that you are fast into a fish of two and a half pounds, and it leaps like a wild thing, shattering the stillness of the pool and causing a tremendous commotion in its fight. This is fishing that I shall never exchange for any other. Its combination of utter stillness and sudden turbulence is unique.

WESTER ROSS

There may be no better way of describing this magnificent area of fishing and mountain and loch scenery than by recalling my own introduction to it. I cycled from Achnasheen along the side of the Bran river, Conon headwaters, and Loch a' Chroisg to the head of Glen Docherty. At last gravity was on my side. I free-wheeled thankfully, and found the

glen unfolding before me the most glorious prospect of Loch Maree. There it was – a long, gleaming blue reach of water with green islands, set between the incomparable Slioch on the east and the magnificent Beinn Eighe on the west, white with its screes in the summer sun.

Maree leads away to the north-west, for, like many of our best lochs in Scotland, it has an inclination from north-west to south-east. It drains towards Poolewe and the River Ewe, another of the short, distinguished watercourses joining a large loch to the sea.

Loch Maree is famous among anglers everywhere for its sea-trout fishing, and for its development of the art of dapping – rolling and dancing a great bushy fly over the fish on a floss-silk line carried by the wind. It is a famous water for big sea-trout. It is not so much that the average is strikingly high, for it is probably not more than two and a half pounds, but many individual fish are big, especially those taken in July. Sea-trout of ten to fifteen pounds are typical of this big class of fish in Maree. One great fish of almost twenty pounds was taken on Maree in 1951 by Mr David McNaught – it was certainly the first sea-trout of twenty pounds ever recorded in Scotland on rod and line, although when in the end it was weighed officially it had dried out to nineteen pounds eight ounces.

Maree is fished from the hotels on its banks, including one at Poolewe and one at Gairloch, but the bulk of the fishings are from Loch Maree Hotel. There is a rotation of beats in the main part of Maree, and strict conventions to regulate the fishings. For instance, the Kinlochewe beat, which is not in the rotation I mentioned, has a special right of salmon fishing at Grudie, but the boat travelling to that beat must motor all the way down from Kinlochewe without stopping. Further, in the earlier part of the salmon season, trolling is permitted at Grudie on this fly-only loch. There seems to be little evening fishing on the main part of Loch Maree, but some is possible at Kinlochewe, where I have enjoyed fishing salmon and char in the evenings of May and June.

There are also good brown trout in Loch Maree, but not every angler would want to spend time during the sea-trout season to fish for them. Further, by July, when the sea-trout arrive, the brown-trout fishings are becoming dour. It is in spring that the browns are well worth attention, and during my May salmon-fishing sorties I have caught several excellent trout of good size and quality.

From about the middle of April, salmon make the most of every high tide to ascend the River Ewe into Loch Maree, but in a wet spring the River Kinlochewe draws the fish out of the loch with hardly any chance of fishing the salmon in the still water. When the usual spring drought sets in, the loch shows great improvement in sport. The Ewe still allows fish through at the spring tides, and these fish move quickly to the Kinlochewe end of the loch and take up their lies along the shores within easy striking distance of the river. When the fish are fresh (and there is always a good proportion of fresh fish in the loch after a spring tide), they rise well to small flies fished near the surface.

I arrived after the start of an early summer fishing trip to Kinlochewe, and found that my fishing partner, Mr C. G. Maclaren, then of Lochinver, had taken four salmon on fly in just over an hour. On the following day I killed one fish, lost another, and (I blushingly admit) lost two others that offered but were not properly hooked. Anyone with experience of salmon fishing in lochs will understand the problems attached to striking salmon in still water. The fish come to the fly with a delightful porpoise movement, and it is suicidal to make any move towards setting the hook as long as you can see the salmon. The fish must be given a full chance to take the fly in and turn down from the surface. Only then ought you to strike. For many the period between the sight of the offer and the strike is an agony of waiting.

The most difficult salmon to hook in a loch is the one that porpoises towards the boat. Even with careful timing, this kind of fish is often hooked only on the forward parts of the mouth, where there is only skin and bone and little hope for a good barb-hold; the smaller the hook the better. On the other hand, the easiest salmon to hook is the crossing fish that you see very clearly and can hook well in the scissors. In both cases, however, the pause is essential.

Excellent early summer sport may be had on Loch Maree, from mid-April until the beginning of July, by fishing salmon during the morning and evening and filling in the rest of the day trying for trout. The trout of the loch are of excellent quality, running frequently to a pound and a half and fighting well after taking the fly. In the course of dapping for sea-trout in the late summer, some very large Maree brown trout of the three-pound class are taken, but normal trout fishing with wet fly for the run-of-the-mill pounders is not widely practised. This is understandable in the months of July, August, and September, when the loch is alive with sea-trout, but in the fresher months of May and June these brown trout are worth anyone's attention.

Without doubt the finest trout fly on the loch is a Soldier Palmer, No. 10, fished on the bob of the cast. Maree, in common with other north-western waters, gives most consistent sport to this fly. Why the trout should take this fly almost exclusively when Olives are hatching, I cannot tell, but time after time they ignored my Dark Greenwell and came to the Red Palmer on the bob.

Maree has another fish that promises some out-of-the-ordinary angling – char. These fish appear from time to time in hotel records, and Kinlochewe Hotel has at least one entry of a mixed bag of trout and as many as four char. Local knowledge stresses that the char are to be caught in good numbers as soon as the air heats up in the last part of May or, more usually, during June. Char take best on fly in the half light of the West Highland night. They dimple gently in the deeps and take trout flies at once, if you succeed in not scaring them with the boat or with a sloppily cast line. A char of eight ounces is average, but slightly larger ones can be taken now and again. Pounders are rare.

The main runs of sea-trout do not seem to come into the loch until July. At Kinlochewe, local people speak of the 14th July as the most likely date. Thereafter in waves, the sea-trout stock the loch from end to end, lying best in water some twelve feet deep, and providing each season some magnificent fish.

The question of depth of drift in fishing Maree is important. Because of the depth, it is all too possible to cover the wrong fish or, worse still, not to cover a fish at all. Salmon lie where six or eight feet of water shelves to a clean shingle shore, and taking fish will on occasion come to the fly from water no more than two feet deep. Brown trout lie and feed in the shallows of six feet or less, either over fly-bearing shingle, or where the rich bottom weeds of the loch contain larvae. Sea-trout are deeper; they may lie in trout drifts, but prefer water ten to twenty feet deep. It is an excellent plan for a stranger without local knowledge to gauge a few depths over what he thinks is likely water. In a week's fishing, many excellent drifts can be discovered in this way and re-membered for future reference.

Loch Maree, then, is a far better general angling loch than is usually suspected. Its spring and early summer salmon run from nine to fifteen pounds and over; its brown trout usually weigh a pound or more; its char add interest. But its sea-trout take the breath away.

A whole range of trout and sea-trout fishing lies in the hills between Kinlochewe and Torridon. There is the salmon and sea-trout fishing of the Kinlochewe river, which fishes best in May and June, when the fish are moving up before summer drought. It is a spate river dependent for best fishing on the right amount of rain. I have, however, seen four salmon taken within two hours in May, and I know that many large sea-trout have fallen to the fly in this water in the later season, when they nose up into its pools from Maree.

Loch Clair and Loch Coulin lie on the headwaters of the western tributary of the Kinlochewe river, which the traveller crosses on the bridge just beside the Kinlochewe Hotel. Loch Clair is a summer sea-trout loch of some merit, although it takes a week or so for the runs of Maree to get up to this water. Its upper neighbour, Loch Coulin, is also a sea-trout and occasional salmon water. It is August and September before the Maree sea-trout are up so far in any great numbers, but sport can be excellent. In September the number of sea-trout in this loch can grow extraordinarily, and some good sport can ensue, even though the fish themselves are often showing colour after a month or so in fresh water.

If you were to travel on down Glen Torridon, the road would run close to the shingly spate stream that gives the glen its name. It is like many small Highland waters, a river begging for rain most of the fishing season and providing a burst of sport for a lamentably short time when the rain falls. The flash flood pattern of these west-coast rivers not only denudes their courses, but makes them very dubious fishing prospects unless you have the luck to bring the right amount of rain with you.

Loch Torridon, the sea-loch, is superb. The road on the northern side peters out just after Alligin, although a rough track takes you over the hill to Diabaig, where a fascinating little fishing hamlet lies beside an almost circular sea-loch sheltered from the south, west, and east by high, steep shores. In the hinterland lie scores of trout lochs, and with permission from the estate it is often possible to walk through the moorland hill country and fish *ad libitum*. This is a great experience not only for the enjoyment of the countryside, but also for the exercise and the fishing. Many of the lochs are undistinguished for fish size, but are charming to fish. They are typical Highland lochs – smallish, well indented with bays, often quite shallow, and as a rule highly productive of rises and of fish. Craig Youth Hostel, standing on the shore of Loch Torridon as the only house for many a mile, is a splendid stopping-place before one sets out again – map in one hand, rod in the other – for Redpoint. I have never seen such sunsets as I saw one August on this walk. Raasay and Skye seemed gigantic against a luminous red sky with shots of flame-like yellow near sea-level. Above, the reds on the clouds deepened almost into purple and merged with the night sky creeping in from the east.

This route would take you to Shieldaig Lodge and Gairloch. This might confuse some people, for the promontory south of Torridon, the spectacular Applecross area, has the village of Shieldaig on it – not to mention the beautiful Loch Damh above. Shieldaig, however, is an area name; it also covers the land between Alligin and Gairloch (that is, Shieldaig Forest), on which so many beautifully-set trout lochs and hill-burns lie. At Gairloch there is a group of waters delighting in the name of the Fairy Lochs. They are all near Loch Clair, the largest water in the area. Their fishing, of half to three-quarter pounders, is good, and local hotel guests find them popular places to fish, not too hard to get to and beautifully placed in the gentler hills of the area.

In this part of Wester Ross there are few large rivers save the Ewe. The small Badachro river and the little Kerry (with a hydro-electric plant on it, which makes it have an erratic flow) are typical of many waters of the west. Each water, but particularly the Kerry, contains salmon and sea-trout in the later season, from July onwards, but no great claims are made for the fishings, save that they are interesting little Highland waters with runs of fish that, if lucky, you might do well with. Loch Bad an Sgalaig, above the hydro plant on the Kerry, is also an erratic water for levels. It has big trout in it, dour as these big fellows always are, but it can give some good days of sport. Pike are also to be found in this loch, and the local Gairloch angling club used to pay a bounty for each one killed; probably it still does so.

Over the River Ewe, with its wide, heavy streams, one comes to an area of good trout lochs with some sea-trout sport in a few of them. In this well-watered area, however, there is one loch of great distinction: Fionn. The loch lies in the hills to the east of Maree, and it drains by the Little Gruinard river into Gruinard Bay. Fionn Loch is famous for its large brown trout. For generations this has been noted as a *ferox* loch with few equals. This idea of *Salmon ferox*, a variety of trout that grow huge and take to cannibalism, is part myth, part fact. Today biologists do not accept the classification *ferox* as properly descriptive, but there can be no denying that some of our Scottish lochs like Rannoch, Shin, and Fionn persistently produce larger brown trout than most other waters. Even if these are merely ordinary browns that have suddenly found a rich source of protein in their fellow trout, they are distinguished enough to be well noted in angling literature, and to be boasted about in the diary of every angler who has been lucky enough to catch one. Fionn Loch, however, actually has more than the occasional large trout. It has big small trout, if I may be Irish about them. It has trout of two to four pounds that you may take on the fly in the ordinary way. Fionn also has salmon willing to come to smallish flies, and the trout fisher there should certainly have a ten-foot rod and a well-filled reel, and five pound or better as the breaking strain of his cast, particularly above the bob fly, for salmon so often take this one in a loch.

In the Highlands everywhere, as one would suspect, there will be many attractive waters not readily available to the public. This is inevitable, for these waters are parts of estates, and many of the owners spend August and September in the north fishing and shooting and generally enjoying their properties. Anglers rich enough may rent some quite delightful waters through the usual channels – estate agents and the like; but anglers who are not so rich might find that lets are cheaper in June and July and are more readily available before the shooting season. Further, an angler, if he makes the right approaches when he is in the district, may find that certain lochs and rivers are available on certain days by chance. I have had some good sport on this basis, often for no more than the ghillie's tip and a letter of thanks to the owner. But, increasingly, fishings come into circulation through newly formed angling clubs and through hotels in Highland areas. Ross-shire has a tourist guide to cover this available water, and booklets for other northern counties are available from the Highlands and Islands Development Board in Inverness. With these for details, an angler attracted to a given area can often know whether real fishing is available, as well as possible rented water through local estates.

Before we leave the county, there are two other areas in this northern part of Ross to be noted: the Ullapool river and the lochs in the area; and the Coigach–Inverpolly fishings in the north-western corner of the county. Visitors will probably reach Ullapool by the main road from Garve; like many a thousand before them, they will find it a whitewashed fishing village lining its sheltered bay and looking out towards the Summer Isles. They will moreover find it, like many a Highland town, straddling its own little river. This is a salmon and sea-trout river that anglers, by arrangement with the local Rhidorrock estate, may take beats on. There is also a local club beat, though it may be much required when the river is in ply. Loch Achall above, from which the Ullapool river flows, is available through the estates for salmon and trout fishing, and it fishes well from the end of May, with a summer peak in July. The predictable variety of hill-loch fishing that Ross-shire usually offers is not absent from the Ullapool district. Local inquiry will lead you to numbers of estate waters available for visitors through hotels and day tickets bought in the post office and elsewhere. Highland post offices, I have found, are usually first-class places to begin a search for fishings.

The Coigach–Inverpolly area is festooned with interesting fishings, such as Loch Osgaig – a splendid sea-trout loch – and the fast river below it. There are several large and good brown-trout lochs, including Bad a' Ghaill and Loch Lurgainn, all fished usually through the Summer Isles Hotel, Achiltibuie. Loch Lurgainn also has summer salmon and sea-trout, and there are plenty of hill-lochs for family fishing (or even for serious fishing of one's own), and they are all set in this great tract of hill country, well fretted by the sea and with some fine beaches and marvellous views.

Those who have fished the River Polly, which drains its own loch in the hills above and takes water out of a burn from Loch Sionascaig, say that it is a remarkable little river. Most of them mean that it is a remarkably hard little river to fish. It is very clear, and very slow, since for the most part it idles through reedy, marshy land. The salmon of Polly are caught in the river, but only by those who take care to fish stealthily. Sea-trout are even more disturbed by boisterous fishers, or those who put more than a judicious half-eye over the top of the nearest cover. It is refreshing to find this problem in the Highlands, for so often the brownish tinge of peat in the waters, both river and loch, helps to conceal the angler. The little river in Glenelg, opposite Skye, is a water like this. The Avon on Speyside is clear like the Polly and some other waters, but generally speaking the waters of Scotland resemble sherry more than gin.

To finish describing this part of Ross, I could do no better than mention one of the largest trout lochs in the west of the county: Sionascaig. It lies backed by three famous Wester Ross peaks: Stac Pollaidh, Cul Beag, and Cul Mòr – all rock-climbing hills. To the west of Sionascaig lie the low lands of the Inverpolly estate and the sea-scapes of Enard Bay. This is a setting of the greatest beauty for the loch, itself framed with multitudes of bays and scattered with islands. To top it all, the loch is full of keen sporting trout of the half-pound order. It is not a specimen-hunter's water, but it is a most agreeable piece of trout fishing in one of the most lovely places in Scotland. Ross is full of beauty, and each water has its particular admirers, but few would grudge the prize to Sionascaig for summing up what Wester Ross trout fishing really offers.

W.B.C.

Chapter Eighteen

SUTHERLAND

From the angler's point of view it would be misleading to describe Sutherland as if it were one county. It is as diverse a region as we have in Scotland, with landscape to the east that reflects a fertile farming scene, with moorland and loch behind, and on the west and north-west what has sometimes been inadequately described as the Scottish Interlaken. All the Sutherland salmon rivers of any length flow east or north. The western waters, usually associated with lochs to give them flow, are short, often spectacular, and radically different from the eastern ones.

KYLE WATERS

If we are travelling north, we enter the county when we cross the Kyle of Sutherland at Bonar-Bridge. This arm of the sea is a remarkable compromise between flowing river and tide. At its head it receives the waters of the Oykel, and at Rosehall the Cassley. Both Oykel and Cassley are salmon rivers of considerable interest. At Invershin, some miles below the confluence of the Cassley, the Shin joins; on the Ross-shire bank three miles further down, the Carron enters, swelling still further the freshwater dilution of the tide. The result is a tidal estuary of unique character that offers good sea-trout fishing, some excellent brackish-water brownies, and an occasional salmon.

Fishing the Kyle of Sutherland is two stages more complicated than fishing an ordinary river, for not only do you have to contend with the effect of freshwater changes like the floods of any normal river, rising with rain and falling with drought, but you have to consider the effect of daily high or low tides and, further, the effect of spring and neap tides. The fresh water of the Kyle, held up by the advancing tide, forms a slow-flowing estuary with long flats, giving loch-like conditions. But, when the tide recedes and the stemmed-up fresh water begins to be released, a changing pattern of streams and pools is formed. Some natural constrictions of the Kyle above the Shin mouth form excellent streams on the receding tide, and the lower the tide falls the faster goes the water. I have fished down the Scart stream, above Invershin, in one state, and have immediately started again at the head of the same stream to find the character quite changed, the depths different, and the fish taking differently.

The fly fishing of the Kyle, practised usually by boat, though at some places by wading, is intricate but deeply engrossing. The Kyle above Invershin seems to do best on a receding tide, and, when it is releasing the pent-up waters of the Oykel and Cassley around dusk in July or August, some really good sea-trout can be taken in the estuary. Below Invershin, there is a long flat running for about a mile to cliffy narrows at Carbisdale – deep, dark waters where few fish are taken; but, immediately below the railway bridge at Invershin the waters of the Kyle broaden out into a tidal loch, with extensive shallows from which the tree trunks that the rivers have washed down stick out like a park of modern sculpture. This loch, receiving the waters of the Ross-shire Carron on its southern shore, is an excellent drifting-place for sea-trout fishing. The sea-trout are not usually large, running to about two and a half pounds, but they are great fun, and there are always finnock and brackish brown trout to keep the sport moving.

Below the road bridge at Bonar-Bridge the Kyle meets the sea proper. At this point it is technically the Dornoch Firth. The waters of the Firth, however, are also good sea-trout fishing, and I have known of some excellent baskets of sea-trout taken by trolling a toby spoon or a remarkable lure made locally by cutting off the handle of a teaspoon and boring it top and bottom.

On the waters of the Kyle of Sutherland, silver and blue are the favourite colours for sea-trout flies. The most successful fly I ever saw there was a No. 6 Teal Blue and Silver, which took several grilse and numbers of sea-trout in one week of July. The larger sea-trout sizes are appropriate for the Kyle. I like a No. 8 Soldier Palmer on the bob, or a Blue Charm or Dunkeld on the tail. I would go as far as No. 6 when the tidal run off was strongest, and reduce to a No. 8 when the water was slacker at full tide and at low ebb. Some anglers use streamer lures, and there is no doubt that the Teal Blue and Silver Ythan lure is very effective at times – especially in the dusk. Bait is also fished extensively, and some locals worm the Kyle well, trotting the bait down the with-drawing races and picking up principally finnock and small sea-trout in good quantities. Spinning is also permitted in the tidal waters, and a Mepps spoon or a 3/8 Toby, both silver, are often successful. One week a young angler of my acquaintance took two salmon on a silver Mepps No. 3. My own preference is for fly fishing the Kyle, and I have seldom found time to spin it. The fish that boil at your flies, and the fish you see leaping, all make you want to continue fly fishing. Salmon there take fly as readily as bait, though doubtless the indifferent caster needs the

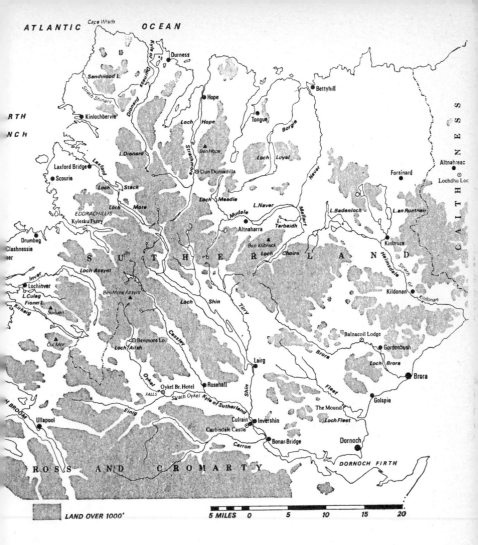

fixed spool reel to cover some of the best water, and some of the lies –
say the Shin mouth – are really long casts even with the spinning rod.

The Oykel is a famous smaller salmon river, known not only because
it is productive with spring as well as summer catches, but also because
it is managed as a hotel and letting water with well-keepered and well-
factored beats available for salmon fishing. It is not a cheap river, but
it can be a good river. The Oykel is entirely under one owner, and the
netting rights of the estuary are also controlled by the estate. This means
that a careful policy of restricted netting has led to a balance of stock
very much in favour of the angler.

From Loch Ailsh up, the Oykel is of little angling interest. There, it is
a sparkling little hill-water tumbling off the slopes of Ben More Assynt.

This upper water is reserved as a spawning area. Loch Ailsh fishes well for brown trout and gives good sea-trout fishing from July onwards, with the chance of the odd salmon thrown in. Usually it is reserved for tenants of the Oykel, so that, if the river falls very much below the level at which fish can run, and at which fish might readily take the fly, there is always a place with some chance of sport.

The Oykel falls have been said to mark the two main divisions of the Oykel itself. The upper Oykel, above the falls, is the Benmore Lodge stretch, and it fishes well from mid-June onwards, although some rods have had good spring fishing there in May. It is superb fly water, and it gives greased-line sport of a high quality. It is a river, generally speaking, of small pools in great variety, with smallish salmon of seven to ten pounds taken in delightfully scenic conditions of hill, rush, and moor. Some pools lie very close to the access road, but others take the angler further into the moor and hill country, and always each pool seems to have an unforgettable character of its own. Many fish the smallish pools of the Oykel with light salmon rods, even with single-handed rods, and find the sport excellent, but there are certain of the lower pools that need something like a twelve-foot double-handed rod for speycasting, although many of the Oykel pools are open and unimpeded from the casting point of view. August is the best month for the upper Oykel, provided there is no bad drought. Usually August provides good small floods. As many as 200 salmon and grilse can come from the upper beats in this month.

The salmon leaping the Oykel falls above Oykel Bridge are an attraction in themselves. Fish rarely run the falls before the end of April, and June is a likely month for the first good runs. The main runs of fish, however, are to be seen coming up in July and August, when numerous grilse may be in the river and memorable leaping may be seen. Guests of the Oykel Bridge Hotel fish the river below the falls, and they may take fish from early spring onwards. There are records of fish in February, but mid-March to mid-June probably covers the best of the spring fishing in the lower river – and excellent fishing it is. Many of the spring fish taken in the lower Oykel are Einig fish, shapely salmon, making for the tributary that joins the Oykel about a mile below the Oykel Bridge on the Ross-shire side of the river.

The summer fishing of the lower Oykel can be marvellous, and there are some records of single-rod takes of 'teens of fish in a day – eighteen salmon and grilse is the best I have heard of recently. This is tantalizing, but anglers would be advised not to think of the Oykel as the duffer's paradise. Salmon are very dependent on water and weather, and they are nobody's fools unless they are very fresh and excited, and even then they can be so keen on running that they will not take a single fly, no matter how well presented. Fishing closes on Oykel usually in the third week of September, when the river is teeming with salmon, spawners for the next generation of fish. The Benmore Estates, who own and run this remarkable little river, have records of fishings that any prospective tenant would find interesting, but even the non-fisher can see that the Oykel is a jewel of a river set in scenery that lifts the heart to a kind of ecstasy, for here Sutherland is in the grandest tradition of the Highlands.

The Cassley river joins the Kyle of Sutherland at Rosehall, mingling with the waters of the Oykel to make the effective beginning of the tidal Kyle. It is a spring water, and in many years its lower waters fish well from early March. Later in the season the Cassley brings into it good runs of sea-trout and grilse; but, being a spate river, it is subject to periods of difficult sport in June and July, when water may be short and few of the fish in the pools can be tempted. Cassley is a rocky river with small pools, many of which are little more than basins in the rock. In the upper waters the riverside scenery is wild and remote (although it is in fact quite accessible), and it seems to me the essence of Sutherland, with rush, heather, rock, and moor in wild profusion.

Although some of the beats of the Cassley are estate lets, taken year after year by tenants, much of the water becomes available through a Lairg hotel for guests, and there is an arrangement also in force by which an angler may take a fishing and rent a small cottage near the river. Those who go north to try the night fishing for sea-trout in Cassley (at its height in July) find the riverside cottage the best arrangement. No hotel welcomes the nocturnal fisher, yet it is in night fishing that a water like Cassley can be made to yield its best bags, especially when low water has made the day fishing virtually impossible.

The third main tributary of the Kyle of Sutherland is the Shin. This short, deep, rocky river was one of the master-features of the Highlands. I remember my first glimpse of it in the 'thirties. It poured down a short course of the greatest splendour. Its pools were terrifying. Its salmon were big, clean springers, powerfully facing the falls of Shin and braving the torrents of the river above. Now the Shin is an apology for its former self. The course is still wild, and the river still flows, but it is a river tamed by hydro-electric water-abstraction. Salmon still run its streams, and the big, clean springer is still caught; fish still leap the falls, giving some degree of spectacle, but the glory of the Shin is departed. Catches are well down. In recent years, however, the decline has been stopped, and it is even being gradually reversed. The re-stocking schemes that the Hydro Board is carrying out are ambitious and, to some extent, effective. But these are apologies for harnessing and diminishing the wildest of the Sutherland rivers. Shin still carries springers, and mid-March to mid-May is the best time for them. Also the river still brings in a reasonable summer run of salmon; but, despite the fish-pass into Loch Shin, few salmon now reach the loch and run the Tirry as they used to do. This is a sad loss, for the fish the Tirry yielded were often enormous salmon, and in the late summer and autumn that small river had tremendous sport. It is now only a trout river, though of some quality, and, as far as I can make out, few salmon reach it, because of the Lairg dam.

Loch Shin itself improved greatly under the first five years or so of hydro activity. As so often happens, a loch whose level is raised suddenly provides for its trout a bounty of food. Shallows rich in feeding are added to the loch, and often a very nutritious diet of earthworms is provided at first. Shallows like these form excellent fly-bearing mud bottoms, and for some seasons the trout grow fat. Then there is often a decline in the fish as the food supply is reduced somewhat. Loch Shin, however, seems to be going on from strength to strength, and it may well become a loch with pound-average trout. Its trout are well-proportioned fish, well marked, and excellent fighters. In small spates they run up the Tirry for distances of as much as a mile at a time, and I have seen excellent bags of fish up to a pound and three-quarters taken on fly on the Tirry. The loch itself usually produces a fairly even bag of fish running to over three-quarters of a pound, but with an occasional very much larger fish.

Loch Shin also produces the large trout some anglers still call *ferox*, and in recent years fish of six, eight, and nine pounds have been taken, some on trolled bait specially used for the larger trout, but (surprisingly) some on ordinary trout flies. It is a water with extensive new drifts, and with splendid sport in late May and June, although the trout fishing goes on right through the holiday season. An endearing feature of Loch Shin trouting is that, in times of calm, dry fly takes some of the best bags of the year.

If one denounces the Hydro Board for reducing the fishings of the River Shin, one must also praise it for improving the trouting of Loch Shin. Further, the Hydro Board and the Tourist Board were instrumental in forming the Lairg Angling Club, whose boats on the loch an angler will no doubt hire. Local club development like this is the hope for the future of Highland angling. Local estates will release waters to the public when there is a properly run club to handle them, but, until such clubs exist, estates are likely to be slow to run ticket waters on their own. Lairg is one of the pioneering clubs of the 'new deal' for Highland fishing, and to my mind it is one of the best examples of how local organization is opening up good trout fishing in the north.

FLEET, BRORA AND HELMSDALE

An area of particular fishing interest in eastern Sutherland begins on the north side of the Dornoch Firth, where the road to Dornoch, Golspie, and Wick turns east and, clinging to the coast, discovers a landscape that is in full contrast with the seascapes of the west of the county. It is not Highland-type country on this coastal strip. For the most part you travel through well-cropped fields with trim and often large farm steadings of the Lowland sort. Fat cattle graze in the fields, and estates with pheasant coverts make you think you are 400 miles to the south. This, of course, is a local illusion, for you have only to travel up a glen of an east-flowing river in this area to find that within a few miles you are again in a hilly region of bracken, rushes, and heather, with rocky rivers foaming over boulders in Highland style.

There is a remarkable estuary at Loch Fleet about four miles north of Dornoch. Here a long sandy estuary floods to give a brackish loch that in summer holds a good head of sea-trout and salmon. The road crosses the waters of Loch Fleet on a causeway 1,000 yards long, which follows a natural wasp waist on the water at the Mound. Here, at a famous old cruive and netting point, visitors can often see great shoals of fish waiting to run through into the smaller loch above and the comparatively tiny waters of the Fleet. As the tide ebbs, the lower estuary forms good currents and pools where there is a tradition of fishing for salmon, and often catching them, with normal angling gear, in the brackish water. This is therefore an exception to the rule that salmon do not take the angler's lures until they are in fresh water. In fact, there are several places in Scotland where a small amount of salmon fishing in esturial waters is done successfully. One thinks of the Dionard, where conditions are occasionally right, and one has heard of grilse that have fallen to sea-trout fishers' rods in Shetland off the burn mouths. All the same, there is no extensive fishing for salmon in salt water. This is in sharp contrast with the Pacific salmon fisheries of the west coasts of Canada and America, where large kills are made at sea by commercial and sporting fishers trolling baits.

The Fleet is probably best known for its sea-trout fishing. From mid-June onwards it can provide some good fly fishing, both in its lower reaches, where the river is slow, and in the faster pools above. It is, however, a tiny river, with a course of only some twelve miles, and it naturally requires rain to make it fishable. While you are waiting for the rain, you may fish for sea-trout in the miniature 'kyle' that the river forms at its mouth, in conditions not unlike that most outstanding sea-trout fishery, the Ythan.

The road to Brora gives a pleasant drive. The sea, often pounding the rocks and (further north) the cliffs of Easter Sutherland, provides views of compelling interest. I have never seen it really calm. Great green waves rear out of the swell and heave themselves on to the shores in cascades of foam, and the roar of their breaking and the hiss of their withdrawal can sometimes be heard for miles. But it is from this sea that the good stocks of salmon and sea-trout come to feed Brora and Helmsdale rivers. For an angler, the scenery and the prospect of sport in combination are irresistible.

On the hill to the left of the road as you travel through Golspie stands a remarkable statue of the first Duke of Sutherland. This statue – erected, it is ironically said, by his grateful crofters – was paid for by public subscription. It commemorates the Duke of the Clearances, the laird who shipped his unwilling tenants in cattle-ships to the New World, burning their crofts to encourage their departure. This scandalous episode in the history of the Highlands has been extensively written about, and the villains of the piece have been well blackened. Yet, as you drive north, you will find your eye drawn to this grotesque statue, a symbol of the worst period of landownership in the north, a monument to pride and brutality and ruthless class warfare that blackened the annals of Scotland over 150 years ago.

The Brora and Helmsdale rivers lie within a comparatively few miles of each other, but are far from being twins. Brora runs from the hills above Lairg, forming above Loch Brora a splendid Highland river of attractive pools and superb scenery. Loch Brora forms a triple loch, which is in effect the holding pool of the middle river. The lower Brora is only four miles long, a lowland stream with the most delightful fishing pools surrounded by farmland and gorse banks, and giving at times remarkable sport with salmon.

Helmsdale is a Highland river, cutting through the Strath of Kildonan – a rugged, small Highland glen, well cared for by the estates and probably preserved to a great degree by the fact that, although the railway to the north goes through the strath, the main road to Wick and Thurso does not follow the Helmsdale, but clings to the coast.

Helmsdale has lochs behind it in the hills, and a section of slowish Highland water in its upper reaches, but for the most part it is a river of good flow, with magnificent fishing pools in a setting of bracken and birches.

The Brora has an early run of salmon, and from its opening days in February there is a chance of fresh fish. In recent years the summer run of grilse and salmon has greatly increased; the May and June fishings, and (given water conditions) the later summer fishings, can be excellent. But the best of the Brora fishings are not on the lower river, admirable in spring; they are on the Balnacoil and Gordonbush waters above. Here the river is divided by a fall about ten pools above the loch.

Above the fall itself, the Black Water fishings are said to be the best as a summer beat, though the Gordonbush water below the fall has the best in spring. Great runs of sea-trout come into the river from midsummer onwards, and there is good sport in the loch and in the upper Brora river, particularly in the pools below the falls.

The Brora has always been well-preserved and well-run, with an arrangement covering the lower river by which the Sutherland Estates tenants and the Gordonbush tenants take half the river each, the upper and lower beats changing in the middle of the day on the lower Brora river. In recent years, and mainly through the excel'ent leadership of Rob Wilson of Brora, the loch has become available on a more general basis. This can be a good summer and autumn sea-trout loch, and there are excellent chances of a salmon on sea-trout flies in the summer months. A leaflet has been produced by the local club describing the drifts of Loch Brora, and visitors would be well advised to ask for a copy when they arrive.

This is a fly-only area, I'm glad to say. Loch and river have traditions of high sportsmanship, and I believe that even double hooks or tube flies with trebles are discouraged on the river. This may be taking the fly-only rule rather far, but the pleasure I have had in fly fishing the Brora seems to make any restriction worth while. I remember fishing the Gordonbush beat and losing a fish in the headstream of the Ford pool. Shortly afterwards I raised another and distinctly felt the hook pluck. A bad sign, I thought – that one would not come again. I changed down in size and took the fish two or three casts later: twelve and a half pounds. My companion, who arrived from the lower river in time to see the fish killed, took over and fished the tail of the Ford pool, raising one other fish. It was fast and furious sport with a small spate running off, but it was sport with large flies. It was August, yet the fly that proved best was a 2/o Hairy Mary. Elsewhere in Scotland I would, under such conditions, have fished a No. 4 to No. 6 fly, perhaps feeling even these too large.

The Helmsdale has always been regarded as one of the earliest spring rivers, and once springers used to be taken at Christmas time. It still opens as one of the two earliest rivers in Scotland, on the 11th January, sharing this distinction with the Thurso. The best fishing in spring is below the Kildonan falls. In recent years, although there have been fresh fish in the Helmsdale from the first day, there has often been a lapse in the spring fishings around late February and March, and the Helmsdale may be changing from what was in the main a very early river to what now seems a normally early spring one, short of springers until April and with the bulk of its fish coming in late May and June. The summer runs can be marvellous fishing, and this is said to date from 1901, with the raising in height of two of the river's headlochs, the

Badanloch and Loch an Ruathair. The former of these is the more important reservoir for the river.

In the lower waters of summer, when there is still enough water for fish to run (and to provide this was the purpose of the dams), a splendid form of fly fishing is practised on the Helmsdale. Local anglers call it dibbling. The fastest necks of water are fished with a cast of two flies, the dropper fly being the larger and dressed in a bushy form with long trailing hackles. The flies are 'dibbled' across the necks of streams; salmon come up to them excitingly and, on the light tackle used, give wonderful summer sport. A technique similar to this is practised on the Thurso and the Naver. I have found it successful on these rivers, but unproductive elsewhere. This 'dibbling' technique appears to be a local or a northern Highland one. The Thurso and the Helmsdale more or less rise out of the same hill, and the Naver is not very far away. There may well be a factor of chemistry concerned with the method, and I would tend to consider the oxygen level of the waters. It is probably the nearest thing to dry-fly fishing for salmon, an art successful with Atlantic salmon in the fast rivers of Nova Scotia and Newfoundland, but notably unsuccessful in Scotland.

The Helmsdale is, like Brora, a well-managed river. The whole river is fished on a rotation system, and proprietors do not have a private beat. The rotation moves downstream, and this is said to make the distribution of sport even more equable, for no angler can follow a shoal of fish upstream day after day. It is a fly-only river, and those who know it well hold it to be the best fly fishing in the Highlands, with first-class bags. In June 1896 a huge bag of twenty-two fish was taken on light tackle in a day by Mr Buckley on No. 5 beat on the upper Helmsdale. It is a story of skill and sportsmanship well told by both Grimble and Calderwood. Mr Buckley first broke his twelve-foot trout rod when he had six fish out, and he walked the four and a half miles to his house for his ten-footer, another trout rod, with which he returned to kill a further sixteen fish. He had no ghillie, and he found that he had to spend more time in netting the fish on his light tackle. At the princely total of twenty-two he stopped fishing, it is said, because he had beaten the previous record of twenty-one. Had he been fishing heavier tackle, the tradition adds, he might have had forty or fifty fish in the day. Calderwood says that this feat of sportsmanship far outstrips the record fifty-four salmon taken in a day on one rod in Grimersta.

In the Kinbrace–Forsinard areas excellent trout fishing is available in lochs. Some of the Forsinard lochs have only recently become available, having been opened up to help tourism. If I were looking for a holiday in remote moorland surroundings, I would certainly try this place, or its continuation on the Caithness side at Lochdhu at Altnabreac. It is wild country, but to me it is possessed of a great beauty.

ALTNAHARRA

Sutherland is a county to make the angling mind boggle. It is full of delightful, but difficult, choices. At Invershin, for instance, should you turn west to Lochinver, with its varied lochs and rivers, or east towards Dornoch and its waters? Of course you could carry straight on, following the valley of the River Shin for eight miles to Lairg, where another Sutherland decision has to be made. You could stay and fish the trout of Loch Shin or other waters in the area, or you could be lured by the hills and moorland beyond, to both north and west. To the west lies Scourie – in profusion of waters perhaps the richest area of loch fishing in Europe. Or once again you could carry straight on, from Lairg up the Tongue road into a region wild and beautiful and rich in angling of all sorts.

A little over twenty miles from Lairg on the Tongue road lies Altnaharra. It nestles behind a long strip of pine trees at the head of Loch Naver, and after the long moorland drive from Lairg it looks like an oasis. If you check your map, you will see that Altnaharra lies almost in the centre of the northern reach of Sutherland, and from it roads radiate to Hope, Tongue, Bettyhill, and their surrounding areas. These spidery roads lead an angler from Altnaharra to such splendid fishing as Loch Hope, the River Mudale, Loch Loyal, Loch Naver, the River Naver, and a multitude of other waters in the hills. Altnaharra is an angler's focusing point in a county that offers a bewildering wealth of sport.

Fishing in this area begins in February with the arrival of the spring salmon in Loch Naver, and they have occasionally been taken on the River Mudale just as early. Loch Hope has its early salmon, too, and there have been cases where fish were taken on fly (it is a fly-only water) in March, but Hope should be thought of as a later spring water, and fished in a mild April and May for its spring salmon and from June onwards for its magnificent sea-trout.

Altnaharra shows the richness of Sutherland in the settings of its loch fishing, and families should think of this type of holiday to combine good trout fishing with picnics. How would you like to be ferried across Loch Naver, to walk about a mile over heather and rushes and fish Loch Tarbhaidh under the shoulder of Ben Klibreck? Or would a moorland loch studded with islands attract you more? Loch Meadie is accessible by road and lies only about eight miles from the hotel at Altnaharra.

The one-inch Ordnance Survey map is scattered with trout lochs fishable from Altnaharra, and with trout waters and burns of real sporting value. Some are fairly remote, but of high quality. There are lochs with gilaroo trout, for example, to which Mr Charles McLaren, the hotel proprietor at Altnaharra, can direct you, or there is the splendid little Mallart river, which flows out of Loch Choire with trout, sea-trout, and salmon in its waters. Those who walk to its fishing have a great report of its stock.

Two of the waters we have mentioned as being in the Altnaharra area, or at least as being accessible from this centre, deserve a more detailed description. One is the River Naver. This charming small river gathers its source waters in the hills above Altnaharra and forms the Mudale river, which feeds the north-western end of Loch Naver. Here, swelled by other waters and by springs of its own, the reservoir that makes the Naver itself is formed. Loch Naver is itself a salmon loch of some note, offering fish to trolled baits in March and April and, from late April onwards, to fly. It is also a sea-trout loch, yielding fish to those who know the best bays rather than as a general bounty to anglers. In the summer and autumn the Mudale river takes many of the salmon upstream, and in the hills above Altnaharra they spawn.

The Naver is a clear salmon river with some of the most attractive fly fishing I have ever seen. The river measures only about twelve miles from the outflow of Loch Naver to the long estuary at Bettyhill on the north coast of Sutherland. It is divided for fishing into six beats, and the agreement is that rods fishing the river take a rotation of fishings; thus a different stretch of the river is fished every day of the week. There is also a somewhat unusual restriction on the Naver. Two rods fish a beat, one a gentleman's rod and one a lady's. This arrangement is strictly kept. There is no point in expecting a son, a guest, or a ghillie to fish the lady's rod. It is either an angler of the right sex or nothing. This curious arrangement must have irritated anglers in the past. Further, there is a rule that fishing finishes before dinner in the evening, and, although it may be argued that fishing is often best in the evening, particularly for sea-trout, this also seems to be a fairly strictly enforced rule. Thus the Naver, already a fly-only river, becomes hedged about by regulations that make its fishings probably a little less productive than they might be.

The river is, however, a most thrilling fishery. Although it is nearing the westernmost margin of true spring fishing in Scotland (the Borgie nearby is said to have the most westerly run), there have been some good spring Naver fishings in recent years. The most experienced of the Naver keepers has assured me that in his time the river first of all grew in stature as a spring water, then declined; he believed that this followed something like a thirty-year cycle. The spring fishings that give a beat five or six fish in a week in March used to double and even treble this in former years. What goes back in this way, of course, may well return. While the river has been declining, Loch Naver, on the other hand, has had some excellent spring fishings. This suggests that the cause of the change has been weather and water conditions as much as variation in the pattern of runs. In fact, it is difficult to be more than speculative about changes of this sort, for seldom are explicit records available, and, even where they are kept, they obviously cannot be treated as information for general release.

What is certain, though, is that the Naver is improving almost beyond recognition in its summer fishings. The huge grilse runs and the waves of small summer salmon in the river from July onwards give a striking indication of this improvement. A beat in August may produce a dozen lively little fish in a day (to two rods), or in days of bounty may double this. I remember asking what the day's bag was, one day in August 1965, and being told that two rods had had twenty-six fish. I assumed they were salmon and grilse and did not include sea-trout. This is stunningly good fishing in a superb water. It shows something of the stock resources achieved by the management, and it may well vindicate what some anglers think are irksome regulations to limit heavy fishing.

One of the tributaries of the Naver, the Mallart, is a worthwhile little stream. It flows down an attractive glen from Loch Choire, and it can be reached by crossing Loch Naver and walking over the shoulder of the hill. This water has not only excellent salmon fishing for rods who have access to it (through the hotel at Altnaharra or through the estate), but also some very exciting brown-trout fishing, well over the pound mark and sometimes much heavier.

The second water in the Altnaharra orbit that we must mention in more detail is Loch Hope. This is one of the finest sea-trout lochs in Scotland, and to my mind it ranks with the best of Loch Maree. It has produced an eighteen-pounder to the dap in the last decade, and has graced many an angler's bag with 'sherry fish' of nine pounds or over. The beats I know best on this water are the top one (No. 1), at the Strathmore end, and the middle beat, both fished from Altnaharra. The water daps well, given the right direction and strength of wind, but it remains in my mind as a water that yields excellent sea-trout to wet fly. This method of fishing also brings in to many a sea-trout rod a salmon or two in the course of the July or August day. The average sea-trout is between two and three pounds, and the average salmon about nine pounds – this is typical of good sea-trout and loch-salmon fishing throughout the Highlands.

I have thought for some time that the loch would fish well for salmon in late April and May. Unfortunately, I have twice been blown off the water in April when I was trying to find out. Beat 1 should certainly fish for salmon by May, and in June I would want some of the larger sea-trout, the typical fish from the first run of the season, to be rising to my flies also.

The Strathmore river above the loch is a very heavily scoured spate water, and it is not usually fished until the late season, and even then only occasionally by the tenants of the shootings. Loch Hope is a holding loch, and the short Hope river that links it with the sea is easy for fish to run. It is thus a well-stocked water and, for good measure, most excitingly set, with Ben Hope towering above the head beats and with a shore of birches and heather-lined bays, essentially Sutherland in their quality.

The head of Hope seems to me also to have the ambience of great antiquity. Dun Dornadilla, the broch by the roadside about three miles up the shingly Strathmore river, adds to the effect, but the sense of primitive splendour really springs from the landscape itself. I was once on Beat 1 in an inky-black thunderstorm. Ben Hope beetled its brows, the air became leaden, and the ripple on the loch died away. As the storm broke, the blue-black waters suddenly reared into cone-shaped waves that hammered the timbers of the boat and spun us hither and thither. I was more awe-struck than afraid, for I had long before then – even in summer sunlight – sensed the primeval power and splendour of the place.

There are many areas in the north of Sutherland where a walker can find exciting wildness and good loch fishing. One of these, Tongue, has recently formed an angling club and has opened up its fishings in the lochs nearby. Using fishings like these as a base, and taking other fishings, or getting permission by approaching the owners or factors, one can have a tremendous fishing holiday – invigorating and at times with memorable sport. Anyone keen to have this kind of holiday will know that tramping the northern moors and hills is not a pursuit for the poorly clad, the inexperienced, or the infirm. There are many waters where all the family can join in the walking and the fishing, but there are also many where a couple of hours' walk are called for, and where a keen sense of route-choosing and, occasionally, compass-reading is vital. Further, anglers who expect to walk miles of moor in waders, carrying large game-bags and loosely slung waterproofs, will be well advised to stay on the lower waters. Walking is walking, and one must have proper footwear, weatherproof clothing, iron rations, and tackle that is easy to carry and yet efficient. But for the hill fisher the rewards are magnificent. Occasionally they can be summed up in terms of fish alone, but more often they arise from something spiritual – a tone, an insight, a contact with experience of a radical kind.

LOCHINVER

This charming little fishing village, with its sheltered sea-loch, is reached by driving up the Invershin–Rosehall road that follows the Kyle of Sutherland, then Strath Oykel, over to the valley of the River

The River Inver, a highly preserved water, tumbles through Inver Gorge.

Inver itself, which wends its way down from Loch Assynt westward to the sea at Lochinver. Loch Assynt is a typical Sutherland combination of salmon, sea-trout, and brown-trout loch. Like any large water, it is a fishery that repays study and – again like many Highland lochs of this sort – is probably less well fished than it deserves to be. I should think that Loch Assynt would fish well for April salmon, and perhaps also for the larger sea-trout that run the Inver as early as the end of March. These great fish, of seven to ten pounds, run each year and are hardly fished for, since the main fishing tenants are not around so early. Further, successful loch fishing for salmon demands an intimate knowledge of the loch-bed and a careful handling of drifts. This needs a local man to work on it, and this is often what the lochs of the Highlands lack.

The River Inver itself is a superb summer and autumn stream, with excellent to superlative grilse fishing and good to very good sea-trout fishing. It is a highly preserved and carefully managed water. Lets of its fishings are sometimes available, but in general the best summer fishings are taken by the proprietor or his guests. Nevertheless, always make inquiries, either through the local hotel or through the local estate office.

Lochinver is sandwiched between the Inver and the slightly less impressive Kirkaig. This smaller river to the south of the village has a massive fall in its middle course, which prevents salmon from ascending to the Fionn Loch, where the Kirkaig gathers its flow. The falls pool on the Kirkaig can be fished, but the experience is hair-raising. A 'steeple' cast is called for, and if possible an observer to tell you whether your flies, fishing round the blind corner of a rock bluff below you, have raised salmon or not. I have heard of six salmon raised in this way and not one hooked. This, of course, is typical of rather stale fish. Walking back from the Fionn Loch, I remember casting my trout flies over the falls pool and watching a grilse rising slowly towards the flies, boiling on the surface of the water below the flies and not even opening its mouth. But the Kirkaig can have salmon very much with open mouths when the water is right. It runs heavier fish than its neighbour, and tends to bring in some very impressive late runs with fish into the twenty-pound class – a rare weight for small west-coast Highland rivers. When I last fished it, the Kirkaig was a well-run and nicely managed little stream with named pools, good access, and well-regulated fly fishing.

Behind Lochinver village lies a little weedy loch called Culag (the same name as the hotel's). Up to this, by way of the manse burn, salmon and some sea-trout run. I have heard of some very successful fly fishing here in July, with a brace of salmon and others moved and lost in two days' fishing. Sometimes Culag can be a dour water, but sometimes, after being slandered by anglers who cannot even raise fish,

A skilful angler may land a keepable trout from a Wester Sutherland burn.

it yields salmon liberally – you might almost say with a thrawn generosity. If you are in the area, don't forget it as a possibility, especially when the Kirkaig is low and unproductive.

The trout fishings of the Lochinver area are prolific. For a few shillings a day you can fish something like thirty named lochs in the Assynt area. Many of these lochs are well worth a visit; some are 'picnic' fishing with trout three or four or even six to the pound. But I know of some excellent bags of good fish, including some of over two pounds, taken from this cheapest of loch fishing. If there is an area in Scotland of better hill and seascape scenery, of more open and happy fishing for trout, I have not heard of it. This is bracing walker's country with hummocks rather than high hills, and loch after loch in the rocky hollows and in the depressions of the moor. On a summer evening, with a sun setting blood-red behind the skylines of hill ridges, trees, and islands, it is unforgettable. In such a gloaming the trout will be on the rise too. Visual and sporting pleasures accumulate and give as pleasant a Highland holiday as you could devise.

Naturally, not all the trout fishing in the area is available in the cheap day ticket. The Fionn Loch, for instance, is a lovely piece of inland trout fishing. You walk up the path by the Kirkaig for half to three-quarters of an hour, and you find lying at the head of the river one of Sutherland's most memorable lochs. The abrupt slopes of Suilven dominate the northern shores. Extensive bays with sandy and highly productive weedy water reach back for miles. This is a water of beautiful trout, often a pound or more, magnificently spotted and golden. It is also a loch of big trout, with occasional three- and four-pounders coming to the fly. Marvellous!

SCOURIE

One of the difficulties of writing a book about much-loved fishings like those of Sutherland is that you never manage to do justice to the sport because of its sheer abundance. Take the Scourie area. This wonderful fishing district lies north of Lochinver, and it can be reached by taking the road across the Stoer peninsula, through Clashnessie and Drumbeg, across the Kylesku ferry and on through Eddrachillis to the hotel at Scourie itself. Most people, however, would approach the area by the main road, following Loch Shin from Lairg, driving down the side of lochs More and Stack to Laxford Bridge and turning left down to Scourie. In either case it is a superb drive. I prefer the 'big lochs' road, for the sight of More and Stack and of the prolific little Laxford river whets my angling appetite enormously. *Lax* is Swedish for salmon, and to this day Laxford lives up to its Scandinavian name. It was over the waters of Loch Stack, as I travelled on this road, that I saw my first eagle. It was impressively harrying a raven, which escaped by flattening itself to the water like a fighter plane, flying lower than its more powerful but less manoeuvreable assailant. I was near enough to see that eagle's eye.

Scourie parish has something like 300 trout lochs. It could be the centre of hill trout fishing – walking and cycling or driving are thrown in – with a range hardly possible in any other area of Scotland, except the similar country to the immediate north and south of this part. The lochs vary from hill-pools with fingerlings (or sometimes monsters that have engulfed the fingerlings) to mixed lochs with good trout and sea-trout, and some top-class waters with excellent high-average bags.

Stack and the Laxford are world-famous as salmon and sea-trout fishings. The river itself is not usually available to the public, except those people who manage to rent some of its fishings. In summer the river is 'stiff' with fish, and it is watched day and night. The lochs above – Stack and More, but principally Stack – are superb sea-trout lochs. Stack daps well and yields to wet fly in some abundance. This is *par excellence* a water for 'bottle' fish (nine pounds plus). There is seldom a year without a fourteen- or fifteen-pounder to top the numbers of sea-trout taken in Stack well over the nine-pound mark. The fish rise enormous to bobbing dapped flies. They open mouths like caverns to engulf the flies and, tantalizingly, they sometimes miss! Dapping on Stack can be heart-pounding work. Oddly enough, I prefer wet-fly fishing here, and several of my friends like it too. In fact, the dap may raise fish that a wet fly fished by the other rod in the boat may take. It is complementary fishing at times – team work. Naturally, sea-trout fishing of this order is expensive. If I say the results are worth it, only those who have experienced them will believe me. This is, after all, virtually unrepeatable sport; and in July and August it is vintage sport.

Loch More, further up into the hills on the same system, has slightly less expensive sea-trout fishing to offer. The fish are sometimes less fresh in More, but they are no less heavy. Sea-trout of eleven and twelve pounds have come off More in recent seasons. For drifting, the dark surface of Loch More can be just as rewarding as the more open waters of its larger neighbour, Stack.

I need hardly mention that the scenery is breathtaking. Sutherland in the west is varied Highland country. It is pre-Cambrian rock, ground down in millions of years to a low landscape with an air of antiquity and a calmness that I have found only in one other place in Europe – the wilderness of Lapland. From above, the scene takes on a complex appearance as loch after loch heaves into view. In some directions of light the whole field of vision seems to glitter, partly from the lochs and lochans and arms of the sea, but partly also from the quartz screes and the rocks.

CAPE WRATH AND DURNESS

Limestone bases for trout lochs in Scotland are rare. One of the most extraordinary and inexplicably-placed of these is the small area surrounding Durness to the north-west of Sutherland and separated from the extreme north-west point of Scotland's mainland, Cape Wrath, only by the Kyle of Durness and the River Dionard. For an incalculable number of square miles around the waters, you find schist, gneiss, or granite based on or lying over peat. Here, by some geological freak, is an outlying basis of limestone – the best water bottom for trout.

The four most obvious lochs for the trout angler in this remote, wild, beautiful part of the mainland are Croispol, Caladail, Borley, and Lanish. In Croispol and Caladail the average trout weighs between one and two pounds, the two-pounders being taken mostly in Caladail. In either loch the newcomer, on getting into a one-pounder or two-pounder, will, until he sees his prey approaching the net, think that he is playing a trout at least twice the size, for it will fight like fury.

Borley and Lanish, however, are in a class of their own for the size of their trout and for the dourness with which they come to the fly. In each loch there exist, have come to the fly, have been played, lost, and occasionally caught, brown trout of fifteen or even sixteen pounds, not of the ugly *ferox* kind but natural and graceful in appearance. Borley has two boats, and, if luck and the wind are with you, you may have a memorable catch.

Lanish is more alluring, more difficult, more dour. It has a two-pound minimum limit, yet it is a mere strip of water some 200 yards long and has no boat. Narrow and shallow, it can be almost completely covered by fly while wading. Here brown trout of good proportions and of fifteen pounds are possible; but they are extremely difficult to lure. One can drift and wade Lanish all day and see no fish or sign of one save the occasional remote large swirl, perhaps not even at your fly.

A local crofter who watched me fishing in Lanish one forenoon volunteered that the biggest trout in Lanish was just over sixteen pounds. 'He's never been brought to the land or the net,' he added, 'but everyone knows him. You can always tell him by his beard.'

'Beard?' I could not help asking, with memories of barbel in the remote Thames.

'Yes, he wears a beard of Invictas. He's worn it for as many years as I can remember.'

This exciting, if hardly credible, piece of information is characteristic of the limestone lochs of Durness. A local writer, who knows the lochs well, has said: 'Let no one go up there [to Durness] thinking that he will be sure to bag a few of these large trout; but the fascination of them attracts people year after year, who pit their wits against these wily monsters in the hope that they will successfully land one of the really big ones'.

He goes on to say that a Lanish or Borley fanatic would be more satisfied with one specimen trout in double figures during his stay in Durness than numerous smaller trout or even salmon. I agree. During my stay a few years ago I saw the swirl of only one monster brown trout, but I did taste the fighting capacity of the one- and two-pounders. I find it difficult to suppose how anyone could on an ordinary trout rod ever begin to hold the Invicta-bearded monster of sixteen pounds.

Visitors staying at the Cape Wrath Hotel at Durness fish these limestone lochs according to a rota; but those staying in the neighbourhood can apply to the hotel for the right, on payment, to fish any of these extraordinary lochs that are not in use by the hotel.

Also in this area is that delightful little salmon and sea-trout river, the Dionard. It is an early summer stream, running fish in May and June. At its head lies Loch Dionard, until recently a hard eight-mile walk from the nearest road. Now special hill vehicles take the angler up to this wild, productive loch. Once they said you had to throw the salmon back, for you could never have carried them all down to the road.

The Cape Wrath peninsula itself, lying stark and remote to the west and north of Dionard, has attracted many a walker and fisher with a taste for the windswept wildness of Sutherland. There are trout lochs in plenty, and several small spate waters that have salmon and sea-trout. The most attractive of these is Sandwood, a low-lying trout and sea-trout loch joined to the sea by a short river. The splendour of Sandwood Bay is something to reward the walker who foots it out down Strath Shinary. Kinlochbervie is a good base for a fisher walking overnight – a man willing to take the far north-west as he finds it. It is one of the most isolated and most stimulating parts of Scotland.

The areas we have touched on above do not exhaust Sutherland; they do not even cover, by sampling, all the fishings available. But they may serve to indicate that I have wandered extensively in Sutherland, fishing and exploring over many years. Like the speaker in Tennyson's *Ulysses*, I find the experience

> ... an arch wherethro'
> Gleams that untravell'd world, whose margin fades
> For ever and for ever when I move.

To devote a lifetime to fishing the county would not nearly be enough. It would take a multiple lifetime. Readers who share the urge to travel and fish there should take this description only as a starting-point, and sample the pleasure of Sutherland for themselves.

W.B.C.

Chapter Nineteen

CAITHNESS

Caithness sometimes seems to be part of another country, north of Scotland. You can stand at Strathmore on the Thurso river, and look nearly a score of miles to the south over low rolling moors to where Morven dramatically rises to mark the beginning of the Sutherland hills. Behind you to the north lies the plain of Caithness – rich, low land reaching to the sands of Dunnet on the north and Wick and Duncansby cliffs on the east. This most northern county of the mainland is split between moorland and field, and the 110 trout lochs that lie on both moor and field provide varied and, in some waters, magnificent trout fishing. Caithness is drained by six rivers, small by mainland standards; but all have salmon in them, and the principal river of the county, the Thurso, is a prolific, well-managed salmon river with a character of its own.

One blessing of glaciation, geologically speaking, is that fertile soil can be deposited by chance on a rock that might not have been so sweet. Caithness has a reach of marl, impregnated with shells from the Moray Firth and surrounding seas, and this forms the basis of good farming on the plain and some excellent trout fishing. Three lochs have benefited greatly from this soil. Watten (known everywhere for its good trout), Loch Scarmclate, and the smaller Loch Heilen are all enriched by it. Watten is said to have provided the first batch of trout for the restocking of Loch Leven in the nineteenth century. It is probable that something of this kind happened, for Watten fish are often well-marked trout of the 'Loch Leven' sort. But Watten also has a stock of thumping big trout, yellow on flank and belly and dark brown above. These big fish run to two and three pounds without raising local eyebrows. In fact, local eyebrows would be hard to move in Caithness. Hardly a season passes without the catching of some enormous brown trout. In 1960 Loch Scarmclate, linked to Watten by a burn, produced one of ten and a half pounds. Mr David Mowat, then of the Northern Sands Hotel, who caught this fish, does not boast about it, I believe, since he found it in rather poor condition, not in the splendid form Caithness anglers expect of their big trout!

Watten was a very much neglected loch in the 'thirties and 'forties, and in recent years a Loch Watten Proprietors Angling Association was formed to run the loch on a proper footing. Now boats are limited to twenty-eight, methods are fly only, and the season is strictly from the 1st May to the 30th September. These measures seem to make excellent sense. The loch fishes really well, can grow fish to a pound average, yield three-pounders, and give numbers too. One angler, Mr William Mackay of Thurso, fishing in 1965, caught fifty-four keepable fish in a day, all over ten inches long. Some anglers maintain that Watten is falling back on its average weight. It once boasted a pound, but it now claims a more modest three-quarters. Under good management, however, there is every reason to expect on this water a return to the pound standard.

Rich waters grow weed; and Watten, and its near neighbour Scarmclate, and (the last of the trio) Heilen grow it in profusion. Watten is the clearest by far, but in recent years weed on Scarmclate has been troublesome and on Heilen a menace. Heilen in August looks like a green field, and I believe that those who take fish from it for spawning and hatchery purposes merely wade through the weed with a hand-net and scoop out trout. It is interesting to think about recent weed-growth problems in Caithness, in Orkney, and elsewhere (such as the efflorescence of algae in Loch Leven), and consider whether this growth results from the way in which modern field fertilizers drain into our lochs from nearby fields. Certainly this seems possible in the case of some Lowland lochs. Trout there have been shown to contain chemicals derived from these fertilizers, but it surprises me that Caithness waters should have felt the effects too. It could be, at its most dismal, that the whole balance of nature in loch ecology is being threatened.

There is one special loch in the north of Caithness that does not fall into any of the usual categories. It is St John's Loch, near Dunnet. This loch is on a raised beach, and it has all the qualities of a machair loch, including magnificent, hard-fighting trout. I spent several happy summers of my childhood in Caithness near St John's Loch, and I can well remember the local postman's stories of its fishing. He regularly brought home fish of two pounds, and he just as regularly lost heavier trout. The best fish to come from the loch recently was a trout of four and a half pounds landed in August 1965 by a visiting Glasgow angler. Local opinion holds that there are far better fish still to be taken. Local opinion also maintains that the waters of this loch are unique, possessing strange curative powers. I think it is right about the fishing, but on the spa side I prefer to withhold judgment.

The local water supply in Thurso comes from Loch Calder, a deep, long loch lying due north to south a few miles out of the town. Like most lochs used for water supplies, it has had the history of a raised water-level. In the case of Calder this has happened twice in recent years. Raising loch-levels seems to help trout at first, then to set them back. Calder has apparently maintained its quality of fish. It is a deep loch with steep, treacherous banks, and local people say that uninformed wading is dangerous. Boats, however, may be hired, and on a good day – of little wind, high white cloud, and warm temperatures – Calder can produce not only reasonable numbers but also an occcasional fish of the two- to three-pound mark.

Loch Shurrery is a pleasant trout loch not many miles from Calder, but, since it is also a salmon loch, permission to fish for trout may be rather difficult to obtain. Local inquiry may help, and at certain times of the year a trout fisher would be more likely to gain access than at others. The average weight of trout is around eight ounces.

The moorland lochs associated with the upper course of the Thurso river above Loch More are fished, largely, from Lochdhu Hotel. In the past few years they have been the subject of an experiment in loch management that has yielded encouraging results. The Hon. Robin Sinclair, now Viscount Thurso, is the man of vision behind this attempt to produce better fishings, and his policies seem to me excellent. Some lochs are best suited to producing their yield per acre in the form of a few very big trout; some should try to produce a good number of fish of three-quarters of a pound to a pound; still others – 'picnic' family fishings – should be left to produce three or four fish to the pound, but dozens of them in the day's sport. On the Lochdhu fishings this pattern has been reflected admirably. The fishings there range from Loch Glutt, a tiny but quite remarkable hill-loch, with fish that reach an average of one pound fourteen ounces, to Loch a' Cherigal, with fish averaging fourteen ounces to one pound, and Loch Caise, where trout run to a quarter-pound average and numbers are plentiful. Lochdhu is as good a centre for trout loch fishing as any in Scotland. There may be areas of more prolific fishing, but I wonder whether there is such variety available elsewhere within such a short radius from a hotel.

The angler who likes remoteness, and is willing to take a map and strike out over the moor, should take the train (or a car) to Forsinard and walk over the moors the seven or eight miles to Altnabreac, and Lochdhu Hotel. The walk begins at the head of Strath Halladale in Sutherland and takes the angler over open moorland studded with lochs. You can carry a trout rod ready mounted and cast a line casually on the lochs you pass. Your bag may well grow too heavy for you on the journey.

This short account of the trout lochs in the Caithness areas of Strathmore, Dalnawillan, Lochdhu, and Glutt hardly does more than touch a very extensive area of trout fishing. There are lochs to the north and west of Altnabreac about which I have said nothing. There is Skyline, with fish likely to run well over the pound; the cluster of trout lochs to the west of Loch More, most of which yield fish of the half-pound average; and, to the south of Loch More, the twin lochs of Thulachan and Sandy, giving half-pounders and better in a delightful setting on the moors.

If I were asked to name a favourite fly for the moorland lochs of Caithness, I should certainly choose a No. 10 Soldier Palmer. Where water is peaty and wind is usually more fresh than gentle, the hairy red and ginger Soldier Palmer on the bob raises fish very efficiently. The

Black Pennel, the Invicta, and that good old standby of most Scottish waters, the Greenwell, would give you a nice selection for a Caithness cast. The sizes (No. 10, and in a high wind even No. 8) may seem unnecessarily large, but it has often been demonstrated that Sutherland and Caithness hill trout want a mouthful. Why not give it them? Smaller flies in Caithness often succeed in catching only smaller trout.

The Thurso belongs to a select sub-class of Scottish salmon rivers; it can be comprehended as a whole sporting unit. You can stand fishing one of its pools and feel conscious of the whole twenty-five miles of its fishing beats between Thurso and Loch More. Better still, you can stand in the hotel at Halkirk after the day's fishing and meet all the other anglers from the fifteen beats. Hearing, like this, what fly took the fish, what luck befell, and how the salmon behaved confirms the unity of the Thurso. It is just small enough to be one fishing experience and not a series.

I was made aware of the smallness of the Thurso one April in a memorable way. I had spent a short afternoon on Beat 15, the highest beat below Loch More, and I had been lucky enough to take two fish and lose a third in a short hour and a half. The fish were fresh springers and were taking deeply. As the sun began to set I fished through the bridge pool again before packing up. I was concentrating, when a head appeared over the bridge parapet. It was one of the fishing tenants who had driven up from Thurso to see how the top pools were doing.

We chatted, and he, a local man, told me of his remarkable luck there the previous evening when the fish had 'taken a gee', and he had caught eight salmon on a large bushy dropper fly on his cast as they rose like trout in a frenzied display of activity while the sun set.

I left the banks of the pool and drew out my fly-box, asking the Thurso man to pick anything like the successful fly. He looked disappointed, but prodded a Yellow Dog as being 'near the right shape and size'. To me it was madness to fish a large dropper in cold April conditions for spring fish, but I did so. Almost at once I rose and missed a salmon. Then I had a superb head-and-tail take and duly killed a tenpounder after scrambling down from the bridge praying that the fish would not swim down through the arch. By this time it was nearly dark, and the 'gee' had worn off. My Thurso friend had glided back to the town. I carried off my three beautiful springers and made a mental note to look up my Jamieson (*Etymological Dictionary of the Scottish Tongue*) to find the meaning of 'gee'. Not that Jamieson could have added anything to the word for me. I know only one context. For me 'gee' means 'mad Thurso salmon whim'.

The Thurso has always had for me a peculiar and attractive quality. As a boy, I was lucky enough to spend several summer holidays near its waters, and, although I did not think of it then as a salmon river, it held a very special place in my fishing life. I discovered that the brackish waters of the town beat had splendid brown trout, which I could take on dry fly at certain states of the tide. One August dusk I remember standing and taking twelve from one run. The best was nearly two pounds. To a boy, fishing his first trout rod, this was unforgettable sport. Perhaps it was the memory of this early success that made me want to return a few years ago to fish Thurso salmon.

In length, the Thurso is not a leading salmon river. Twenty-five miles of water is of little account. In flow, it is unimpressive, and even in appearance some would say its 'linns' were dead waters. No one should be misled by these negatives. The Thurso is not only a highly significant river, but in some ways it is a symbol of what well-managed salmon fishing might be elsewhere.

The last sixty years have seen a most remarkable change in the Thurso. Sir Tollemache Sinclair, the laird of the river at the beginning of the century, decided that he would like to add science to nature by impounding the waters of Loch More and regulating the flow of the Thurso by a system of sluices. Thus he could combat drought and select a good fishing height for his whole river, improving salmon runs and salmon fishing. As one might have predicted, many anglers thought this was a sin of the gravest order. Augustus Grimble, the salmon authority of the time, strongly disapproved and told Sir Tollemache that he would ruin Loch More as a fine salmon loch, and would do better to employ the money in buying off esturial nets. Grimble, however, lived to see the first improvements. The summer and autumn fishing increased almost at once.

The returns from the Thurso make fascinating reading. Not only are they among the most detailed and careful salmon records available in Scotland, but they cover a whole salmon river, and one can see a profile emerging, especially in recent records kept for years by Mr David Sinclair of Halkirk, the river superintendent. His excellent chronicles have played no small part in the success of the river. Management policies based on the returns have made the Thurso a paragon of productivity.

I suppose many Scottish anglers sigh for the unspoilt days of Edwardian fishing. Well, let them sigh. In 1909 I can trace, in a good year, only 338 fish (Grimble). By 1920, another good year, the Thurso yielded 1,111 fish from all its waters in the season (Calderwood). By 1927, the best year that the river had then enjoyed, 2,265 fish were recorded. But 1965 broke all records again, when 2,312 fish were caught in a year that one might have predicted would be lean after extensive sea netting off Greenland and previous drift netting elsewhere off our coasts.

Drift netting around Scottish shores is now banned, of course, but during the past few years grave doubts have been expressed over the possible effects of the sea netting that takes place – mainly by Danish boats – in salmon sea-feeding grounds off the Greenland coast. Tagging experiments have shown that 'Scottish-based' salmon have been taken in some numbers in these Arctic regions, but the difficulty in determining the extent of the danger lies in our inability to establish, even approximately, the number of 'Scottish' salmon that are being captured, in relation to salmon from other countries in the United Kingdom, Canada, Norway, and so on. So far, attempts at international level to halt the Greenland netting activity have not met with noted success.

Since the record 1965 season Thurso salmon catches have fluctuated considerably, dropping to only 523 in 1967. But in 1970 the annual total had risen to 1,240.

As a fisherman's river, the Thurso rewards those who take the trouble to know it. It has fifteen beats between Loch More and Thurso. The top beats, 10 to 15, have most of the broken, streamy water of the river. Beats 8 and 7 amble along, and to the untutored eye at times look dead. Beat 5 takes on a pleasant stream and pool character, while the lower waters have much more the appearance of 'linns', as the local people call very slow pools. Certainly there could be no greater contrast than Beat 12 and Beat 8. Beat 12 is set in a dramatic little gorge with rocky streams and pools. The Queen Mother finds this her favourite beat. The water is very lively, which makes it easy for an angler to read off the position of lies, and the best taking-places for salmon.

Lower down on Beat 8 the river meanders between peaty banks, like an inscrutable dark canal. Yet these 'dead' waters are far from dead if you care to study them. Beat 8 gave me my first springer of 1965, and has provided me with sport at other times of the year. Slow water is not dead; it is merely different. Instead of reading off easily where salmon would lie in it, you have to seek finer clues and change your tactics in the light of what you discover. I watch for a narrowing of the river, and I fish these necks very slowly and carefully, and in spring very deeply. It is only when you try to achieve depth with a salmon fly that you discover that apparently still water is moving with some power.

Hand-lining helps the presentation of the fly, and Thurso fishers often put a considerable speed into fly-retrieval. It is a splendid feeling when the hand-lined fly suddenly stops, and there is a tremor, followed by the first strong pull of a fresh salmon. In spring, fishing slow waters on the Thurso is an art in itself; in summer it becomes an extension of loch fishing. The upstream wind can ripple the surface and give the slow reaches a splendid wave for a fly fished cutting into the surface. Bob flies work well under these circumstances.

Above Loch More the Thurso is as long again as it is from its estuary to the loch. This is a region of wild grouse moors, trout lochs, and hill-burns. The Rumsdale Water has a good salmon beat on it for about a mile above the loch, but the water soon takes on the character of a hill-stream. As one walks up its banks, it dwindles to a trout burn, and, although (as an angler would view it) the stream is far from its source, it loses itself in an ocean of moorland.

Caithness is a county of fish, with salmon and trout figuring largely in its returns. One odd lack is sea-trout. The Thurso has some sea-trout in its waters, and the boys on the tidal water catch finnock, but no significant run of sea-trout exists on the river. I know of no parallel to this in Scotland. The only explanation seems to be that the Thurso is unsuitable in its lower reaches as a spawning river for sea-trout. It is peaty, and sea-trout like gravel. Salmon also like gravel, and they find it in the Rumsdale and the hill-waters above. This may be too far for sea-trout, and the small stock exists on such spawning as they can find in tributaries on the lower reaches of the Thurso system.

One attractive feature about the modern era of Thurso fishing is that it is reasonably easy to get fishings on the river through hotels. The river is entirely owned by Ulbster Estates, and beats are often available for renting direct. Some beats are available through Lochdhu Hotel and other hotels in the area. Rates vary according to the months of the season, and a careful rotation system is operated to give tenants a share of the best beats. All in all, it is a remarkably well run fishery, an agreeable little river of great sporting possibilities, and a locality that grips you with its peacefulness and charm. I should say that April and May saw the best of the spring fishings on Thurso, and August brought the best of the summer fishings. In the bumper year of 1965 one beat produced fifty fish in one day, and on the same day the whole river produced 100. This is outstanding, and anglers should not expect it every year. A brace or two, a single fish or two, and even a blank or two make up the run of spring fishings, and summer sport depends heavily on the right floods, the right skies and temperatures, but it can give exceptional catches of smaller fish.

The Berriedale is a river only recently made available to the public. It flows east to the North Sea, and it follows a scenic glen in one of the hillier parts of Caithness, flowing hard by the lower slopes of Morven and Scaraben, both of which rise to over 2,000 feet. This is a little river, providing three double beats over some twelve miles of fishable water, with rather more than forty named pools. Fish run from February onwards, dependent on the water, but as with the Thurso, April and May make the best months of the season. Berriedale fish average under ten pounds, usually nearer seven pounds for the spring, but in a river of this size and character these fish offer excellent sport. Sea-trout run in July and August, and there is the chance of some good brown trout, if you want to fish them, in the lower river. The fishings are available through Mr R. I. Mowat of the Portland Arms Hotel, Lybster, and he can often make arrangements for day tickets. Access to this attractive little salmon river is possible only until the 10th August in each year, because of the proprietor's shooting arrangements, but after that date fishings may still be had by special arrangement with the estate.

Of the other salmon rivers and streams in Caithness, the Dunbeath and Forss waters are not usually available to the public. They are small and entirely dependent on rain. When they are in ply they are almost certain to be reserved for the estates concerned. However, a third small water is available: the Wester Water. It drains the shallow Loch of Wester, and meets the sea near Keiss, north of Wick. This is one of the true sea-trout waters of Caithness, a comparative rarity in the county. It is a summer and autumn water, and is most productive after the Loch of Wester has filled with rain. It is probably the latest salmon fishing in Caithness, with good catches in late September and even into October. Local anglers fish trout rods on this small river, and they take salmon up to ten pounds, with occasional larger fish. The loch also fishes for salmon and sea-trout, and, although some people spin this shallow fly-fishing water, it is usually fished from bank and boat with a fly. Permits are available locally by the day.

One other river remains: the Wick. This water is again a fairly small stream, but the Wick Angling Association, which has the fishings, is intent on developing and improving its migratory ones. They have taken off the estuary nets, and they have a restocking programme in hand. There are some good brown trout in the reedy, slow pools of the middle river, and in summer grilse and salmon are taken on flies and spinners. Some tidal sea-trout fall to anglers right in the middle of Wick itself. Anglers staying in the neighbourhood should inquire about terms of tickets and extent of fishings available both in the Wick river and in local lochs, which can add trout, for there are also trout lochs that can bring variety and good sport to a fishing holiday. Hempriggs and Sarclet come at once to mind.

Some have said that Caithness is an acquired taste. I don't doubt it. I merely record my good fortune in having been able to acquire the taste for Caithness in my boyhood and to develop it further – almost to the level of an addiction – in my recent fishing years. Anglers who like spinneys and fat cock pheasants on the bank as they fish may find Caithness not up to scratch; those who like grouse in heathery moors, peaty waters lapping moss-covered stones, fresh clean winds on their faces, and (above all) expansive moorland landscapes will find the taste of Caithness at once heady and satisfying.

W.B.C.

Chapter Twenty

INTRODUCTION TO THE ISLANDS

The 787 islands scattered about our coasts, and occasionally in the estuaries we call firths, represent a truly astonishing number, hardly surpassed by any other country. In the larger of these islands, and in a few of the smaller, the lover of inland waters will find lochs, and occasionally streams and near-rivers, to hold his eyes by their subtle beauty and to give promise of splendid angling.

I cannot call such sport unique in Scotland, but there are differences between fishing for trout, sea-trout, and salmon in the islands and angling for them on the mainland. These differences are alluring and can be exciting. Some anglers who fall under their spell return year after year to the same island or group of islands – dedicated for life, it seems, to Scottish island angling.

Its allurements are these: the seclusion in which you can practise your sport, the plenitude of the fish, and the high average sporting quality of the fish.

The family helicopter has not yet proliferated like the motor-car, and, until it has, those islands that are not all but attached to the mainland by a daily or hourly motor-ferry service seven days a week keep a reasonable degree of seclusion. You may be fishing one of the famous and expensive waters of the Outer Hebrides, or you may be wandering at will by the lochan sides of a small island in which the angling is free; in either event you will not suffer from crowds. Island fishing in Scotland, of whatever degree, still keeps much of the quality that fishing had on the mainland before the First World War and before invasion by the motor-car. Either because of this, or because natural conditions for game fish are so favourable on so many islands, trout, sea-trout, and salmon breed prolifically in the island lochs and in the short streams that connect them with the sea. The average weight of brown trout is equal to that on the mainland (in some instances exceeding it); the sea-trout on an average equals but does not surpass its mainland weight. The salmon can run to a good weight, but never reach that of the monsters in Tay, Tweed, and the other great rivers of Scotland. The Hebridean salmon is a fine fish indeed, but he very seldom reaches the twenty-pound class. Yet he exists in plenty.

When, however, it comes to the sheer fighting capacity of many game fish in the islands, their average beats that of the mainland. This is not a matter for debate or statistics or of pious belief; it is a question of experience. Of course, not every brown trout, sea-trout, or Hebridean salmon will, pound for pound, beat in fighting capacity their opposite numbers on the mainland of Scotland, but frequently they do.

The islands of Scotland can be divided thus. There are only a dozen islands or islets off the east coast of Scotland, ten of which are in the Firth of Forth. Some of these are impressive to look at (particularly the Bass); some are rich in history and red with its blood. In angling value they are of no note. We then move first to the other side of Scotland and to the enormous number of the group known as the Hebrides, which runs for 205 miles north and south off Scotland's western coast. These are divided into the Inner and Outer Hebrides. Nearly all the inhabited Hebridean islands are well, some plentifully, endowed with inland waters. From the Hebrides we move to the northern islands, which lie north to north-north-east of Scotland. These islands are also divided into two groups, Orkney and Shetland. Neither is attached to shires in the body of Scotland; each is a county in itself. Their many fishing waters (and here one must specially mention their estuaries and voes) are as famous for angling as any waters of the Hebrides.

Scenically and for the angler, these groups have much in common, but they have also many differences arousing local loyalties. Before we come to them in particular division, I must say what the angling waters of these famous Scottish islands do not share with those of the mainland.

There are few rivers in the islands, and the longest of these cannot be compared with Tay, Tweed, Dee, Spey, or many other mainland rivers. Except for some of the Inner Hebrides (particularly Skye), their scenery is not often impressive in the obvious manner. It holds no great sweeps of water, no gorges torrentially filled, no resounding waterfalls, nothing of that Highland water-scenery which Landseer and his contemporaries used to paint for the delight of the Victorians, and which the railways still plaster on their posters in the hope of luring trippers to the 'Land of the Mountain and the Flood'.

The lack of this sort of riverscape in the islands is easily explained. Except for a few places in Lewis in the Outer Hebrides, there just is not enough land between the lochs and the sea for outgoing water to accumulate to river size. For the most part, the lochs in the Hebrides and the northern isles reach the open sea through burns and rivulets.

Among the almost innumerable lochs in the islands, there are some fair-sized sheets of water, but nothing that approaches Lomond, Ness, or the greater lochs of the Scottish mainland. Again there isn't enough land to hold together a Loch Lomond; but there certainly is just enough

The Suisgill Burn in Helmsdale once yielded gold as well as fish.

land on Benbecula, for instance, to hold between narrow strips of rock or peat a Loch Lomond split into 100 parts. The result is that from the air Benbecula looks like a great heathery shawl.

The scenic appeal of most of the outer and some of the inner isles is subtle: soft colours, long beaches of silver sand, and (on fine days) apparently limitless horizons. Before we come to the famous inland waters, we must glancingly mention the obscure ones on some of the less visited islands that have their own appeal. Small lochs or lochans lie sheltered in little hollows within the sound of the sea yet secure and harboured from it.

It is most satisfying to fish from the bank of such a lochan on one of the lesser islands and be content with a moderate basket of sporting brown trout. At intervals you will listen to the waves on the western beach, and the sound of them will assure you of your seclusion. There aren't many people on the island; few of them are anglers; and there is the sea to guard you against the rest of the world. That is part of the appeal of all islands everywhere; but it is particularly potent if you are an angler and by the banks of such a lochan on such an island – Coll, for instance, in the Inner Hebrides.

When I describe the islands as secluded I do not mean they are difficult to get to. The air services from Glasgow, Edinburgh, and other towns are prompt and (save when a deep mist interferes) can be relied on. By boat and land-journey it may take nearly a whole day to reach the Outer Hebrides, but the voyage in and out the lesser and larger islands until your goal is reached can, in fine weather, be so full of enchantment that it is in itself a part of the pleasure of island-fishing. The Gaelic speech begins to insinuate itself the moment you are aboard; by the time you disembark it predominates.

The mention of Gaelic leads to the other great attraction of the islands – the people who live there. Some anglers just go out after the fish and take no interest in the people they meet on their expeditions. The ghillies are just rowing-machines; the crofters, farmers, ministers, and (in some islands) the Catholic priests just 'locals'. Such devoted anglers miss a great deal of the pleasures of their sport.

The people of the islands are, despite bombardment by our mass-communicative age, intensely individual and varied. In the Outer Hebrides the Gaelic strain predominates, and nearly everyone is bilingual in Gaelic and English; they are not shy of speaking their ancient native tongue, far older than English, and you will hear it everywhere – on the loch-side, at the landing-stage of the boats, on steamers from the mainland, and even sometimes at the airport, particularly at the natural airport on the flat sands at Barra. We constantly hear about the imminent death of Gaelic, and certainly it has declined on the mainland; in the Outer Hebrides it lives – vigorously in,

The River Thurso has fifteen beats; the Long Pool is Beat 12.

M

for instance, Stornoway (population over 5,000) in Lewis.

The Gaelic strain is softer in the southern and Catholic isles, rather sterner in the northern ones, especially in Lewis and Harris (more especially in Lewis), but everywhere you meet with the same natural courtesy. The Gaelic language or Gaelic-accented English softens extremes of religious difference.

Kindliness rather than obvious courtesy is the characteristic of those Norse-descended people who live in the Northern Isles, and it is a kindliness that warms the heart. If the weather is against you and the fishing not as good as usual, you will find much compensation in the company of the island folk. Merely to write about them is to evoke the memory of their voices, their humour, and their native dignity.

But let us no longer generalize. Here follows some more particular information upon our theme of Rivers and Lochs – or, more appropriately in this instance, Lochs and Rivers – in the islands.

M.McL.

Chapter Twenty-One

THE INNER HEBRIDES

SKYE AND COLL

The Inner Hebrides, extending some 150 miles north to south off the west coast of Scotland, are officially composed of three groups: those around Islay to the south, those in the neighbourhood of Mull, and Skye and its few satellites. Here, however, we take them in personal rather than geographical groups, since each of the present writers has selected as his province the islands he knows best.

Generally speaking, the Inner Hebrides have a more dramatic though a no less subtle beauty than that of the Outer Hebrides. Their angling waters are indeed often striking to look at; but the fishing, though varied and attractive, has not the pre-eminent quality of the Outer Hebrides or the Norse isles of Orkney and Shetland. We must in fact omit certain of the more than thirty islands in the Inner Hebrides, for only on some of them are the inland waters worthy of special mention. Let us move from north to south. This will enable us to begin with the most famous of all Scottish islands, scenically and historically: Skye.

The largest not only of the Inner Hebrides but of all Scottish islands, Skye is just short of fifty miles from north-west to south-east and nearly forty-five miles at its greatest width. Its surface area is 411,704 acres. Its indented shape and wide, wing-like projections, coupled with its appearance on the map of leaping off from the body of Scotland, gave it the Gaelic name of the Flying Island from which the English name Skye is derived.

Skye, made familiar to us in legend, song, and pictorial art, is so celebrated as a tourist island that the visitor may well feel he knows it before he has been there. When he does come for the first time, or even if he has visited it in youth and not seen it since, he is soon liberated from the idea of false familiarity. Skye's spectacular beauty is irresistible whether seen for the first time or re-encountered. Its great Cuillin range of hills in the south-west centre are famous for their proud dominance, and are known all over the world to climbers – some of their rocky peaks were scaled for the first time only at the end of the last century, by

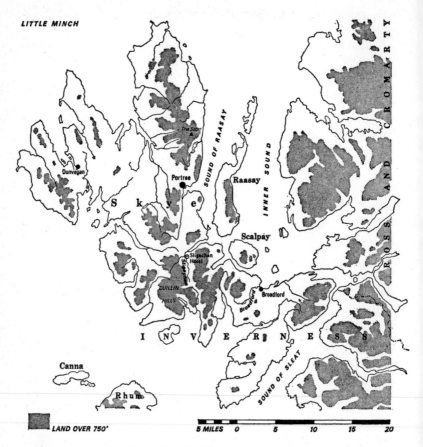

LITTLE MINCH

Dunvegan

The Storr ▲

Portree

SOUND OF RAASAY

Raasay

INNER SOUND

S k y e

Scalpay

Sligachan Hotel

CUILLIN HILLS

Broadford

Broadford

I N V E R N E S S

SOUND OF SLEAT

ROSS AND CROMARTY

Canna

R h u m

LAND OVER 750'

5 MILES   0   5   10   15   20

which time nearly all the Alps had been conquered.

For its Jacobite and late nineteenth-century fights against eviction, Skye has a notable history. It lives on in the tenacious inhabitants, whose love of tradition in their way of life and worship is not yet, or likely to be, overcome by tourist popularity. Even the most dedicated angler cannot visit Skye without feeling the influence of the island's beauty and its past. He will find sport there that is an agreeable addition to a holiday, but it is not the prime reason why most people visit Skye.

The Sligachan river is available through the Sligachan Hotel. The average weight of sea-trout is a pound or over; of salmon, six pounds. The biggest Skye salmon caught in the last twenty-five years weighed fifteen pounds. The Broadford river, also containing salmon and sea-trout, can be fished by arrangement with the Broadford Hotel. The

Dunvegan Hotel in the north-west also has loch and river fishing, available to residents and to those who apply for tickets.

There are some brown-trout lochs. The most accessible and most rewarding are the Storr lochs on the north-eastern wing of the Flying Island. Tickets and permission can be obtained on inquiry at Portree, the capital. Angling visitors to Skye will, if they inquire at hotels in Portree, find easy access to waters available to the public. They should not expect outstanding angling facilities but they will enjoy the fishing if there has been a spate, particularly on Sligachan, where in normal conditions the water is very clear.

Coll, with its close neighbour Tiree, though near to Mull, is among those Inner Hebrides furthest from the mainland of Scotland. It is flat, but not so much a plain as Tiree, which is known in Gaelic as the 'island under the waves'. Twelve miles long, south-west to north-east,

it is nowhere more than four miles wide. You can easily cycle round it in half a day. There are few cars on this, alas! depopulating island, and a bicycle is the best way of getting about. The road has no hills, and the island's highest peak (avoided by the road) is only 339 feet.

Its east coast, when you approach it by steamer, looks formidably rocky; but its west coast is filled with multi-coloured sandy bays Between east and west much of the land is green and fertile. It is indeed strange that an island that not so long ago supported over 1,000 people (200 years ago it contained well over 2,000) should now have under 200.

For those who are prepared to put up with this (humanly speaking) melancholy fact, the island scenically has great charm of a quiet kind. Coll today would be one of the least celebrated of the Hebrides had not Dr Johnson and Boswell been all but shipwrecked on it and had they not spent a memorable ten days there. The island's minute capital of Arinagour now has one hotel. Occasionally lodgings may be found elsewhere, including caravans that are let on the west coast.

For the unambitious angler who likes to fish easily accessible lochs full of sporting brown trout, Coll has considerable attractions. There are between twenty and thirty lochs and lochans in which the trout rise freely. Their average weight is half a pound, and there is a surprising lack of really small fish that bother one by coming to the fly. The largest brown trout I have caught on Coll was a pound and a half, but I have heard of two-pounders and, occasionally, of specimens of slightly greater weight.

Save for the Mill Loch near the southern side of the island, which can on occasions boil with rising fish, there is little point in naming the lochs and lochans that lie scattered about. All contain trout that are of keepable size and good fighters (their feeding is rich) and, owing to the paucity of anglers on Coll, are not usually afraid of the artificial fly. The Mill Loch has one boat; the other lochs must be fished from the bank. If you are staying at the hotel, the fishing is either free or inexpensive. The Coll Estate Office at Arinagour can provide details.

Coll is a grandstand seat for the beauties of the west Highlands and the Hebrides, enabling you to see vast stretches of mountainous and enisled scenery. All this adds to the pleasures of angling there. You move from lochan to lochan catching half-pounders galore, and occasionally larger fish. At each movement you will have glimpses of fresh and fascinating scenery around the island. Flat, and thus a paradise for the youthful cyclist, Coll has, with its slight population, a touch of melancholy for those who like the Gaelic way of life. This is relieved by the fact that Coll has become increasingly a holiday island for the summer months, with peace, relaxation, and plentiful brown-trout angling easily accessible.

The brown trout of Coll have been described as 'never too small, never too large'. Most of the fish, however, are in the smaller class. They are well fed from lush, grassy land that covers the greater part of the island and grows (within limits) rapidly. This explains why they are never too small.

For the truly contemplative fisherman, angling on Coll has unique attractions.

M.McL.

MULL, EIGG, AND TIREE; COLONSAY, ISLAY, JURA

Of the islands covered in this chapter, I take Mull as my centre; and, radiating to the north, consider Eigg; to the west Tiree; to the south-west Colonsay, Islay, and Jura. I do not apologise for making my island world revolve around Mull, since I have spent by far the most island fishing hours on this largest of the inner isles. I have lived on Mull, and worked there for varying periods at different seasons of the year, and I believe I have a reasonable knowledge of its fishings.

Mull is almost two islands. Between Salen and Gruline, it has a kind of wasp waist that separates the northern part from the rougher southern one. East part has fishings of note, although the best of the loch trout fishing seems clearly to lie in the north, while the best river and loch fishing for sea-trout and salmon lies in the southern half of the island.

To many, Mull means the trout fishing of Frisa and the Mishnish lochs. Frisa is about four miles long and lies in the middle of the northern part of the island, running from a point not far north of Salen to one not far south of Dervaig. It is a deep loch with the main shallows confined to the ends. For most of its length the sides of the loch rapidly drop away to give depths of twenty or thirty feet and more, reaching 150 feet in the centre. From the trout-fishing point of view, depths of over twenty feet are of little use. Generally speaking, fly life centres on water under ten feet deep, and on Frisa I have had my most consistent trout sport on the shallows at the southern or Ledmore end. Here there are pleasant drifts, an island, productive little bays with promontories and reefs, and a nice contrast of banks. The Dervaig end also gives extensive shallows and good bays, but I would argue that the Ledmore end has better trout. One can fish close in to the shore all the way up from Ledmore to Lettermore, and my best bag ever on Frisa came from the very margins of the loch in this area. That was a bag of twelve fish weighing eight pounds, and all were taken in about an hour and a half from the Aros Estate boat in a high wind that later blew us off the loch. Frisa trout usually run to about half a pound average, although there have been complaints that in recent years the average and the numbers have been dropping. Frisa also carries runs of sea-trout and herling – fish that run up the Aros river and take the little branch tributary that Frisa contributes to the main stream. It is a small feeder, and it is remarkable that sea-trout run it. Even salmon run it, and there are records of odd single fish that have been taken in Frisa, mostly grilse size. It is not really a salmon and sea-trout loch, but the trout fisher may fairly often find that he has a sea-trout of two or three pounds to add to his catch of brownies.

At one time the Mishnish lochs were regarded not only as the best trouting on Mull, but the best trouting for many miles around on the mainland. In the 'fifties, they were still yielding smallish bags of trout of half to three-quarters of a pound. Every so often a brace of two-pounders would appear from nowhere. They were beautiful fish and had clear, delightful spot markings, and often a glowing yellow that suggested good gravel-bottom conditions. There have again been depressing reports in the 'sixties that these lochs are going back rather badly. One becomes wary of over-pessimistic anglers' reports, especially when these arise from an unlucky day or two that seem to colour the whole prospect of fishing a given water, but there appears to be some genuine concern that lochs as good as the Mishnish ones should be allowed to slip back. I had the impression several years ago that the lochs were subjected to far too much casual roadside fishing, and I am sure that a proper policy of access would greatly improve the distribution of the sport. To some extent the same is true of Frisa.

Trout fishing on Mull is held in a surprisingly unconcerned way by many local people. Some local hotels can tell you little about the fishings. It is hard to find a well-kept game book, and in short there appears to be a view on the island that trout fishing is hardly worth the effort to manage well and preserve. How wrong this is! Trout fishing is the staple sport of the game-fishing public, and it can bring in good revenue at times of the year when ordinary tourism is at a low ebb. The proprietors of one Mull hotel once told me they were not interested in their fishings, since anglers sometimes came in wet. They took the fishings with the shootings as a matter of course, and they hardly used their boats. I asked for a boat on one of their trout lochs in mid-September, and found that they had been taken off for the year. This laxity of management is changing now that the island has a splendid car-ferry operating on it. Further, if trout enjoy legislative protection in the near future, will not this raise the possibility of proper direction of the Mull troutings?

The Aros river is a small spate stream joining the sea just north of Salen. It is a gin-clear river not much larger than a good-sized burn, but I have seen in its pools excellent sea-trout and a scattering of

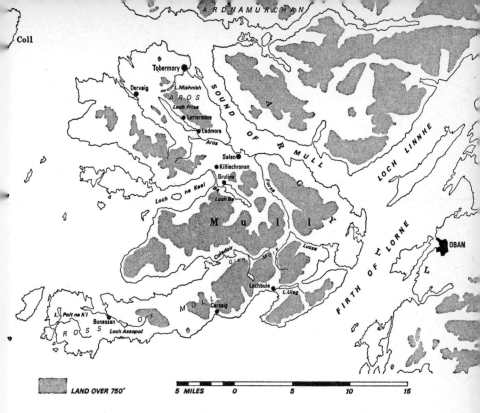

LAND OVER 750'   5 MILES   0   5   10   15

salmon. I have found the sea-trout difficult to take except in flood conditions, but on a flash river like the Aros small floods, and even sustained floods, are not infrequent. There is an interesting, but small
sea-pool, where in the past I have at times found excellent sport with
finnock and sea-trout of an average pound and a half. Get the high tide
coinciding with July darkness, and you have ideal fly-fishing conditions.
Two of the Mull estates have salmon fishings on the Aros, and one at
least, the Killichronan Estate, lets fishings by the day. This estate has
fishing on Frisa, on the sea-pool of the short river Ba, and a varied
week's fishing can be taken for an all-in fee. It is also sometimes
possible to fish the Aros by arrangement with a landowner, but this is,
like all fishings, a matter of personal contact and arrangement.

The River Dervaig is another small spate river, and it attracts sea-
trout and salmon in summer floods. There is an extensive estuary, which
at times teems with sea-trout, but, like most Mull salt-water sea-trout,
these prove very difficult to catch. I do not know of any public water
on the Dervaig, but here again local inquiry and arrangements with
the proprietor may be worth while.

The southern part of Mull has one really good sea-trout and salmon
loch, Ba; an often productive salmon and sea-trout river, the Forsa;
a chain of salmon and sea-trout (and brown-trout) lochs at the head of

the Lussa river; and a smallish spate salmon river flowing west, the Coladoir, which includes an interesting lower mile or two with a fine estuary for sea-trout and finnock fishing. Loch Uisg, at Lochbuie in the extreme south of the island, is said to be a good sea-trout loch, but I have little information on this water.

The River Forsa once yielded me a sea-trout of four and a half pounds when all I was trying for was a brace of brownies to fry for breakfast. I also remember seeing the lower pools of the Forsa very well stocked with salmon in July, and many times seeing the estuary splashing with sea-trout that ran to three pounds and better. The Forsa is like all the Mull rivers, dependent on rainfall for its best fishing. It may be less dependent on rain than, say, the Coladoir, for the slower middle reaches of the river can be fished like a loch, provided the wind ripples the surface enough. There are miles of moorland pools on the Forsa, water that some would call 'dead'. I think it is interesting and productive fishing, so long as you study the best taking-places (which only local help can give you), and try deep fly tactics no less than loch-style fishing through the ripple. Salmon and sea-trout will be taken by both methods. There is hotel access to the Forsa and local inquiries as to the best times would improve your chances. July is probably best, but August also provides sport with later sea-trout if the rains oblige.

I think of the Lussa river merely as the excellent channel by which salmon and sea-trout reach the three Glen More hill-lochs. This defames the Lussa, for it is one of the most attractive island rivers I have ever seen, with pools and rocky runs of good fishing character. There are one or two large pools below the lowest of the lochs, and there the sport with summer salmon is well worth noting. Fishings on the Lussa are available through the Department of Agriculture and Fisheries for Scotland, and there is a chance through a hotel of fishing the upper part of the river and at least one of the lochs.

The last time I fished these lochs I found them well stocked with good sea-trout, some of them running to seven and eight pounds. There were splendid brown trout in the lochs as well, some of them reaching a pound; and as fighters they were without equal on Mull. All three lochs would dap well, given the wind, but the chance of salmon would tend to keep me on the wet fly. Fish a cast with something about the size of a No. 8 Dunkeld on the tail and a No. 8 Soldier Palmer or Black Pennel on the bob. There is also a wonderful fly on which I have had salmon in Mull; I would strongly recommend it for the bob position on the sea-trout or salmon cast. It is Dickson's Dark Mackerel, a fly not unlike the Grouse and Claret, but tied with Mallard wing and a Palmer-style hackle down its body. Fish this in Dickson's No. 6 (the sea-trout size in outpoint hooks).

The Glen More lochs seem to me the best salmon fishing in Mull, although Loch Ba may run them close. Further, there was often a chance of taking fishings on the Lussa lochs, where Ba would be let with the lodge. Ba is something of a specialist loch, with dapping as a favourite method. On the short river connecting Loch Ba to the western sea opposite in Loch na Keal, there is a famous sea-pool on which one can take a rod by the day. It is expensive estuary fishing, but, if two reasonable rods take the pool together and fly-fish it at the right height of tide in the late evening and in the right conditions of light, it can be a splendid piece of fishing. Sea-trout mill in the estuary of the river, and any date from late June onwards would be productive for fishing.

On the Ross of Mull, apart from the little loch near Carsaig, there is little fishing except for the sea-trout loch of Assopol, near Bunessan, and Loch Poit na h-I (pronounced 'Potee') which means 'stew-pond of Iona'. This last water is a pleasant trout loch with trout of the quarter- to half-pound order. I have had better fish too, but not in any great number. Assopol is potentially a good salmon and sea-trout loch, but, like other waters on Mull, it is either misunderstood by the local people or ignored by them. No one seems to know where the salmon lies are, and there are poor records of the sea-trout catches. I fished it one September and took brown trout (very poor in size), and some finnock – good fish running to perhaps fourteen ounces in the late season; I saw some better sea-trout moving, but not very many. I also took a nine-pound salmon on my sea-trout cast (the amazing Mackerel), and raised local eyebrows a bit. The general opinion was that it was surprising that the burn up from the sea could carry salmon of this size, because it was so choked and overgrown. "Why not clear it out?" is my immediate question. If I had the loch, I would make the two-mile run up from the sea as easy as possible for sea-trout and salmon. There are excellent numbers of salmon returning to the bay. The local nets have some wonderful summer catches, and I believe unmentionable others also share in the salmon and sea-trout take. Why not make it possible for more salmon to reach Assopol?

In a way, the Assopol question of developing a potentially good fishery is the whole Mull question. There is a clear choice for the island now that so many more anglers are coming over in cars on the new car-ferry from Oban. The choice is: come to grips with the management of the fishings or let them waste away until they are in total disrepair. Management would take work and a small outlay of money, but – with some of the waters I have mentioned – would more than justify the trouble. Salmon lochs are not ten a penny. Mull could greatly help its own tourist trade if it improved the fishings it already has.

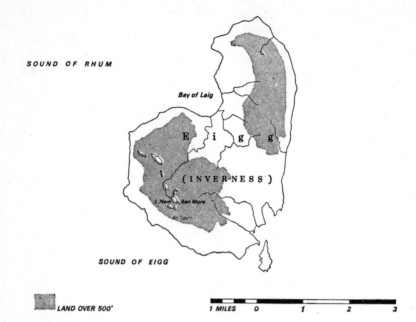

LAND OVER 500'   1 MILES   0   1   2   3

Eigg is an island as different from Mull as one could imagine. It is small and fertile, the capital of the small isles, and its southern profile is famous to all sailors and all scenery-lovers from Ardnamurchan north. The amazing Sgurr of Eigg rises 1,200 feet in a great scarp before plunging just as suddenly back to the moorland plateau behind, making a shape like the crown of a high hat. It is dramatic and beautiful island country, but for general angling is really inaccessible. I have been lucky enough to fish the lochs of Eigg, and they are difficult but very rewarding, with big trout of two and three pounds. Loch Nam Ban Mora is the best water, if not for maximum size, at least for fishing area and baskets. One of the smaller lochs, which I called the Boomerang, has nice fish running to a pound each. However, the small reedy loch, the 'Kindney', has trout of three pounds, even if they are hard to catch. Eigg is, to me, an island of the greatest charm, and its loch fishings are, in miniature, like the bigger loch fishings of the Highlands. One thing it does lack is a machair loch. That is a loch like Bhasapoll on Tiree, or like the famous shell-sand lochs of South Uist. But Eigg has a ruggedness in its sgurr and a mountain charm that the flatter islands do not possess.

Tiree has sometimes been called the market garden of the isles. It is a mild, sunny island, low-lying and green; on its machairs the fattest of

the island cattle graze. Tiree cattle command a high price on the mainland and (it is said) Tiree farmers are among the most prosperous of the
Hebrideans. In recent years an attempt was made to establish Tiree as
the centre of a bulb-growing experiment, and for some years Tiree
daffodil and tulip bulbs took prizes wherever they were shown; but for
some reason the trade has slowed down and is hardly worked at all
today. Both fat cattle and fat bulbs derive from one thing – machair
soil; and it is the same factor that makes Tiree trout just as desirable in
their own way.

The machair loch is usually a low-lying water, set on a raised beach.
Loch a' Phuill, set low on the turf behind Balephuil Bay, is a perfect
example; on the northern side of the island, Bhasapoll, lying almost
close enough to spill over into the sea at Bhasapoll Bay, is another. They
are lochs on a soil rich in calcareous material made from sea shells
pounded into sand by the waves. This shelly sand gives the water an
alkaline character, and in such environments shrimps grow big, snails
thrive with hard shells, and there are good colonies of fly larvae for the

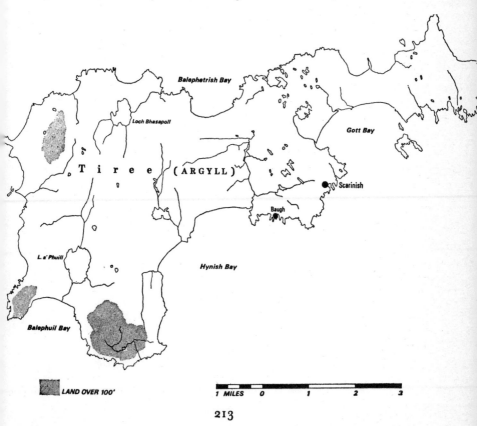

LAND OVER 100'

1 MILES   0   1   2   3

213

trout to feed on. Oddly enough, these conditions are usually poor for trout spawning, with the excellent result that you get smaller numbers of really fine trout in your water. By smaller numbers I mean plenty for the angler, but not so many that the loch becomes infested with tiddlers, as so often happens in a Highland or Island acid loch where there is perhaps a good spawning burn and a poorish food supply.

Tiree has other small waters. There are three lochs behind Scarinish, of little note as fishing waters; there are two lochs behind Gott Bay, one of which is stocked by a local hotel; and there is, running into the sea just south of Baugh, a remarkable machair burn, clear and sandy and really looking like a sea-trout water. Strangely enough, it does not flow from a loch, and it is said to carry no sea-trout. I have seen sea-trout in the bay there, and I cannot believe that in autumn the fish do not run up and spawn, yet local people say Tiree has very few sea-trout indeed.

Apart from fishings taken through a local hotel, Tiree is more or less a closed island for the casual fisher. True, an interested angler may be able to rent fishings from the Argyll Estates, or by arrangement with a tenant take a sub-let, but this is probably the only way in which he will get access to the better trout lochs – and these, one should hasten to point out, are really good fishings, with trout running to two pounds if you are at all lucky. The average is about a pound, and they are lovely fish, highly coloured, white on the belly, and very clearly spotted. They fight well, too, but perhaps fall into the second class as table fish, as many big-boned alkaline water fish do.

Colonsay is an island more like Coll than Tiree in its general configuration, which is of the Highland type with rushy and rocky hills and a cliffy coastline of great beauty. Its lochs are few and greatly contrasted in their characters. Scoulter, the laird's own loch, lies near Kiloran. It is a charming round hill loch with a quaint little arbour on an island. You could fish it all day and hardly touch a trout, but suddenly you would be playing a fish of two or three pounds. Scoulter trout are very big and have run to several pounds – six, seven, even eight. The smaller of the Scoulter trout (and by that I mean the two-pounders) do come to the fly. If you take two in an evening, you have been lucky. The larger fish have often been taken by spinning. Several attempts have been made to reduce the population of monsters on this water with a view to re-stocking and making the fishing more productive, but none of these attempts have really worked. I hold Scoulter to be as thrilling a water as I have ever fished, and I would travel far to fish such a loch again, particularly in June or early July, when the larger fish rise well.

In complete contrast is Loch Fada, the long chain of lochs that almost cuts the island in half. These are good waters, the smaller

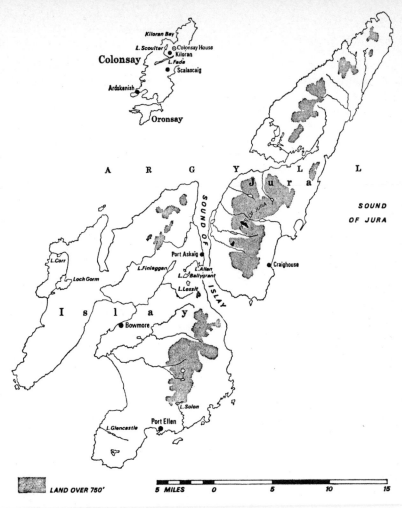

eastern member of the chain being regarded as the best. Fish average about a pound, and on a good day can provide excellent sport; but they are dour fish, and some anglers find they have to spin for their trout. This does not in any way appeal to me as a method of taking loch trout. I'd rather spin for mackerel from the new Scalasaig pier. The island hotel, just behind Scalasaig, has boats on Loch Fada and can provide records of the catches. It is often possible, by special permission from the laird, to fish one other water: Touramine. This is a little hill dam, specially made as a trout loch by, I believe, the present laird's grandfather. Once it was extraordinary, but today seems to have reverted to a trout loch with a half-pound average. I like half-pounders, but as I hook them in Touramine I often think of the reels of other generations of anglers screaming as six-pounders were hooked.

Colonsay has only a very few sea-trout, and they feed in and out of the sandy bays where the small burns fall into the pounding green breakers. I know of one sea-trout guddled out of the Ardskenish burn, and I have seen what appeared to be herling in the lower pools of this same machair water. At Kiloran Bay a good burn runs in, and I would swear it must carry sea-trout. Behind Colonsay House the burn has a splendid character, well suited to migratory fish. It seems not improbable that sea-trout might run up right into Fada by this route, but I have heard no details of catches. Colonsay, however, is a delightful island with the usual sea-fishing bounty to add to the pickings of the lochs. It is an island where cottages are readily available for rent, thanks to the policies of the owner, and often fishings can be arranged in both fresh and salt water when the house is taken. I have the happiest memories of the island, and, without becoming lyrical over the trout fishing at present, regard Colonsay as an island that could produce bags of big trout in surroundings of great peace.

Islay is the most southerly of the Inner Hebrides and one of the largest. It is an island famous for splendid malt whisky and, from another gastronomic angle, for excellent cheeses. It is also an angler's island of some repute, with a variety of good trout lochs available for the trout fisher and several sea-trout and salmon waters in which sport can be brisk. If we take the trout lochs as representative of the fishing the visitor might enjoy, we could consider three lochs: Finlaggan, Ballygrant, and Corr – all in their way excellent trout waters of great island charm.

Finlaggan lies ten miles from Bowmore and three miles, or slightly more, south-west of Port Askaig village. The loch itself, lying among heathery hills, gives the impression of great remoteness, although it is perfectly accessible, even to the angler relying on Macbrayne's buses and his own two feet. It is a loch with islands sprinkled over its northern and south-eastern ends, adding greatly both to its charm as a scenic water and to its fishing potential, for a loch with islands is a loch with shallows, generally speaking, and shallows spell fly-bearing fishing water. Finlaggan Castle, sitting on an island close to the north-western shore, adds a touch of drama to the wild surroundings, for it was the site of clan battles between the Macdonalds and the Macleans.

The western shore is weedy at many points, and this at once suggests shallowness, but also the difficulty of fishing the fly well without snagging. Take care in your casting, however, and the western shore will yield you trout, red in the flesh and well marked in flank and back – Islay trout of great sporting value. You should expect trout of three-quarters of a pound from Finlaggan, but you should hope for trout over the pound mark. Wading down the western shore, fishing over the weedy and boulder-strewn bottom, may well produce more of the smaller fish; but the eastern shore, with its single island, and its several promontories that have reefs running out beyond, are likely places for the bigger fish. Permits to fish Finlaggan are readily obtainable from the Islay Estates office at Bowmore.

Within a few miles of Finlaggan, to the south-east, lies a very well-known and highly regarded Islay trout loch, Ballygrant. Again either shore or boat fishing is possible, and the northern shore and the eastern 'narrows' are good drifts. Ballygrant can produce baskets of fish of the fourteen-ounce order, and ten or a dozen daily to a rod is reasonably likely. Finlaggan, its neighbour, has the reputation of not needing much wind (a reputation that I for one very much doubt), but Ballygrant responds badly to lack of breeze, and it fishes poorly in conditions of summer sun. It may seem strange that I should mention this, for lochs generally do not fish well in hard sunlight. Some Hebridean lochs, however, positively revel in sun, particularly in the Outer Hebrides. Further, June sun is often highly beneficial and, if it is in the wind's tail (that is, shining in the same direction as the wind), all might be well on the loch; but, if the sun is in the wind's eye, things are likely to be very unproductive indeed. Ballygrant seems typical in this respect.

Loch Corr is in the northern part of Islay and is a very different water from Finlaggan and Ballygrant (both fairly 'big-name' waters). Corr is a small hill-water, but one with some splendidly proportioned trout in it. I have heard of half a dozen fish of between one and two pounds taken in one evening off Corr. There are some magnificent trout in this water, but, like many other outstanding small lochs, it is unpredictable, and can be dour. Evening is best, and June and early July are probably the best months, although – if May is mild rather than a drought month, as it so often is on the islands – late May could provide still more free-rising trout of good size. I should say that I have also had many reports of empty baskets off Corr. Such is the price we often have to pay for the chance of a really good Islay two-pounder.

These three waters do not in any way exhaust the trout fishings of Islay. There are for example Lochs Gorm, Lossit, Solon, Glencastle, and Allan – all fished from hotels or by arrangement through the estates concerned. No angler should fish Islay without asking the advice and assistance of his hotel or of the Factor's office of Islay Estates. Tickets can be obtained without much trouble, and, in the main, are cheap.

Islay adds salmon fishing to its other attractions for the angler. Like any west-flowing rivers on the mainland and the islands, Islay waters depend heavily on rain for their sport. But it is good in June, July, and August. By September the fish are tending to become potted, and to splash about tantalizingly in their small pools and be virtually uncatchable. In a late season, however, where water has been scarce in the high summer months, a late angler may well find September is of the greatest interest for salmon and sea-trout.

Henry Williamson – the author of a whole range of delightful books on the natural scene, including the unforgettable *Salar the Salmon* – has a charming description of Islay fishing in his *A Clear Water Stream*. He describes the wildness of the moors, the darkness of the burn waters; and, in a passage I have never forgotten, he speaks of how he waited for weeks for the burn to rise, until on his last afternoon it did, bringing the salmon up immediately from the sea. He attached a Black Dog salmon fly to his trout cast, and on his very first cast took a five-pound grilse. Islay is not always so kind, but the essence of the spate river is in this tale. One day it is hunger, the next it is surfeit. Not that spate rivers are really generous; they are, rather, concentrated and sudden in the sport they give.

Jura, with its Paps rising enormous out of the western sea, is hardly a 'public' island for angling. Its estates are principally sporting ones, and that means stalking and grouse shooting in late summer, with fishing thrown in when the rivers are right or when the lochs seem to be in good ply. Jura also has the distinction of being developed as a low-ground (pheasant) shoot, one of the few in the islands. Sporting interests of this sort very often tend to close islands to the general angling public. Jura of course is not – as Rhum once was – a place on which landing is forbidden. In fact, recent development of the hotel business in Jura has marked the beginning of a new era for the island. Through the Craighouse Hotel certain loch fishings are available, and there is no doubt that trout fishings would be available from the estates for lets in the earlier summer months and possibly later. Salmon fishing, however, is not likely to be easily obtained.

The islands we have mentioned in the Inner Hebrides do not exhaust the possibilities of fishing. Unless we are to write a scarcely portable book on the details of each island (details that would in some cases be out of date as soon as written), all we can really offer is characteristics. There is no fishing area in Scotland in which some angler has not found a secret and much cherished little water of his own. The Hebrides make the richest possible area for 'personal' finds of this sort. Usually they are scenic finds as well as sporting ones. The angler creates a highly personal map of the islands. Landscape is enjoyed subjectively; so is fishing. Every man can build his own Hebrides.

W.B.C.

Chapter Twenty-Two

THE OUTER HEBRIDES

These are usually called the Outer Isles (as if Shetland were not still further out); but the Inner Hebrideans who are accustomed to looking at the apparently unbroken stretch of them across many miles of sea laconically throw them all together as the Long Island. In doing so they perhaps unconsciously testify to a geographical unity. The Outer Hebrides were once a single piece of land, which was, so the scientists tell us, the 'oldest known splinter of the continent of Europe'. Since that splinter broke off, the sea has eaten into it, leaving a little over half a dozen indubitable islands and a very large number of islets.

The Outer Hebrides run roughly parallel to the west coast of Scotland, from between forty to thirty miles out in the Atlantic. The most northerly point is the Butt of Lewis on the biggest island; the furthest south is the lighthouse on Barra Head in the Barra group. The eastern side of the Long Island is largely peaty, but the centre and the western side have cultivated soil lying on rock of almost wholly Archaean gneiss. This – combined with sand, rather than peat, and with the grassy fringes – provides admirable bases for the far-famed Outer Hebridean lochs. The sea-trout love returning to them; the brown trout flourish in them.

Most of the land, compared with the mainland opposite to it, is flat, but at Clisham in North Harris the mountains rise impressively to 2,622 feet.

Moving this time through the islands from south to north, our interest in the fishing waters must begin on the large, long body of South Uist. This unfortunately compels us to neglect Eriskay and Barra, for their lochs and burns are few. These islands have, however, alluring beauty and delightful inhabitants. Any visitor to South Uist, separated only by a narrow channel from Eriskay (a channel in which took place the real-life fantastic event on which Sir Compton Mackenzie's *Whisky Galore* was based), is recommended to take a day off from angling to have a look at Eriskay and Barra.

SOUTH UIST

Certain inland waters on South Uist are famous for their unique sea-trout angling. The sea-trout in some lochs on the west side of South Uist are not only large but are the most sporting fighting fish of their species on fresh water in Scotland, and therefore in Europe and probably in the world.

Waters of interest to the angler may be said to begin near the south of the island of South Uist. They continue north right up the twenty-two miles of the island's length to the large Loch Bee, which contains some fine brown trout and occasional sea-trout. In between these two extremes lie a number of sea-trout lochs celebrated throughout the angling world, and a few brown-trout waters, one of which is in my view outstanding. There are said to be over 190 lochs on the island, if you count some small but game little lochans. It is believed that some of these have not been fished in living memory.

For many years the hotel at Lochboisdale had the rights over certain lochs. Some other particularly famous lochs were in private hands; of the rest of the 190, many were almost free for all. Recently this divided and sometimes, in the remoter lochs, undefined status has been unified, and the position made clear. The estate landlords have acquired the fishing rights all over the islands, and are doing their best not only to keep the reputation of South Uist fishing at its high level, but to improve it. They have first rights on certain lochs, though permission can be obtained.

The local South Uist Angling Club has rights from the proprietorons certain lochs that they share. Visitors may avail themselves of the angling club facilities.

Passing north from the Sound of Eriskay, the first loch worthy of mention lies just to the west of the main road: Loch Dun na Cillie, commonly known as Dunakillie. It is not even in part a machair loch, and it has the reputation of dourness. One angler I know comes to Dunakillie from the neighbouring island of Benbecula; he denies this dourness, and examination of his records supports his view. It is not a sea-trout water, and the brown trout (now much more easily got by boat) are of a good size, some just under the pound, some well over.

The next loch, on which we must pause before coming to the great waters of South Uist, is the only one under survey here that is connected with the eastern side of South Uist and with the waters of the Minch, the channel between the Outer Hebrides and the inner isles and the mainland. Loch a' Bharp lies behind and east of the port of Lochboisdale, and is worthy of mention as a good (though not characteristically South Uistan) sea-trout loch. It is also the only water on South Uist in which salmon run regularly, if sparsely. Salmon do appear in some of

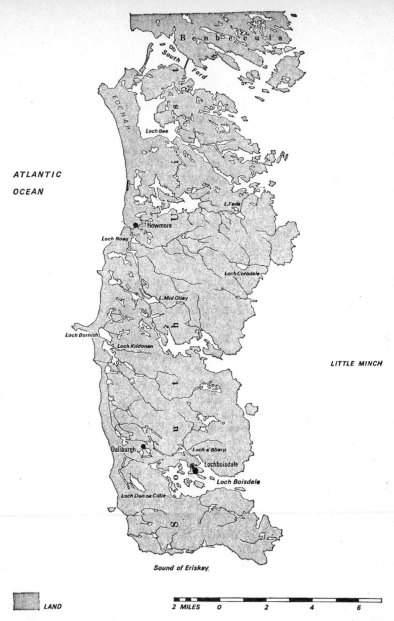

ATLANTIC
OCEAN

LITTLE MINCH

LAND   2 MILES   0   2   4   6

the northern and western lochs that we shall come to, but Bharp is the
only one in which salmon are known every year. The present management has encouraged this by the deposit of salmon ova in two fair-sized
burns running into the loch from the hills. It is very easily approached
from Lochboisdale and the hotel there.

The road from Lochboisdale joins the main road north at Daliburgh, the little capital of the island, and it is just north and west of here that we approach the machair and machair lochs.

The machair is a wide stretch of flat, springy, sand-based turf running well up the Atlantic side of South Uist. In spring and summer it is bright with small, many-coloured flowers; the birds wheel above it, and its western beaches are pounded by Atlantic rollers. The machair has many attractions, as readers of popular Hebridean books may already be well aware. But to the angler it offers, besides beauty, its unique machair lochs.

The inland waters, whether great or small, that lie upon the machair have firm sandy bottoms, safe for wading and (what is more important) holding clear alkaline water free of peat and acidity. It is this fresh water, lying so close to the sea, that is responsible for the world-famous South Uist sea-trout.

His average size is very good, and he can on occasions run to considerable weight, but it is his quality as a fighting fish that is the chief cause of his fame. His sporting quality, his at times almost reckless gameness, is the product of the water in the machair lochs. Everyone knows that in salt water the sea-trout is lively. It is unexpected, however, to find that liveliness not only sustained but apparently increased when he comes to fresh water; yet this is what happens on the South Uist machair lochs. Why?

It is because he meets the exhilaration of the fresh water in which he was born, yet doesn't have to face those debilitating factors so often present in fresh water. Above all, there is no acidity, no dulling peat. Moreover, coming to the fresh water in these lochs, he finds himself swimming over sand exactly like the sand of the sea he has just left. In such circumstances fresh water acts on him like wine, but leaves no hangover. He will at times take freely, even recklessly – and always he will fight to every last ounce of his considerable strength when hooked. A two-pound South Uist machair sea-trout is an unforgettable experience – and two to three pounds and more is the average in the lochs that we shall be considering.

The sea-trout of the machair lochs on this island have none of the burrowing habit you see in the fish of some big mainland lochs. This may be partly because the machair waters are not deep, but is more through the character of the fish. They take you, jump, and then dash off at high speed near the surface, varying these rushes with skittering hops or huge take-offs maybe far from the boat. They seem to be as much at home in the air as in water. Only dry land, your own dull support, is beyond them.

The machair lochs of South Uist under consideration here are as follows.

First, about five miles north of Daliburgh there is Kildonan, lying west of the main road and just between the road and the Atlantic. Once a single stretch of water about a mile long, it is now separated about half way by a controlling lock carrying a small road. This lock enables the manager of the estate to hold the incoming sea-trout at one end. The other end of the loch is being vigorously developed as a brown-trout water. The Mill Loch always had a tenuous connection with Kildonan. This connection has now been strengthened and carefully grid-controlled. At the latter end of the season, the grid to the Mill Loch is opened and the sea-trout encouraged to explore further up and seek breeding-grounds in the streams and burns.

Kildonan, with the Mill Loch as a useful satellite, is probably the most famous South Uist sea-trout water. This is not to say that these two are superior to the Howmore group further north; it is merely that at present the Kildonan waters retain from the past a wider following of enthusiasts. Kildonan was always accessible to residents at Loch-boisdale Hotel under the genial proprietorship of the late, much lamented Major Finlay Mackenzie; indeed, even if you were not stay-ing at the hotel but had access to Finlay Mackenzie's hospitable com-pany (and who that was worthy hadn't?) you could usually manage a day on Kildonan.

Generations, then, of sea-trout fishing visitors to South Uist, visitors who came to Lochboisdale during Finlay Mackenzie's long life, and before him during the even longer life of his nonagenarian father, have carried the name and fame of Kildonan all over the United Kingdom and far elsewhere. There are other places in Scotland called Kildonan, but for the lover of sea-trout there is only one Kildonan on the map of the world; it is on the west side of South Uist.

The two principal Howmore sea-trout lochs lie about half a dozen miles north of Kildonan. They are Roag and Fada; their satellites are the Schoolhouse and Castle lochs, to which sea-trout access is, as between Kildonan and the Mill Loch, controlled by grid. A short but considerable stream, the Howmore River, connects Roag with the sea immediately by it; there is also controlled connection between the two major and famous waters of Roag and Fada. It is man's decision alone when the sea-trout should gain Fada.

The Schoolhouse Loch is connected by a burn with the Howmore river, but under control. Finally, the Castle Loch has been connected with the Schoolhouse, but fish are not let up into it until August or even later.

The whole fish movement between these great sea-trout waters is as meticulously managed as if it were a traffic scheme on a popular part of the mainland among various close-lying towns. The final movement of the breeding sea-trout who escape the angler is, of course, towards the spawning-beds in the hills far above. It is interesting to note that recently the management of the South Uist waters has carried by helicopter, up to the heights where the beds lie, the gravel that encourages fertilization because fish are so fond of laying upon it.

The Howmore lochs have not, as has been explained, the world fame of Kildonan, for until recently they were in private hands. The trouble and expense that the estate management are taking with these great sea-trout waters, and the fact that (at a price and at agreed times) the public at last have access to them, should make them equally if not more famous. What we know of their potentiality even in private hands should ensure that.

If you take Kildonan waters and the Howmore group together, the average size of sea-trout is from two or two and a half pounds to three pounds or more. Any sea-trout angler on the mainland of Scotland will know that these are remarkable averages, especially considering the quality of the fish. Let him be prepared on these waters to obey his boatman in putting back fresh-run sea-trout of a weight and size (reaching a pound and a half) that he would gladly consider 'keepable' anywhere else.

Up to now the largest recorded sea-trout came from Loch Roag in 1965; it weighed fourteen pounds and was caught by a schoolboy of fourteen. One pound of silver, fighting sea-trout strength for every summer of the boy's life! I sadly reflect that I have long passed the age when I can ever hope to catch a sea-trout or even salmon (though this is just possible) whose poundage is the equal of my own racing years.

The mention of salmon reminds me that – though Bharp is the only regular, if sparsely visited, salmon loch on the island – salmon do appear at intervals in the Howmore lochs.

A word about the manner of fishing these machair lochs.

In a boat on the South Uist sea-trout lochs, there is little of the customary drifting downwind sideways with two rods, one in the bow and one in the stern. This would be too rapid a progress over likely fish. The more usual system here is to sit on a cross-plank in the stern (two of you if you like, sharing the rod in turn), while the ghillie works the boat with the bow into the wind slowly over the suitable spots.

Very properly, only fly fishing is allowed, two and sometimes three flies to the cast, which must be strong, as strong as you like in these often dark waters. I have found the Black Pennel efficient, but other flies in use are the Silver Zulu, Blue and Black Zulu, Watson's Fancy, and Greenwell; also other well-tried favourites. Sea-trout grow very fast on the west of South Uist, and there is a strict limit on the boat-bearing lochs of not killing any fish under sixteen inches; that is, about one pound six ounces. But on days when the bigger ones are coming up well, we have seen fish a good deal over that weight returned to the water.

Of the 180 or so lochs on South Uist that I have not yet mentioned, some are scarcely more than pools; some are considerably larger; one, which I shall deal with later, is very large; some are extremely accessible; and at least one, Loch Corodale, is highly inaccessible. I have fished it, and I know that it has big trout, but I never wish to go through the experience again of getting to it. Anglers on the island have said that, before I fished it, this loch had not been fished within living memory. It may well be true.

There are very many lochs lying just beside the road or within 100 yards of it. Strictly speaking, of course, these are the property of the people who own the land. Among the smaller of these lochs the proprietors do not take a strong line. If a loch has not been fished for many years, and it happens to lie accessible to one or two of the many campers who now come to the islands through improved motor and ferry facilities, the proprietors would not object to the occasional casting of a line provided that reports are made to the Factor. So much water on South Uist is unfished and unknown that any information must be welcome.

Among the inhabitants of South Uist there exists a flourishing angling society. The proprietors have come to an arrangement with this society by which they have given to it, or share with it, many of the lochs – apart, of course, from the great sea-trout lochs mentioned above. Visitors to the island who cannot afford the best of the sea-trout lochs, or who have no residential qualifications in the hotels, may join this local angling society temporarily for a reasonable fee. Including the ones on Benbecula, there are eighteen of these angling club lochs. I have already mentioned Loch Dunakillie in the south; I should also mention Loch Mid Ollay, which contains brown trout of considerable note. There is no need here to list the other lochs; I shall confine myself to two that are outstanding: Loch Bee and Loch Bornish. Bee is the more famous loch, and is indeed well known all over Scotland. Bornish is less well known, but I have a particular affection for it.

Loch Bee is, for island waters, very large – about six miles long (north to south) and nearly three miles at its greatest breadth (west to east). It contains brown trout of size and strength. Two-pounders are by no means uncommon, and three-pounders and still larger fish have been taken. Owing to its great size, it is strictly speaking not a machair loch, though its western fringes do touch the machair. Its eastern half lies in the peaty district, and the dark-coloured water from this is apt to infiltrate all over the loch. The trout of Loch Bee, therefore, are certainly brown trout and lack the silvery qualities produced by the pure machair lochs of which Bornish is the supreme example. It should be added that, recently, Loch Bee lost some of its former glories. This was due to a failure in the sluice-gates that admitted brackish or even salt water; the seals following this sea water did considerable damage. However, the sluice-gates are now mended, and other steps have been taken to protect this famous water. It is now coming back into form.

There is, and always has been, one extreme north-west arm of Loch Bee that is largely machair in type. It does not appear to have suffered from the other recent ills attached to this loch. This is known as the Priest's Pool, because it is just beside the Catholic Presbytery at Eochar. Many priests – including in particular a recent incumbent, now moved to the mainland – have taken advantage of the Priest's Pool and, following St Peter (though not in his own manner of fishing), have great sport there.

We must now turn to Loch Bornish. As a pure trout loch, this water, lying just about half way up the island of South Uist, is outstanding.

Why? The average weight is a little under that provided by Loch Bee – though a five-pounder was caught there some years ago. It is not the possibility of hooking the five-pounder's mate or successor that allures one on Loch Bornish; it is the quality, appearance, and extraordinary vigour of the silvery pounders that makes one devoted to it. Incidentally this wide, fair-sized basin of fresh alkaline water upon a sandy floor is most attractive. It lies close to, but is not connected with, the Atlantic; hard by the landing place is the most beautiful, small Catholic church in the Hebrides. To put out upon Bornish is invigorating even before you have made your first cast.

In my opinion, these natural trout (the loch has never been stocked) are unbeatable in all Scotland for their dash and courage. Nor is this an individual point of view. Many trout anglers of wide knowledge have said the same; and the opinion has been set down in reputable books. I set it down here again.

When you are into your first fish of a pound or three-quarters or even half a pound on Bornish, he will have your line out before you are prepared for it, and you will believe he is twice as big as he is. If he hasn't jumped to show himself before you get him to the landing net, you will almost be disappointed by the first sight of him – but only for a moment. If a pounder or less can fight like this, what will the two-pounders (and we know there are some there) do to you?

On one singularly happy occasion, I introduced Bornish to a young nephew from the south of England who had had no experience of Scottish loch fishing. We embarked at half past ten on a perfect morning in May, the perfect month. At the somewhat delayed luncheon interval the boat contained twenty-two silver beauties, all of which were up to Bornish standards in size and game fishing.

'Is it always like this, fishing on lochs in Scotland?' the lad asked zestfully as he thought of the future.

'Always,' I lied with equal zest. Who was I to spoil a morning of shared perfection, to anticipate in words the possible disillusion of experience? And my Saxon-bred nephew might never fish another loch and never find out.

'If Youth but knew.' This is perhaps the place to point out that the second half of the familiar French lament, 'and Age but could', does not apply to the angler. It is the angler's unique gift among sportsmen that he can go on hoping to the end. The golfer knows when he has driven his longest drive, the mountaineer when he has scaled his most difficult peak. Not so with the angler. So long as he can stand, walk, and move his arms, he may hope for the biggest and best to the last day of his life.

From these lofty speculations we descend to the fact that for Bornish one does very well with the usual rather small flies of the Loch Leven type – that is to say a cast of three, with the usual variations upon Teal and Red to imitate the freshwater shrimp, and upon the Butcher and the ever reliable Greenwell. The alkaline water of Bornish is clear and calls for fine casts. An unusually big fish might break you on fine nylon among the occasional patches of weed on Bornish, but it is better to lose one trout in this way than to frighten many away on a cast that is too thick.

BENBECULA

This, the smallest of the angler-worthy Outer Hebrides, has since the Second World War been linked to South Uist by a road-carrying causeway. But, by a ford (wadeable at low tide, sometimes crossable all but dry-shod), Benbecula was always within South Uist's orbit. Half the inhabitants share the Catholic faith of the South Uistians, and half belong to the Church of Scotland. Complete harmony – an example to much of the Christian world elsewhere – exists between the Benbecula Protestants and Catholics.

No one has attempted to estimate the number of lochs on Benbecula. This is partly because it is less notable an island than South Uist and considerably smaller (roughly circular, it is nowhere much more than seven miles in diameter), and partly because there is almost as much water as land. There are no famous machair lochs, as on South Uist, or notable salmon or sea-trout inland waters, as on North Uist and Harris; but for an angler – not necessarily one after great records or great sizes, but one who wants a variety of easily accessible sport – Benbecula must be nearly unbeatable.

There can be few places in the United Kingdom, or in the world, where it would be more delightful to be at some age between fifteen and twenty, to have been bitten by the bug for trout and occasional sea-trout fishing, to have a bicycle and freedom of action. I might add that I have

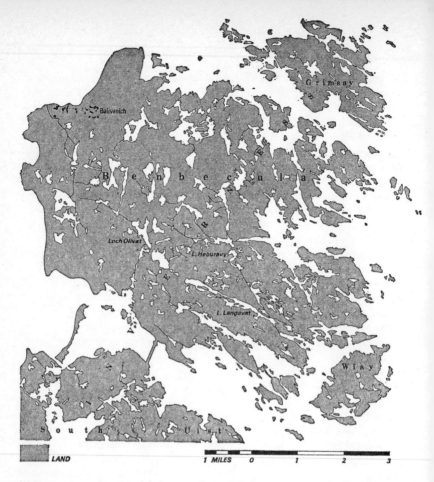

LAND   1 MILES   0   1   2   3

known some who are, in the number of their years, very far from being boys of fifteen to twenty, and yet have become boys again on Benbecula by the mere possession of a bicycle and the love of angling.

A bicycle on Benbecula! To begin with, the island is almost flat; then you can, if you are active, cycle the island south to north and take in the western circular road in one morning. In the afternoon you can easily cope with the dead-end road of a few miles taking you to the south-eastern wing, an ideal spot for lochan-hopping.

It should be added that, largely, Benbecula is part of the South Uist Estate, and on a few waters you have to seek permission from the estate Factor or the one hotel on the island, with which the South Uist Estate has joint ownership. For the rest, as on South Uist, the proprietors have no objection to the honest angler's casting his flies on the unnumbered minor waters, so full of sporting sizeable trout. As on South Uist, it is courteous to let the Factor or proprietors know the result of your fishing in these free waters.

The cyclist should aim mostly at the fretted south-eastern wing mentioned above. Let him just wheel away until he finds himself surrounded by little lochs; then let him drop his machine into the heather or peat (everyone is honest on Benbecula, and it will be quite safe) and start lochan-hopping. But it is as well to have some landmark near the place where you have left your machine. The landscape here is rather confusing, and one lochan looks very like the many others.

You won't get anything enormous – a rare pounder, or a fish of a pound and a half if you are lucky, and a possible wandering sea-trout. But for the most part your basket will average half a pound or sometimes less. At any rate, if you are a boy with a bicycle, or are of any age between eight and eighty, and if you are bitten by the trout-angling bug, you will have immense fun – fun, indeed, that is probably unique. It is unlikely that anywhere else in Scotland has the quality of this south-eastern wing of Benbecula. Though they do not have the extra-ordinary spirit of the South Uist machair lochs, all trout in the Ben-becula lochs fight well.

The reserved waters for which you have to seek permission – and, if you are not staying at the Creagorry Hotel on the island, pay a moderate price – are these. First, Loch Olivat, plumb in the centre of the island and bisected by the main road north and south into eastern and western Loch Olivat. Both sections have boats, and there is a good average of brown trout from three-quarters of a pound to a pound. One of nearly three pounds was taken on the eastern loch. Also Loch Heouravay and Loch Langavat contain sea-trout (now rather neglected), and permission to fish them must be sought.

The other guarded waters are the pools in the south and north fords, which separate Benbecula from South and North Uist. At low tide these fords leave pools in which the sea-trout linger. They give good sport in the sheltered sea-voe fashion. The time to go for them is an hour or two before low ebb, and for a brief period afterwards.

Benbecula has no established seaport connecting it with the main-land, but there is easy access to it by road over the causeways both from South and North Uist. There is, however, an airport at the north-west of the island at Balivanich. You could be on the island in under an hour from Glasgow airport. If you are interested in human beings as well as trout, you will note that your fellow passengers are likely to be Gaelic-speaking native islanders, nuns, ministers, priests, and anglers.

NORTH UIST

With North Uist we come to an island much more notable for its waters than Benbecula; and, though it has in part some machair lochs, it does not have sea-trout lochs of that world-famous kind on South

Uist. Yet it is, indeed, as notable for its angling as its southern sister, not only in the Outer Hebrides but in all the Scottish islands.

North Uist does certainly have good sea-trout fishing, but its main inland-water claim to fame lies in the splendid run into its lochs of those very sporting fish, the Hebridean salmon.

These, as has been stated, do not run to the huge sizes and weights you get on the mainland in Tweed, Tay, and such waters, where fish of sixty pounds have been caught on rod and line. The usual Hebridean salmon is under ten pounds; even if he is only a six- or seven-pounder, he puts up as hard a fight in a different kind of way as the celebrated South Uist sea-trout. But by no means are all the North Uist Hebridean salmon only in the 'ten pounds and under' class.

In 1932 Colonel Craven established a record by landing from a boat in Loch Skealtar (see below) a salmon of thirty-two pounds eleven ounces. In 1961 Father John Morrison, on a visit from his own South Uist, approached the Colonel's feat by grassing from the same loch a salmon of twenty-nine pounds two ounces. Casts of these giant Hebridean salmon are displayed in the Lochmaddy Hotel.

From the air, or from a glance at the map, the island of North Uist (twelve miles by sixteen) is seen to be almost as loch-besprinkled as Benbecula. It is, however, by no means as flat as that smaller island, and, though its higher hills never exceed 1,000 feet, they are impressive. There are good brown-trout lochs, of which I shall mention one or two. None attain the splendid status of Bornish in South Uist. But that, perhaps, is an unfair comparison: Bornish is, I think, unique in Scotland. Keen brown-trout anglers on North Uist have good sport in May and June. This, however, is surpassed by the fishing for sea-trout and (above all) Hebridean salmon, which, of course, come on later in the season.

The first and most important water to mention is Loch Skealtar, quite close to the island's leading township, Lochmaddy, with its hotel and its sea port to the mainland. Skealtar is entirely a salmon water connected by the briefest run to the sea; during a dry season you may see hundreds of Hebridean salmon at the mouth of this run waiting to get up. The loch is large enough for anyone, but suggestions are being considered for connecting it with Loch Scadavay to the west. If this were done, there would be twelve square miles of salmon water. As on South Uist, a helicopter has been used to deposit spawning gravel in local tributary burns.

Painfully, on North Uist as on other islands, we have to miss out many fishable waters to concentrate on the main ones. Apart from the splendid Skealtar, these are chiefly on the north and west of the island.

On this north-western circular tour, the first is the large Loch Gerrin Mill. It is big enough and varied enough to contain salmon, sea-trout,

ATLANTIC OCEAN

SOUND OF HARRIS

Haste Loch

L. na Clachan

L. Garrin Mill

Loch Eval

Loch Skealtar

Loch Scadavay

Lochmaddy

L. Hovisary

Loch nan Eun

L. Dusary

L. na Morach

N o r t h   U i s t

Loch Eport

LITTLE MINCH

Baleshare

SOUND OF MONACH

North Ford

Ronay

B e n b e c u l a

LAND

2 MILES 0   2   4   6

and brown trout; different species are inclined to use separate bays and spawning-grounds. Still, there is no doubt that the presence of salmon is threatening the sea-trout. As at Skealtar, there is a short run to the sea, but here it is controlled by a sluice-gate. There are also sea-pools further out, as at the ford between Benbecula and North Uist, where sea-trout lie accessible at low ebb.

Loch na Clachan, further to the west, is small – ideally small for a boat on a windy day – and is solely a sea-trout water. It is not altogether a machair loch, but has machair features. It is one of the most famous North Uist sea-trout waters, and contains a man-made and controlled entry to induce and hold water in dry summers.

Hoste Loch and Loch Eval are more obvious machair lochs containing both sea-trout and brown trout. They are connected with Grogary, where the Hebridean salmon are taking over.

But the most attractive sea-trout water, a few hundred yards from the coast road as it turns southwards and eastwards back to Lochmaddy, is the very small Loch Horisary. One can smell its sea-trout qualities even out of season. In full season (July to October), unless the

231

weather is intolerable, no one ever fails to get sea-trout from Horisary. Though not in the least a machair loch, it has a rocky bottom, and the water is not too peaty. The average size of fish is two and a half pounds, and the record is twelve and a quarter pounds.

Back to Lochmaddy, you pass the larger Loch Dusary, again sufficiently remote from peat to avoid being acidulated; it contains larger sea-trout than Horisary, but they are more elusive. Loch na Morach, and at a further distance Loch nan Eun, are both notable for heathery-type brown trout running to a pound and over. These, however, are only two out of almost unnumbered lochs and lochans in which brown trout of varying sizes abound. It is not difficult for the camper or casual visitor to gain permission to cast a line on these many remote brown-trout waters. It is a different matter, of course, with the famous Hebridean-salmon and sea-trout lochs. Here you have to do something about the right to fish, and do it well in advance.

The island for the most part (including the hotel at Lochmaddy) is owned by the Earl of Granville. Other parts of the island are under the control of the Department of Agriculture and Fisheries, and fishing permits are available.

Lord Granville is very much a resident landlord who has the interests of the island at heart. A keen angler himself, he has reserved only one loch close by his house for his private use. For the rest, he is willing that as many of the public as possible should come to North Uist and avail themselves of its outstanding angling for sea-trout and salmon. But, as he spends much time and money in maintaining and improving the fishing, he naturally cannot open a free-for-all angling system.

If you stay at the Lochmaddy Hotel, you have certain rotatory rights on the waters. Incomers, too, can gain access by approaching the estate authorities and paying a fee. The same applies to other visitors to the island. But they should remember two things – the hotel residents have prior choice, and it is desirable for any who wish to try the more famous waters mentioned above to book well in advance. If you are attracted by the obvious sea-trout qualities of Horisary, and by its fame, and wish to get on it in September (about the surest month), you should think rather of the September of the year following than of the current year.

Not all waters of Hebridean salmon quality are quite so heavily booked. If the great Skealtar is conjoined with Scadavay, and there are in consequence more boats, it ought to be easier to get on at shorter notice.

Long notice (though again with prior claims to hotel residents) is not needed for the more well-known brown-trout lochs. The less well-known and remoter lochs and lochans containing nothing but brown trout can be fished with scarcely any prior notice at all. One must stress, however, the value of courtesy in asking permission from the estate Factor or at the hotel at Lochmaddy.

North Uist, then, is the island that (to paraphrase Barrie) 'likes to be fished'. Nevertheless its angling facilities must be maintained and, if possible, improved. The expense involved is considerable; and those who avail themselves of this beautiful island's highly accessible fishing should recognize that what they pay goes to maintain and improve North Uist's Hebridean-salmon and sea-trout lochs.

You can sail direct from the mainland or by Skye (now for practical purposes a part of the mainland) to Lochmaddy three times a week. On every day except Sunday there is an air service from Glasgow to Benbecula. As North Uist has since 1961 been linked by a road causes way with Benbecula, you can travel by car from the Benbecula airport to Lochmaddy in less than an hour. Thus you can leave the centre of Glasgow in the morning and (if you have arranged it in advance) be on a Hebridean-salmon loch in the afternoon.

HARRIS

The island of Harris is in one sense more of an island than any we have considered in our journey northwards through the Outer Hebrides; in another sense, it is less of an island. 'More' because you cannot approach it from other islands to the south by means of man-constructed road causeways, but must come to it from the mainland by boat or by air to Stornoway in Lewis, and thus down south by road – a long journey. 'Less' inasmuch as it is firmly attached to the island of Lewis over a width of about seven miles. The broad and formidable rampart of hills that stretches between the sea-lochs of Resort and Seaforth became, in Gaelic antiquity, a boundary-line between the two 'islands'.

Geographically, therefore, Harris and Lewis (the largest single piece of land in the Outer Hebrides) is one island. But historically, scenically, and perhaps ethnologically they are separate.

Harris's island status is further complicated by the fact that it is itself nearly split into two islands at Tarbert, its capital, where the narrowest of isthmuses connects the mountainous North Harris from the milder but by no means flat South Harris. The island of Harris is sizeable. It is about twelve miles from south to north and about twelve miles at its widest from west to east.

Harris has a great appeal to the lover of fine scenery and of Highland and Hebridean humanity. Our immediate concern, however, is its inland and eminently fishable waters.

Most of those that are available to the public lie in South Harris. The first ones that visitors are likely to encounter are attached to the Harris Hotel at Tarbert and are known as the Lacisdale chain.

The word Lacisdale is an anglicized derivative from Laxadale, the name of the largest loch. Laxadale (frequently found in the Hebrides, Highlands, and Norse islands) comes from the Old Norse *lax*, meaning salmon – or, for that matter, sea-trout. Laxadale is the most northerly of the chain of lochs; the other two connecting it with the sea are known as Torasclet and Urgha Beg or, more generally, the Mid Loch and the Lower Loch.

The Lacisdale chain is easily accessible from Tarbert; and from the peak of the road that runs by the west side of the main Loch Laxadale can be seen the whole of the linked lochs from Laxadale to the sea.

The lower loch is naturally the first in the season to offer sport. It has a projection of rock that an informed ghillie will point out to you with pride; it is known as Salmon Point, and, if there is a fish to be caught in the loch, it is here. Near Salmon Point the record fish for the Lacisdale chain, a sixteen-pounder, was caught (it is said) by a schoolboy of sixteen. On the Lacisdale chain a ten-pounder on the Middle Loch fell to an English schoolboy of ten.

On this natural chain of lochs, needing no man-made contrivances, the Hebridean-salmon season lasts from about midsummer till late September or even later. As in North Uist, if you wish to have a real 'go' at these splendid lochs, you must lay your plans and make bookings at the hotel well in advance – preferably the year before.

Southward by the east road, so weirdly beset by outcrops of silvery gneiss or Hebridean granite, you pass through the one part of Harris in which brown trout predominate. I eschew the mention of private waters here, but some of the best brown-trout waters, notably Loch Drinesheader with its fine fighting trout, do just come into our category. The average for Drinesheader is three-quarters of a pound, but the fish have fighting capacity of well over that weight. Brown trout of between two and three pounds have occasionally been known there. These lochs go with the Lodge at Horsacleit, which is sometimes let for as little as two weeks. If the Lodge is not let, permission for angling is obtainable with the payment of a fee. There are many minor lochs and lochans on the Lodge property.

The southernmost tip of Harris contains the famous small village of Rodel, with a pier for a somewhat prolonged ferry trip over the intricate Sound of Harris to North Uist, and a hotel that has the fishing rights.

It is impossible to speak of Rodel without mentioning the incomparable church of St Clement, set on a hillock nearby. Small and now unused for public worship, it is the most striking and least damaged of all Scotland's pre-Reformation churches. It was probably built in the early 1500s as a burial-place for the MacLeods of Dunvegan, who then owned Harris. It contains a magnificent tomb and arch designed before the death of the seventh Chief. In it you will see Celtic craftsmanship

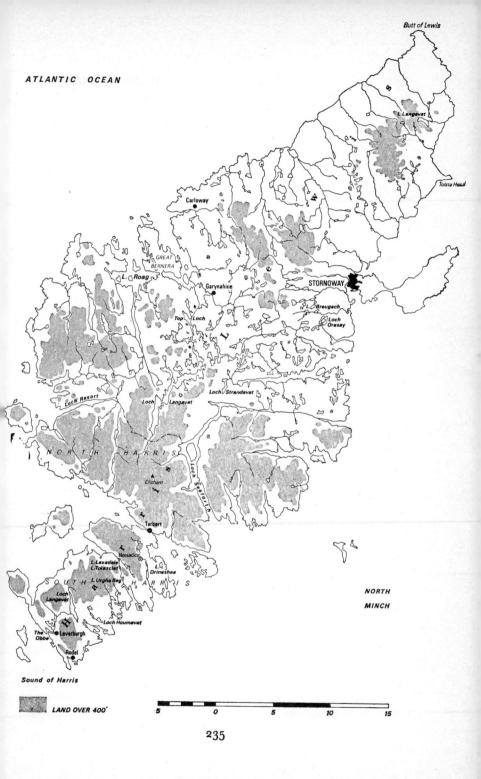

Butt of Lewis

ATLANTIC OCEAN

L. Langavat

Tolsta Head

Carloway

GREAT
BERNERA

L. Roag

Garynahine

STORNOWAY

Breugach

Top *Loch*

*Loch
Orasay*

Loch Strandavat

Loch Resort

Loch *Langavat*

NORTH   HARRIS

Clisham

Loch Seaforth

NORTH

MINCH

Tarbert

Horsaclet

L. Laxadale
L. Torasclett

LQ
Drineshea

L. Urgha Beg

SOUTH   HARRIS

Loch
Langavat

Loch Houmavat

The
Obbe   Leverburgh

Rodel

Sound of Harris

LAND OVER 400'

5   0   5   10   15

235

at its most luxuriant. You can easily gain access. And, if you feel inclined, you may say your prayers there undisturbed.

The lochs at this southern end of Harris are under the control of the hotel at Rodel. For the most part they are Hebridean-salmon lochs, but the interesting little waters of Corrie and Creagh a few miles north of Rodel contain both species. They are in a sense man-made lochs, with runs constructed to convert them from small granite-enclosed waters into genuine sea-trout and salmon lochs. There are two boats, one for each.

The Houmavat loch, with a short run to the sea, contains a sea-pool where both salmon and sea-trout linger. Here you can fish (up to three rods) in fresh water, brackish water, or enclosed sea water as you like. The average for Hebridean salmon, about seven and a half pounds, is maintained.

The Clachan run through Loch Strumore, still on the eastern side of South Harris and in the Rodel property, is very fruitful of both salmon and sea-trout, but on some occasions the sea-trout have been known to lose all caution. In the early 1930s Lord Cardross in one day and on this run alone killed 160 sea-trout.

To the west on this property, at Leverburgh, lies the Obbe loch, which leads into the river to Loch Langavat. The hotel proprietor has recently been introducing salmon ova from Thurso to breed larger salmon in these deeper waters.

Loch Langavat, over a mile long, has sea-trout, salmon, and brown trout. The averages are the usual, the brown trout being about three-quarters of a pound. But the unexpected feature here is the presence of *ferox* trout, which have been caught on Langavat up to fourteen and even fifteen pounds.

Maybe it is the influence of the Gulf Stream, which flows so strongly through the Sound of Harris, but the grass here seems greener than anywhere else in the Hebrides, and the peat and granite less obtrusive. The hotel has an internal greenhouse rich with plants that seem almost tropical – a delightful place in which to sit and discuss with the proprietor the prospects of salmon, sea-trout, brown trout, and marvellously large *ferox*.

LEWIS

Lewis alone – apart from the island of Harris, to which it is geographically attached – is by far the largest unit in the Outer Hebrides. About forty-two miles from south to north, it is at its widest some thirty-four miles west to east. Its population is over 20,000, and its lively sea-port capital of Stornoway contains over 5,000. Practically everyone in Lewis and its capital uses Gaelic as his or her first language.

In Stornoway you can enter the local branch of a world-famous international store and hear the salesgirls chattering to each other in the language commonly said to have been spoken by Adam and Eve in the Garden of Eden. But those who do not understand Gaelic need have no fear of isolation. Everyone also speaks English.

Lewis, humanly speaking, is full of vigour, but much of its hinterland between the populated east and west coasts is a brown and often wet expanse of peat. In this hinterland lie about 1,000 lochs and lochans – or, as was said to me during a recent visit to Lewis, 'a loch for every rod on the island'. Practically all these lochs and lochans contain brown trout of varying sizes, and access to them as a rule is either free or obtained through the various angling associations on Lewis. On the many lochs that are all but free you have to pay only if you hire a boat.

A young man with a love for trout fishing could spend a wonderful few weeks exploring the trout lochs of Lewis. He would require, however, transport rather more far-reaching than the bicycle suggested for Benbecula. Some 1,430 square miles need covering by car and bus, sometimes with heavy walking where the roads do not go. But the water would be such as he could find practically nowhere else in Scotland. Here, moreover, the visiting brown-trout angler is likely to have an open field, not only through its remoteness from the towns, but also through the preponderant excellence of the Lewis salmon fishing. Though there is a certain amount of sea-trout fishing, it is not the equal of that on South and North Uist. As soon, then, as the salmon start running in June or July, sometimes even the end of May, the Lewis angler appears to lose interest in anything but salmon and leaves the 900 or so brown-trout waters alone. This concentration of the native-born Lewis angler on salmon is understandable. In the Grimersta chain of lochs and in the Grimersta river he has what is often described as the 'finest salmon waters in Europe'. But, apart from the waters of Grimersta, there are various other lochs and (rare in the islands) rivers that would be outstanding anywhere for salmon. The brown-trout angler who comes to Lewis at the same time as the salmon need fear no local competition; he will be left alone.

Confronted by an immense amount of brown-trout water, the visiting angler could hardly do better than consult the various Lewis angling associations, the Tourist Association for the Western Isles at Stornoway, or the Stornoway Trust Estate office. Let him also call upon the main fishing-tackle merchant in Stornoway; he will find him generous with advice. He does not neglect the trout.

Some few indications are called for. Loch Orasay, for instance, lying off a side road some eight miles south of Stornoway, is an accessible and attractive loch of medium size containing one very large island and some smaller ones. The big central island has pasture for sheep and is a nesting-place for innumerable birds. Their droppings have enriched the soil, which in turn enriches the water around the island, providing excellent feeding for the trout. In consequence their average size is good – about a pound and running up to two and a half or three pounds. You will seldom get a big basket from Orasay, but the weight is all you could wish for. Orasay, too, is one of the few lochs in the Outer Hebrides that contain that highly edible rarity, the char, ancestor of all the salmon and trout tribe.

For an almost certain good basket (I have known thirty to one rod in a day), Loch Strandavat lies twenty miles south-west of Stornoway and immediately beside the road. The average size of fish is half to three-quarters of a pound. They rise very freely to the fly. On the loch there is always one boat, and usually there are two.

Twenty miles north of Stornoway is an exciting cluster of brown-trout lochs and lochans, some so small as to bear no name on the map. They lie an hour or more of hard walking away from where the Storno-way–Tolsta road ends on the east side.

The Tolsta road was an ill-fated experiment of Lord Leverhulme's when attempting to connect Stornoway round the north of Lewis with the road on the west of the island, which goes up to the Butt of Lewis at the far north-west. The new road peters out in heather and grass. The result is that the largely uninhabited ten miles or so of the north-east of Lewis can be reached only on foot. The walking is not hard, but if you are carrying gear you must be prepared for vigorous exercise.

The cluster of lochs referred to above lies four miles across country from the ending of the Tolsta road. The biggest is Loch Langavat (not to be confused with the still bigger and more famous Langavat in the Grimersta chain); but it is the little surrounding lochans, scarcely ever fished, that provide exciting sport.

On my last visit to Lewis in the month of June, I arrived the day after an angler had landed a brown trout of just over five pounds. Short, fat, deep, and with a small head, it was caught on the fly, played, and landed from a sheet of water close to the sea and too small for the map to name. It was no *ferox* or lonely cannibal. There must be others like him. But you must make an effort to get at them.

A fourth water worth mention for its close proximity to Stornoway is Loch Breugach, filled with sporting trout from three-quarters of a pound to one and a half pounds.

A word more about the trout lochs of Lewis. I have referred to them as being scattered in an expanse of peat, yet the angler will often note that the waters are unstained, and therefore not highly acidulated. The reason for this is that many Lewis lochs lie on the original rocky or granite soil. Moreover the prevailing wind from the south-west has had its effects.

The waves of countless ages moving the waters to the north-east and beating against the north-east shores have dissolved the soil and pounded the stone and rock. The returning under-currents have carried the sands at the rate of an inch a year to the south-west shores. You may thus expect to find shallow, sandy beaches on the south-west shores and a deep, rockbound or boulder-strewn shore on the north-east. This is where the trout usually live. The wind and waves bring a harvest of dead and dying flies. There is shade under the rocks and boulders, and the eddying waters stir up the little currents that the trout delight in.

We must leave the subject of brown-trout lochs and turn to the finest part of angling in Lewis – the salmon waters. Of these, unquestionably the most famous are the lochs of the Grimersta chain. As they are also the most characteristic, we may concentrate upon them here and deal but lightly with the others.

The Grimersta river, which begins the chain, flows into one of the Roag sea-lochs on the west and Atlantic side of the island facing the island of Great Bernera. The river, with natural pools made more fish-holding by man-made obstructions, flows out of the first loch in the chain. It is usually called the Top Loch.

The river is about a mile long and can on occasions provide good sport; but in the running season the hordes of fish are usually so anxious to reach the lochs and the eventual spawning-grounds that they go through at a great pace. The river, short though it is, would be notable anywhere. It is particularly notable here as one of the few, and without question the best, of the salmon rivers on the islands of Scotland, which usually do not provide enough running-space for fishable rivers.

From the first loch through the second, third, and fourth, the Grimersta chain, always animated by the running waters of the river, ends in the head water, the great Loch Langavat. Although it culminates among the mountain peaks of North Harris, and part of its fishing rights lie outside the Grimersta Estate (the river and the four lochs just referred to), Langavat is geographically a part of the Grimersta chain. Nearly all salmon coming into the Grimersta connection go to it eventually to spawn in its hill-burns.

Only seven miles from north-east to south-west, Langavat has by reason of its winding at least forty-five miles of shoreline. The west Highlands, and particularly the Hebrides, have many Loch Langavats – whose name, derived from the Norse, means long or great waters. There is a far less significant Loch Langavat at the north end of Lewis; and I have already referred to the notable Langavat at the south end of Harris. The Langavat that ends the Grimersta chain so triumphantly is, for the angler, the most important of that name in all Scotland.

On its rocky bottom and between sandy shores, it contains all over its length a fine breed of sporting brown trout. A friend of mine recently grassed eighty-five trout on his own rod alone in a loch branching off Langavat. They averaged just under a pound, though many were well over. There are occasional sea-trout in Langavat, particularly at the junctions of the chain, but more than anything there are the salmon. These can be found in any of the smaller upper lochs early in the season and at the beginning of each run; but when the runs are fully completed all the Grimersta lochs, including the mighty Langavat, are filled with salmon.

It is this profusion of the fish, together with their fighting spirit, that has won Grimersta its fame. The Grimersta salmon have not in size beaten the North Uist monsters; twenty pounds is about the limit. But a man I know, who could not give the whole day to his pleasure, grassed twelve salmon on one outing. This figure is far from uncommon and is usually beaten once a season. On one occasion it was beaten impressively. Near the beginning of this century one rod from one boat killed fifty-seven salmon on the fly. It is said that the angler was reduced by exhaustion to trying the most outlandish flies in the hope of finding one that the salmon would not take; he was unsuccessful. If you are lucky enough to see the salmon waiting to get up into Grimersta, you will hardly believe that there could be so many in the sea, let alone at the entry to one single chain of Hebridean waters.

It would, however, be unfair not to mention the difficulties that lie in the visitor's path if he wishes to tackle Grimersta. Let me be quite explicit.

I have rigorously eschewed mentioning even by name any water that is owned and maintained by one landlord for himself and his friends. Grimersta does not quite come into this category.

Grimersta river, and the upper, middle, and lower lochs, as well as part of the mighty Langavat, are owned by a syndicate whose members do not live in Lewis; they have little connection with the island, and they stay for the most part at the Lodge by Grimersta river when they come to exercise their rights from July to the end of the season. No amount of writing to any member of this prosperous oligarchy can get you half an hour's fishing on the Grimersta estate during that period.

A syndicate, however, is not a thing fixed in eternity, nor do its rights pass of necessity from father to son. If members retire, die, or otherwise give up their rights, places fall vacant. Then, if you can afford the entrance fee, and are approved, you can become a member of the syndicate. Strictly speaking, therefore, anyone can hope that under present conditions he may possibly fish the Grimersta waters as by right. But there are other methods by which one can gain access, particularly before the full flood of the season begins.

Lewis has for long been lucky in its landlords. For generations there has been an understanding between landlord and tenant here that the waters of Lewis are part of the Lewisman's birthright, if he claims or asks for it with courtesy. Something of this tradition lives on at Grimersta.

There is a late spring run of salmon before the great spates of fish in July and the autumn; and in June, even in May, there are fish in the waters – anywhere else they might be considered plentiful. The syndicate does not usually clamp down exclusively until the July run. The Factor and the keepers by the Lodge are then empowered to let keen anglers on Lewis, mostly in Stornoway, know that the waters of the estate and even the Lodge can be hired at a price. It is therefore possible for Lewismen to fish their splendid waters of Grimersta before the full flood of the season.

The people of Lewis are not only courteous but hospitable. If any angler of repute arrives in Stornoway in May or June, and wishes to taste the 'sacred waters of Grimersta' before he leaves, he may be able to join in as a guest or paying guest. It is also possible, at the beginning or very end of the season, to apply to the Secretary of the estate, with your cheque-book ready. You may be lucky. This gives a further reason for including Grimersta in this survey. Hardys in their *Fishing Map of Scotland* include Grimersta and list it in the index.

In writing about Grimersta, I have presented not only Lewis but Hebridean-salmon fishing at its outstanding best and in its most characteristic form. There are, however, less important salmon lochs and rivers as well as a few sea-trout waters (some quite close to Stornoway) that are fed from the eastern coast; and there are some in the centre of the island, some on the west.

These are not free for all, as most of the 'thousand' brown-trout lochs on Lewis are, but access can be obtained at varying prices and without having to book far in advance. The sources for access are, first, the Secretaries of the following:

1. The Stornoway Angling Association, Stornoway, for lochs and rivers near the island capital.
2. The Soval Angling Association for the 'Lochs District' on the east side of the island north of the sea-loch of Erisort.
3. The Carloway Angling Association, Carloway, for the waters on the west side of the island.

For the waters of the Garynahine estate, mostly in the centre of the island, application should be made to Mr C. Scott Mackenzie, County Buildings, Stornoway.

This book, as the reader will have seen, is not entirely about angling. I cannot end without some expression of my pleasure in revisiting the Outer Islands.

I have known some of the Western Isles since boyhood, and the Outer Hebrides since early youth. The fortunes of war, the pleasures of peace, and now the easy burden of work have brought me there again.

The beauty of the scene upon this ultimate edge of Europe has been much praised – too often in words with the colours of a cheap picture postcard. Moreover the courtesy of the Hebrideans and their devotion to their faith, whether Protestant or Catholic, has been much remarked on – too often with an unmannerly surprise. Unusual, however, these qualities are indeed. I can well imagine a mainlander or Englishman being startled to discover communities in which all classes have the manners of gentlefolk, and where nearly all the people accept quite naturally the practice of the Christian faith.

I was not startled. What I did find a surprising consolation was how much of what I remembered, even from a good many years ago, remains. 'Never go back to a place you have loved' is an aphorism much in use by the elderly. I found no use for it on this visit to the Western Isles. I was glad to have gone back because I found I had caught again something of my own vanished years.

On my return by air to the south mainland of Scotland from Lewis, I was lucky enough to have a day of flawless sunshine. I could see almost the whole line of the Hebrides stretched out below me – the map made visible in earth, stone, sea, loch, and river. I will go back yet again to these islands that this uncomfortable age of ours cannot destroy. The scenery, the brown trout, the silvery trout, the sea-trout, the salmon, and above all the people remain as they ever were. One could ask no more.

M.McL.

Chapter Twenty-Three

THE NORSE ISLANDS: ORKNEY AND SHETLAND

Much of the attraction of Scotland for the lover of inland waters and of angling lies in the abundant variety it offers. The Hebrides, we have seen, have their subtle and innumerable differences. But no internal Hebridean difference is equal to the difference between them and the Norse islands of Orkney and Shetland. That difference is most strikingly discovered in going from the Hebridean west on to the mainland of Scotland, thence direct to Orkney, separated by only the seven miles of the Pentland Firth from the mainland county of Caithness.

ORKNEY

'County' – that word is significant. Orkney is a county set in the sea; so is the archipelago of Shetland. But Orkney comes first, not only by the geographical approach from south to north, but because the difference between it and all other island groups, the difference from the rest of Scotland, demands this treatment.

Unlike all other island groups, it is largely a farming and agricultural archipelago and provides some of the best farming in Scotland. It is as if the richer lands of East Lothian had been enisled in the northern seas; and this particularly applies to the biggest island, which contains the capital and is called the Mainland. In Orkney and Shetland this word is used solely in that island sense. What the rest of us call the mainland is dismissed as Scotland in these Norse islands, which joined the Kingdom of Scotland only 500 years ago. The inhabitants think of themselves as Norse people attached politically to Scotland and, by consequence, to Great Britain.

This has its effect on our theme of inland waters and the angling therein. Nearly all the Mainland of Orkney belongs to the people of Orkney – in this case farmers who have too much to do to bother with fishing for brown trout. Generously, and in collaboration with the Orkney Angling Association, they allow their fellow Orcadians and their friends, and the visiting tourists who help the economy of the country, to fish for trout free. If you want a boat, you must of course hire it. But, from the banks of nearly all the brown-trout lochs (among the best in Scotland), you can fish to your heart's content throughout those long summer days without paying a penny. The brown-trout fishing in its better waters is the most democratic in Scotland, in the United Kingdom, or maybe in the world.

Traditional landlordism of the Celtic Chief type found in the Highlands and the Hebrides can be beneficent, particularly in safeguarding the waters from ignoble methods of angling. It can also, in the hands of syndicalized proprietorship, be far from beneficent. But, for good or ill, it does not exist here. Of course there are a few private waters in the archipelago in general, and one or two on the Mainland. But practically all the best waters, which are large and not of the numerous lochan types common in the Hebrides, are the angling property of the Orcadians and their friends, including the visitors.

The intensely agricultural nature of these green and purple, rolling islands, particularly the Mainland, also influences the trout angling. The large Loch of Harray near the centre of the Mainland (just over four miles long, one mile at its widest) is entirely surrounded by rich pasture land or land devoted to other farming uses. This pours excellent feeding into the waters from every point of its shore length of some fourteen miles. At its best, Harray abounds in well-fed fighting fish.

It is a shallow loch, dotted here and there with some skerries round which the trout love to linger, and by which they are easily got at, easily tempted. The Harray is well fed with burns, and its trout population must be enormous – as many keepable trout to each square yard of water as any loch in Scotland. This means that the average size of fish is less than in some of the other well-known Orkney lochs – say, a half to three-quarters of a pound.

But large trout do exist there. Two-pounders are not uncommon. In recent years five-pounders have been taken; and there are giants. A fish of ten and a half pounds held the record until 1966, when a monster of seventeen and a quarter pounds was grassed by Mr Douglas Blyth. You may see its cast in the Merkister Hotel; it is palpably an honest-to-God brown trout and not a *ferox*.

The natural agricultural feeding of the larger Orkney lochs is, of course, mostly beneficial. But at intervals it does raise problems. Until we come to these, let it suffice to say that the great Harray, the slightly less great Boardhouse and Swannay, and the smaller Hundland provide free brown-trout waters unique in Scotland. In Harray the trout at their best take freely, but they are of a better average weight in the other three lochs.

These are the prime examples. But there are up to a dozen lesser waters (carefully looked after and encouraged by the Orkney Angling Association) in which the true Orkney brown-trout sport can be

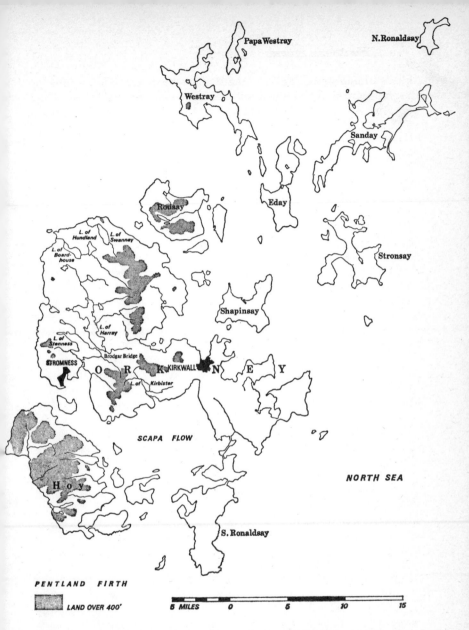

PENTLAND FIRTH

LAND OVER 400'

5 MILES   0   5   10   15

enjoyed. Anyone in this hospitable and friendly island, with its distinguished sub-capital of Stromness, will tell you how to get to them.
Often he will be good enough, unasked, to give you a lift to the waterside and even call back for you at the end of the day.

I have not yet mentioned the large and well-known Loch of Stenness.
This is because it is largely a brackish water connected with the ocean

245

by a small sea-arm and a running trickle influenced by the tides. This provides good, though not superlative, sea-trout fishing – at any rate, the brown trout, not the sea-trout, is Orkney's prime offering. But a controversial point does arise about the brown trout that manage to get down from Harray into Stenness by the small aperture at Brodgar Bridge.

Known in Scotland as slob trout, they are ordinary trout that have accustomed themselves to brackish water, but, while assuming the silvery coats that usually belong to sea-trout, do not have the sea-trout habit of going out to sea. In Stenness, if they can endure the brackish water (variable in parts of this, the second longest loch in Orkney), they receive very rich feeding from the agricultural shores and have every temptation to stay there.

They grow very large. Seven- and ten-pounders have been caught there on the fly. But all records for Stenness – and for Orkney, if you allow that it is originally a brown trout and not a migratory sea-trout – were broken by the famous Loch of Stenness trout caught on a set line in 1881. It turned the scale at a staggering twenty-nine and a half pounds.

A good many trout anglers (but not on Orkney) are unwilling to accept this monster as a brown trout. Maybe it was a slob trout that had spent nearly all its adult life in brackish or, at the southern end of Stenness, almost completely salt water. How do we know that it had not indulged in an occasional migration of the sea-trout type to the nearby sea? In short, may not it have been a brown trout that, over its long life, was turning into something like a sea-trout? This point is enforced by the fairly recent scientific decision on the origin of sea-trout. Long thought to have been a separate species of the salmon tribe from the brown trout, they are now held to be descended from brown trout that, either early or late, have developed migratory habits.

I have minutely examined the twenty-nine-pounder preserved at the Museum at Stromness. Apart from the shock of seeing a thing of this size claiming to be a trout, I was struck by three other facts. This cast is of a salmonoid in excellent condition, with small head, no projecting lower jaw, and a large, fat, deep body. Here was no kelt or *ferox*. The second point I noticed was that the skin was darker, browner than that of lesser but indubitably brown or slob trout, belonging to the seven- and ten-pound class, also preserved in the Museum. These were pure silver, but bore the brown-trout spots all over their bodies. The third point was that, among its rare spots, there were here and there some that were faintly red, of the kind that one associates with brown trout but never with sea-trout.

Among all Orcadian anglers it is an 'article of faith' that the Loch of Stenness trout (that is the only name it bears) was a brown trout. If you start qualifying this by talking about a slob trout, you will be courteously brushed aside with the statement that a fish does not change its species by changing its habitat and feeding. This is as may be, but it conflicts with the latest view about the origin of sea-trout. While not accepting the Orcadian article of faith that the twenty-nine-pounder of Stenness was essentially a brown trout, I do in the theologians' phrase regard it an allowable act *de fide*.

Earlier I said that the rich agricultural feeding provided for the Orkney lochs does at intervals raise problems. Weed has grossly over-proliferated in certain lochs, notably in Boardhouse. This not only makes angling difficult, but, through decay in the overgrowth of weed, has deoxygenated the water to the detriment of the trout beneath.

In Harray the trout behaved in a most peculiar manner during the mid-'sixties – though not for the first time in Orkney angling history. They rushed to the northern and upper end of the loch, almost over-crowding it. The water, even at the upper end, was discoloured. It was alleged that trout had been seen jumping out of the loch on to the stones beside it.

All sorts of reasons were put forward for this unusual state of affairs. Inevitably the modern chemical fertilizers used by farmers, and their methods of silage, were blamed. On this I can make only two comments. The democratic condition of trout fishing on Orkney owes its existence to two factors: the goodwill of the riparian farmer owners and the assiduity of the Angling Association. Clearly the Association is in no position to dictate to the farmers how to farm their land, but they can and do advise the farmers. The farmers do not want to damage Orkney trout fishing, and they act on this advice. There is no bad feeling. Moreover the Association has bought small amounts of land on the sides of the better lochs to become a riparian proprietor itself.

In any event, while modern chemicals undoubtedly do interfere with trout fisheries on occasion, the answer at Harray was more old-fashioned – salt water. The salinity of the loch became excessive because high tides were pushing salt water from Loch Stenness through into Harray. Algal growth was intensified to such an extent that trout became affected. In the late 1960s the Orkney A.A. fitted flaps to the ducts joining the two lochs to control the water flow and reduced the salinity of Harray to about ten per cent of its worst level. Trout fishing improved immediately.

I have mentioned that traditional landlordism on other islands can prevent the more ignoble methods of angling. It is, alas! a drawback of the democratic system that under it such safeguards don't exist, or are, as in Orkney, confined to a few waters where the rule of fly fishing only is in force.

It is a prejudice of mine to dislike the fixed spool reel. One of the greatest pleasures in angling lies in playing a good fish on a fly rod. It is a straight contest between you and the fish, with your nerves, muscles, and mind extending down the rod and line right into the fish's mouth. Dare you give him more line? Dare you exert pressure now? It is all your decision. With the automatic fixed spool you have virtually surrendered that decision. You have set the reel at a certain pressure, and by its slipping clutch it cannot exceed that. The machine in your hands does the rest.

Undoubtedly the fixed-spool spinning reels kill many fish, and many big fish. And, no doubt for this reason, the shores of most unrestricted waters on Orkney are lined in the long summer evenings by anglers whom one suspects, in view of their numbers, to be fishing for the pot rather than for sport.

There is, however, one form of angling that all true lovers of loch fishing for trout will surely deplore. This is the use of the fixed spool reel combined with a bubble float. The float rests on the water while, far below it and attached to it, a hook worm or bunch of worms lies just above the bed of the loch. All the 'angler' has to do is to keep a languid eye on the possible movements of the bubble float and then, if necessary, take action.

One Sunday, on a well-known Orkney loch (Sunday fishing for trout is allowed on Orkney) I saw a good many boats engaged in this operation. In one family boat, with three rods out bubble floating, I noticed that paterfamilias was reading aloud from yesterday's newspaper, only glancing between paragraphs at his own – I was glad to see – motionless bubble. Scottish anglers for game fish have often been heard to pour scorn upon the canal fishers of the English Midlands. But is this sort of thing any better?

I cannot end on this note. Orkney angling for trout is outstanding and, in its democratic nature, unique. All true angling Orcadians keen on their sport stick to the fly or, occasionally, the minnow or spoon, and would deplore as much as I do the bubble float and other disagreeable inventions. Justice, however, compels one to note that visitors to Orkney, drawn by its outstanding reputation, are almost exclusively fly fishers. Otherwise they would not be there.

The brown trout are Orkney's prime glory, but there are also sea-trout and, in very recent years, some salmon. Sea-trout, as already mentioned, come into the Loch of Stenness; some of these make their way up into Harray and further up late in the season. There is also angling for sea-trout in the open bays and in pure sea water. Unlike the sea-trout voe angling in Shetland, it is more properly sea angling, bearing no relation, for instance, to the angling at Benbecula at the north and south ponds in the stranded pools left at ebb tide. As far as Stenness, Harray, and a few connected waters are concerned, the

Orcadian angler by no means neglects the sea-trout. But the brown trout come first.

Most publications in Orkney say that, owing to the shortness of the rivers, there is no salmon fishing in the county. Recently this has been modified. There is a smallish water on the west Mainland, the Loch of Kirbister, that abounds in strongly fighting brown trout that as a rule are of a modest size. Traditionally, if you wanted to take a boy or novice out in a boat and teach him the art of fly casting, with the hope of a reasonable basket, you took him to Kirbister. But in recent years the situation has been complicated by the fact that the novice on a light trout rod and cast might well find himself stuck into a salmon of seven to ten pounds. Unfortunately, in most cases of the past year or two this unexpected monster would turn out to be a kelt or a landlocked, decayed salmon that had spent too long in fresh water.

The reason is this. There has always been a short, easy outlet from Kirbister to the sea, and salmon did occasionally use it. Recently, however, the County Council built a dam on this outlet to raise the water of the loch for pumping. Aware that salmon come into the loch, they built a fish ladder. Salmon coming in to spawn are positively encouraged by such devices. Unfortunately their urge to go back to the sea is less strong, and in Kirbister they don't feel like using the ladder for return. Therefore they loll about through the seasons, turning more and more deplorably into poorly conditioned kelts.

A scheme is afoot to construct an easy outflow from Kirbister through which salmon, having spawned, may drift back into the sea. If this scheme materializes and is successful, Orkney may well have what it never had before, a reliable and regular salmon water.

The people of Orkney, very distinct from the Hebrideans, are mostly of non-Celtic Norse stock. Independent, down to earth, plain-spoken, they yet have the courtesy and leisureliness of island folk the world over. Though most are fair-haired, a few have dark hair and complexions. There is a strong tradition in Orkney that the dark strain in the population is of Spanish origin. This may be. A ship from the Armada of 1588 was wrecked at Orkney, and the crew, which was saved, nearly all stayed there. The Spaniards are a grave and dignified people whose manner would not clash with the *gravitas* of the original inhabitants.

Gravitas is not here used to imply pompous gloom. Your Orcadian, fair or dark, can talk well. He lacks the ebullience, however, of the Celt and, above all, refrains from the occasional Celtic way of telling the visitor what he wants to hear rather than what he ought to be told. He is downright and forthcoming. The young women have distinctly good looks and, as their sudden flashing smiles display, are also forthcoming. But they are more difficult to lure than the Orkney trout.

The scenery of Orkney that the angler is most likely to encounter is quite different from that of the Hebrides. There are, of course, magnificent rocks and cliffs, especially on the island of Hoy, but the central, south, and west Mainland, where trout angling is best, is pastoral.

More than pastoral, it seems to get the best of various scenic worlds. There are parts that in their vivid greenness remind you not only of the lusher districts of southern Scotland in East Lothian and Galloway, but even of southern England. Devon comes to mind and, as in Devon, the green has the contrast of purple heather on the mild uplands. At midsummer the loch-sides are bright with many-coloured wild flowers.

I can recall from my youth one remarkable trick the colours around an Orkney loch played on me. I was fishing a central loch for the evening rise at midsummer. Up till well after eleven-thirty at night (G.M.T.) the colours by the loch-side held strongly and indeed even seemed to grow brighter. Then the evening rise fell off, and with its departure the colours on the land lost their strength. The grass grew grey, the purple of the uplands took on a slightly different grey, and even the bright yellow blooms gave up the struggle to display themselves; the few red flowers just drained away their blood. It was a monochrome landscape.

Being young and contemptuous of sleep (it is almost impossible, anyhow, to sleep in a small rowing-boat), I decided to sit it out, or rather float it out, till the early morning rise of which I had heard so often. I was richly rewarded, not so much by the morning rise, which was fair enough while it lasted, as by the sight of the colour returning to the Orkney landscape all around me. The grass slowly regained its verdancy, the purple on the small hill-sides its pomp. The red flowers enjoyed a painless but patent blood transfusion. Colour was back.

At about three o'clock in the morning a contented youth rowed back to the shore with a reasonable basket of average-sized Orkney trout. Half of them had been caught on the evening rise just before the colour had gone, half during the brief period of its return.

With advancing years, there are some things that you know you will never do again. I strongly doubt if I shall ever again fish and float and fish once more a midsummer night all through. But I shall never forget the time that I did it, and that it was in Orkney.

SHETLAND

This string of nearly 100 closely connected islands running straight up the map looks like a sword flourished by Scotland at the North Pole. This is really not too fanciful a notion when one reflects that at the Gord of Herma Ness – the most northerly point of Unst, the most northerly island – there is no intervening land between it and the ice and snow of the Pole.

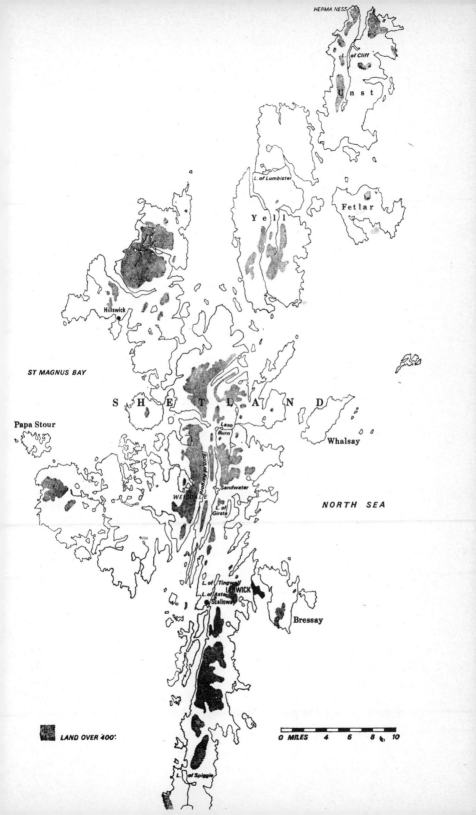

HERMA NESS

L. of Cliff

U n s t

Fetlar

L. of Lumbister

Y e l l

Hillswick

ST MAGNUS BAY

S   H   E   T   L   A   N   D

Papa Stour

Laxo
Burn

Whalsay

WEISDALE

Sandwater

NORTH SEA

L. of
Girsta

L. of Tingwall
L. of Asta
Scalloway
LERWICK

Bressay

LAND OVER 400'

0 MILES   4   6   8   10

L. of Spiggie

Purely Norse, and quite unlike the Hebrides in appearance, Shetland also differs from its fellow Norse island county of Orkney. It is much more hilly, and less pastoral. Its folks are great seagoers. The Orcadian, it has been said, is a farmer or crofter who possesses a boat; a Shetlander is a fisherman who possesses a croft.

Shetland has excellent brown-trout fishing in certain lochs, for the most part confined to the island called the Mainland – as in Orkney, the largest island in the county and the one containing the capital. She has a certain amount of salmon, which has been increasing, but her greatest glory is her sea-trout, often caught in the burns and lochs, but more famously by the Shetland speciality of voe fishing in the long, narrow arms of the sea.

Strictly speaking, this work ought to bypass voe sea-trout angling. But, as anyone who knows Shetland would surely recognize, that would be not only undesirable but impossible.

At any rate the voe fisher for sea-trout is not in a boat; his feet are planted on Shetland soil even though it may be under salt water, and he casts out to sea or sideways and not towards land, as is the habit of sea-trout anglers in the more open bays of Orkney. Finally, the voes are real inlets into the body of Shetland and are accounted part of Shetland. There is nothing else like the voe sea-trout angling elsewhere in Scotland or her many islands. The freshwater sea-trout angling in Shetland is also remarkable, but for sheer excitement it cannot compare with the more arduous sport of voe fishing.

Sea-trout begin to display themselves in the voes and at the mouths of the small rivers and burns in the spring, but they are not seriously considering a return to fresh water, and are seldom voe-fished deliberately until much later on. In July, August, and September merging into October, the sea-trout gather in the voes waiting for the spates to allow them up into the fresh water and their spawning-beds. You cannot tell when they will gather, or in which of the voes they will predominate, but when you do spot them it is an impressive sight.

You may be on a roadside fairly far up above a voe, and you may just glance at the water, but if the sea-trout are gathering in force a glance will suffice. They are there, and you can see them in their hundreds, maybe thousands. If you are lucky enough to have your voe sea-trout tackle with you, or can lay hands upon it and get back again in time for the suitably flowing tide, you can start operations while they are still there and available at the right conditions.

It is not a delicate or, be it admitted, highly skilful form of fly or lure fishing, but it can be very productive. In the voes the sea-trout are still sustained by the power of salt water; moreover they are in a highly impatient mood that often makes them reckless. The average weight of the voe sea-trout is two pounds or a bit over, but he is two pounds of muscular torpedo. As the fresh water has not yet hardened the flesh of his mouth, he is liable to break loose, but if he comes at all he does so with such determination that he is likely to take firmly and with a deep grip.

The method of voe fishing is this. You wade out, preferably over sand, not necessarily very far and certainly not beyond the limits of comfortable safety. You then cast your fly, usually a silver and blue 'terror' or other coloured variety of the same half-fly, half-lure; or you may choose a more openly admitted lure in the form of a small sand-eel, real or imitation. You cast out into the flowing tide as far as you can, and then reel in with as many tempting jerks, hesitations, or side switches as you feel inclined for. There is no question of casting over a rising fish, for the simple reason that in the voes they do not rise. Their thoughts are on other things – the return to fresh water and spawning. You know from previous sight of them that they are in their multitudes. Your chance of hooking one lies in your capacity to excite one of them to anger or a possible last-minute appetite by the blatancy of your silver and blue 'terror' or your lure.

If you succeed, you are usually aware of it several seconds before the fish bites. At the end of one of your casts, and often a good distance from where your fly or lure has hit the water, you will see a V-shape moving rapidly across the surface in the direction of your lure. It is a thrilling sight; for there is no question about his coming to examine what you have offered. Whether you like it or not, he has made up his mind to kill, chew, or eat the impudent silver and blue object or the flashing sand-eel that is disporting itself in the midst of a shoal of seatrout gathered for entry to fresh water.

The V-shape on the surface of the water accelerates until you are taken with what is, compared with ordinary fly fishing, violence. And then, if he is properly hooked, the fun begins. But here again it must be admitted that there is not very much you can do to control events. If he is a two-pounder or over he takes charge.

His tactics are immediately to leap high into the air – a delicate time when you must be careful not to lose him – and then make a dash, putting as much distance between himself and you as he can. Unlike the South Uist machair loch sea-trout, who, aware of their comparatively limited space, continue to jump, this first leap will possibly be the voe trout's only airborne expedition; he is too intent on getting out into his own element the sea as quickly as possible.

If he dashes straight out into the open sea; if you are not too impatient with him and do not put on too much pressure; if your tackle is good and you have adequate backing to your line; if – and all the other ifs that go to make an experienced angler; then you may bring him to the net, or employ that other way of landing a sea-trout in northern waters, by backing slowly towards the shore and inducing him to come flapping on to the dry seashore sand. It is surprising how often a sea-trout so vigorous in his own element will allow this tactic; but you must back slowly and steadily.

On the other hand, if he digs deep into a clump of seaweed, you have lost him. You can't wade or even swim to his retreat and disentangle him. If you tug or put heavy pressure on him, he'll only go deeper into the almost unbreakable cluster of weed, and in the end you will just have to give him up by hand-lining and pulling so that the cast breaks.

I need not designate the various voes worth trying. The sea-trout are capricious, and will gather in any voe that leads by burn or river to fresh water and spawning-beds. News travels rapidly in Shetland when the sea-trout are gathering in the voes; you will soon hear where the fish are.

Though not quite as democratically owned as the fishings on Orkney, there are – besides the voe fishing, which is free for all – some hill lochs in which brown-trout angling can be practised, and no one bothers to interfere. Again, it would be almost impossible to indicate where the fishings lie. They are scattered all over the archipelago, but mostly on the Mainland. The Shetland Anglers' Association at Lerwick will give any information required. Anyone in Lerwick or Scalloway (the old capital) will tell you where to apply.

It should be made clear that, apart from innumerable hill and peaty lochans that, strictly speaking, are under the control of the Anglers' Association, there are others of greater angling value on which the Association asserts its rights, on some of which it keeps boats, and on some of which it practises stocking and breeding. These are not free, but it will cost you little to fish them.

The most accessible loch of this kind, both from Lerwick and Scalloway, is the Tingwall. It is half way between the two towns and only a few miles from each. About a mile long, it is at its widest scarcely half a mile. The average size of trout in it is one pound going up to two pounds, though fish well over that weight have been taken. Like all trout in northern islands, they are determined fighters. It has attached to it, by a very short burn towards the south, the much smaller Loch Asta. This is strangely ignored, although it too contains sizeable and sporting trout. It can easily be fished from the bank. Tingwall, however, has boats, which of course must be hired, though at a reasonable cost.

Tingwall has at its north end a very small peninsula, which should interest any angler with a sense of the past. The word Tingwall is derived from Old Norse and means parliament. Almost 1,000 years ago, on that peninsula, around which the trout gather and proliferate, sat one of the first parliaments in what is now part of the British Isles. Westminster is a newcomer.

Apart from the innumerable hill lochans, in which sporting small fish not exceeding half a pound are free takers and free for all, there are other waters besides Tingwall that are well worth considering and are directly controlled by the Anglers' Association. Having taken Tingwall as one of the best and certainly the most approachable and representative loch, there is little point in listing the others. The Association in Lerwick, Scalloway, or Hillswick to the north will be only too pleased to give advice and help to anyone who buys a temporary or more long-term, reasonably priced ticket.

Hillswick provides characteristic Shetland brown-trout and sea-trout fishing in the far north-west of the Mainland. In one of its smaller lochs, a resident at the local hotel landed a sea-trout of nine and a quarter pounds a few years ago.

Practically all the outstanding waters are on the Mainland. Mention should be made, however, of the good sea-trout lochs Lumbister, on Yell, and Cliff on Unst. I have seen some fine sea-trout in Cliff, and there is, added to its angling possibilities, a fascination in its beautiful and lonely surroundings. Throughout the British Isles, there is no place further north in which one can angle for game fish, or indeed for any fish.

As I have indicated, by far the majority of lochs in Shetland are controlled by the Anglers' Association; there are, however, certain exceptions in private hands. This does not mean that it is impossible to get on to them. The Shetland landowners are generous, and will either freely or for a not excessive fee allow the visitor access if he applies by writing in advance. The Anglers' Association issues a card that lists the waters outside its control and states to whom the visitor should apply. I shall mention but two, on both of which I have had considerable sport.

In the far south of the Mainland there is the large Loch of Spiggie, celebrated for its brown trout running up to three pounds and over. Spiggie is also well known as a nesting place for rare birds.

The Burn of Laxo, with its deep holding pools and some sizeable small Lochs of Laxo at the head of it, lies about three-quarters of the way up the Mainland on the eastern side. It is entirely in private hands (information about it can be obtained from the Anglers' Association), but, if the fishing is not let as it sometimes is, courteous application to the proprietor or through the Anglers' Association will usually get you a day's fishing for its admirable sea-trout. However, throughout most of its length of little over a mile, the Laxo burn really is just a burn, and the sea-trout on their rapid passage to the lochs and spawning-grounds have little temptation to linger in it. You may possibly hook a notable sea-trout in the middle and upper reaches of the burn, but it is a matter of luck. Moreover, there is not much sport in playing a good sea-trout in shallow, running, narrow water.

But near the mouth of the burn, in clean as well as brackish water, there are good, deep holding pools that can give you all the fun you want on a fly rod. Below the bridge that carries a side road to the east, there is a large pool almost divided in two, and influenced by the tides – plenty of scope for playing and fighting there. Above the bridge, there is a rather long, narrow pool between steeply shelving banks, which add the spur of difficulty to the netting or landing of a sea-trout no matter how firmly he is hooked. This bridge pool is distinctly higher than the wider and longer lower pool, and is connected with it by a short but powerful waterfall. This is the only definite obstacle (a surmountable one) to the ascending sea-trout; a fish that overcomes it means business. He has made a distinct effort, and is likely to linger briefly in these narrow depths before attempting the easy task of running up the shallow burn to the loch.

I well recall my first and, as it happens, last essay at this formidable water above the bridge pool. The pool looked almost stagnant; and, finding what footing I could on a difficult bank, I cast a moderate-sized Greenwell without much hope. It was instantly taken by a peaty brown trout of under a quarter of a pound, which was returned. Another cast, and immediately another pluck; probably, I reflected, the sea-trout had not come up yet, and the pool was no doubt filled with hungry little brownies who would take anything. But no, this pluck did not come from a brownie.

Two or three seconds passed, and it became clear that at least one sea-trout had forced his way up the waterfall. A bar of silver, subsequently proving to be a fresh-run sea-trout of well over five pounds, leapt high into the air, falling back with a considerable splash. Oddly enough, he didn't leap again but tore up and down the narrow pool, causing much disturbance in even its deep water.

I scrambled to the foot of the pool by the waterfall and prominently displayed myself. I realized that my only hope of grassing this strong, fresh fish in such constricted circumstances was to keep him in them and prevent him from flying for safety down the waterfall, under the bridge, and into the wider pools well below. I knew that if he did this I would lose him.

He didn't. He just dashed backwards and forwards threshing the water until at last he showed signs of exhaustion near the head of the pool. I crept up on him, reeling in as I did so, with much difficulty keeping my foothold on the steep, muddy bank.

I shouted to my wife to bring the landing net, which she did from about fifty yards away. In the act of shouting my heart sank. I recalled that the only net we had brought with us (we had started only with the thought of brown trout) would be far too small. How idiotic of me even to have attempted the Laxo in passing, and so ill prepared!

But womanly cunning saved the day. My wife put the little net flat down into the water, directly under the fish's nose.

'Is he well hooked?' she asked.

'Yes, he must be – he's tried everything.'

'Well, then,' she said, 'slacken your pressure on him.'

Doubtfully I obeyed, but at once saw what she meant. Free from having his nose strained to the surface, the fish immediately turned to dive into the deeps below. But he didn't reach those deeps; he went head first into the contemptible little net, which would never have held him laterally.

'Heave!' I shouted. She heaved, and the noble sea-trout was drawn with some effort on to the bank, where he at once spewed out my Greenwell.

There was only one thing to do. Flinging the rod aside, I lay flat on top of him on that memorably muddy bank. I continued to lie there until I was certain the life was out of him. Then I pushed him somehow uphill on to safe ground.

This is but one personal recollection of the famous Laxo burn pools, which, be it repeated, are for the most part not brackish but are filled with clean, fresh water. I have the happiest memories of an afternoon on the small, shallow Sandwater, which with caution is wadable nearly all over. It too is in private hands, but is accessible. The average sea-trout I got from this loch were three pounds and just over.

I have already referred to the small loch near Hillswick in which was taken a sea-trout of nine and a quarter pounds. This notable weight has on occasion been surpassed in various other lochs, or in the running water briefly connecting them with the voes. Mention should be made of the Loch of Girlsta about half way up the Mainland. It is the deepest and longest water on the Mainland of Shetland, and the only one to contain that capricious rarity, the char.

Mention should also be made of the waters of Kergord, in the district of Weisdale on the west side of the Mainland. These are in private hands, but permission is readily obtained by approach through the Anglers' Association. The Kergord burn is by some considered the equal of the Laxo burn, and it regularly supplies excellent baskets when the runs of sea-trout are on. Salmon occasionally appear, and a few years ago a friend of mine grassed one in excellent condition weighing ten pounds three ounces.

To conclude on matters of fact, I must repeat the advice to angling visitors to get in touch with the Anglers' Association, whose secretaries will tell you which waters are free, which require a permit, and which an application through private owners. Finally, the best brown-trout waters of this loch-besprinkled archipelago yield an average of a pound or just over. In the voes the sea-trout yield an average of two pounds;

in the inland waters distinctly over two pounds. The record sea-trout of which we have knowledge is fifteen pounds, taken at the Loch of Cliff in Unst.

Salmon do run in Shetland, and for some time have been encouraged in those waters where their presence does no damage to the sea-trout spawning-beds. On the whole, however, the rivers (or rather burns) in Shetland are not long enough to lure salmon in any quantities. But this does not really matter. The brown-trout angling from the humble hill-lochs to such carefully supervised waters as Tingwall is good, though it does not reach the outstanding excellence of Orkney. But the sea-trout, whether in the voes or in the inland waters, is Shetland's proudest possession.

In the course of writing these chapters on the islands, I visited all those that I could, not only to acquire the latest information and impressions, but to recapture earlier experiences. I have spoken of the good luck I had in flying back from the Outer Hebrides in flawless weather. After a brief spell of windswept, cloudy gale, the same luck held for my visit to the Norse islands. On the day I flew south to Edinburgh from Shetland there was not a cloud in the sky above or below. Once again I had the exhilarating experience of seeing much of Scotland's real map – not on the printed page but in earth and water – rolled out and slipped beneath me as the plane slid through the skies.

An angler, a lover of the inland waters of Scotland, can take a special pride in the sight of Scotland and her many islands from the air. I have long known that Scotland has some of the most historic rivers in Europe and some of the most individual lakes. I have also known that, from an angler's point of view, she has a richer variety of game fishing than any other European country, large or small.

I knew this when I walked, rode, motored, or in any other way crawled about the surface of the land. Knowledge is immensely re-inforced by looking at the lochs, rivers, streams, burns, voes, and arms of the sea from the air. Doing this has given me an experience that is a permanent part of memory. No one can take it away. I have fished all over Scotland, and I have seen the waters of Scotland from far aloft.

M.McL.

GLOSSARY

---

n., noun
v., verb

baggot, *n.* Hen salmon that has retained her eggs through the winter and is caught, still unspawned, in the spring.

brandling, *n.* Small red worm with yellowish rings round its body, usually found in dung or compost.

braws, *n.* 'Best clothes': related to *braw*, handsome or beautiful.

cauld, *n.* Weir across river; dam wall.

corrie, *n.* High, glaciated valley, usually in the shoulder of a mountain.

cruive, *n.* Migratory-fish trap, usually of wickerwork and timber. The fish, most often salmon, are directed to the cruive by a cruive-dyke, a dam across the stream.

dap, *v.* Fish a fly, natural or artificial, by making a floss-silk line billow out in the wind before a drifting boat and bobbing the fly highly over the water.

dibble, *v.* Dap with live insects or occasionally artificial flies, which are dangled over trout, usually when they are lying close to the bank, under trees or the like.

finnock, finnoch, *n. See* herling.

grilse, *n.* Small mature salmon returning to the river after one year of sea-feeding.

guddle, *v.* Grope with the hand for trout in lies under stones.

haugh, *n.* Low-lying, flat alluvial ground beside a river, usually liable to flooding.

herling, *n.* Young sea-trout returning to fresh water after one year of estuarial or sea-feeding. Other of its many common names are whitling and finnock.

hodden (from hodden-grey), *n.* Peasant cloth originally woven out of undyed wool; now the name given to any coarse, utilitarian woollen cloth.

parr, *n.* Young salmon or sea-trout during its nursery years in the river. After about two seasons as a parr, the fish changes to a silvery colour, becoming known as a smolt, and migrates down to the sea.

redd, *n.* Gravel in which salmon, sea-trout, or trout lay their eggs.

skerry, *n.* Stony beach, especially in the Hebrides.

slick, *n.* Line of spin-drift, spume, froth, or bubbles made by the wind on a loch.

slob trout, *n.* Brown or silver trout that has taken to feeding in the brackish waters of the river estuary.

smolt, *n.* Young salmon or sea-trout at its sea-going stage. Smolt usually migrate in May. *See* parr.

spoon, spoon-bait, *n.* Flashing lure, often very like the bowl of a spoon, but in fact any non-natural wobbling bait with a flat profile.

thole, *v.* Endure.

troll, *v.* Fish by drawing a bait or lure behind a rowing boat.

weil (well), *n.* Deepest part of a pool in a river.

whaup, *n.* Curlew.

whitling, *n. See* herling.

CONCISE BIBLIOGRAPHY

The editions referred to are those used by the authors in writing this book.

Calderwood, W. L. *The Salmon Rivers and Lochs of Scotland.* London, Edward Arnold, 1921.

Crosseley, Anthony. *The Floating Line for Salmon and Sea Trout.* London, Methuen, 1948.

Grimble, Augustus. *The Salmon Rivers of Scotland.* London; Kegan Paul, Trench & Trubner; 1913.

Hall, John Inglis. *A Highland Stream.* London, Putnam, 1959.

Regan, Gunther and Tate. 'Salmo Levensis' from *The Freshwater Fishes of the British Isles.* London, Methuen, 1910.

Scrope, William. *Days and Nights of Salmon Fishing on Tweed.* London, John Murray, 1943.

Stoddard, Thomas Todd. *Anglers' Companion to the Rivers and Lochs of Scotland.* Edinburgh, Blackwood, 1853.

Studies on Loch Lomond. Glasgow, Blackie, Vol. 1, 1957; Vol. 2, 1967.

Taverner, Eric. *Salmon Fishing* (especially the included essay by A.H.E. Wood). London, Seeley Service (Badminton Series).

Williamson, Henry. *A Clear Water Stream.* London, Faber, 1958.

Williamson, Henry. *Salar the Salmon.* London, Faber, 1961.

INDEX

Page numbers in *italics* refer to illustrations.